LITERACY STRONG
ALL YEAR LONG
2nd Edition

Other ASCD books by the authors

Literacy Strong All Year Long: Powerful Lessons for Grades 3–5
by Valerie Ellery, Lori Oczkus and Timothy V. Rasinski

Reciprocal Teaching at Work: Powerful Strategies and Lessons for Improving Reading Comprehension, 3rd ed.
by Lori Oczkus

LITERACY STRONG

ALL YEAR LONG
Powerful Lessons for Grades K–2

2nd Edition

VALERIE ELLERY
LORI OCZKUS
TIMOTHY V. RASINSKI

ASCD
Alexandria, Virginia USA

INTERNATIONAL LITERACY ASSOCIATION
Newark, Delaware USA

1703 N. Beauregard St. • Alexandria, VA 22311-1714 USA
Phone: 800-933-2723 or 703-578-9600
Fax: 703-575-5400
Website: www.ascd.org
E-mail: member@ascd.org
Author guidelines: www.ascd.org/write

INTERNATIONAL LITERACY ASSOCIATION
PO Box 8139
Newark, DE 19714 USA
Phone: 800-336-7323 • Fax: 302-731-1057
Website: www.literacyworldwide.org
E-mail: customerservice@reading.org

ASCD Staff: Ranjit Sidhu, *Executive Director and CEO*; Stefani Roth, *Publisher*; Genny Ostertag, *Director, Content Acquisitions*; Julie Houtz, *Director, Book Editing & Production*; Darcie Russell, *Senior Associate Editor*; Judi Connelly, *Senior Art Director*; Georgia Park, *Senior Graphic Designer*; Keith Demmons, *Senior Production Designer*; Kelly Marshall, *Interim Manager, Production Services*; Shajuan Martin, *E-Publishing Specialist*

Copublished simultaneously by ASCD and the International Literacy Association.

Copyright © 2020 ASCD. All rights reserved. By purchasing only authorized electronic or print editions and not participating in or encouraging piracy of copyrighted materials, you support the rights of authors and publishers. Readers may duplicate the reproducibles, as marked, for noncommercial use within their school. All other requests to reproduce or republish excerpts of this work in print or electronic format may include a small fee. Please contact the Copyright Clearance Center (CCC), 222 Rosewood Dr., Danvers, MA 01923, USA (phone: 978-750-8400; fax: 978-646-8600; web: www.copyright.com). To inquire about site licensing options or any other reuse, contact ASCD Permissions at www.ascd.org/permissions, or permissions@ascd.org, or 703-575-5749. For a list of vendors authorized to license ASCD e-books to institutions, see www.ascd.org/epubs. Send translation inquiries to translations@ascd.org. Please note that it is illegal to otherwise reproduce copies of this work in print or electronic format (including reproductions displayed on a secure intranet or stored in a retrieval system or other electronic storage device from which copies can be made or displayed) without the prior written permission of the publisher.

ASCD® and ASCD LEARN. TEACH. LEAD.® are registered trademarks of ASCD. All other trademarks contained in this book are the property of, and reserved by, their respective owners, and are used for editorial and informational purposes only. No such use should be construed to imply sponsorship or endorsement of the book by the respective owners.

Common Core State Standards © 2010 National Governors Association Center for Best Practices and Council of Chief State School Officers. All rights reserved.

All web links in this book are correct as of the publication date below but may have become inactive or otherwise modified since that time. If you notice a deactivated or changed link, please e-mail books@ascd.org with the words "Link Update" in the subject line. In your message, please specify the web link, the book title, and the page number on which the link appears.

PAPERBACK ISBN: 978-1-4166-2819-4   ASCD product #118046   n12/19
Quantity discounts are available: e-mail programteam@ascd.org or call 800-933-2723, ext. 5773, or 703-575-5773. For desk copies, go to www.ascd.org/deskcopy.

Library of Congress Cataloging-in-Publication Data

Names: Ellery, Valerie, 1964- author. | Oczkus, Lori D., author. | Rasinski, Timothy V., author.
Title: Literacy strong all year long : powerful lessons for grades K-2 / Valerie Ellery, Lori Oczkus, and Timothy V. Rasinski.
Description: Second edition. | Alexandria, VA : ASCD, [2020] | Includes bibliographical references. | Summary: "40 ready-to-use lessons are complete with teasers, strategies, and reproducibles to help students in grades K-2 build comprehension, fluency, word work skills, and vocabulary"-- Provided by publisher.
Identifiers: LCCN 2019023075 | ISBN 9781416628194 (paperback)
Subjects: LCSH: Language arts (Primary)--United States. | Literacy--Study and teaching (Primary)--United States. | Reading (Primary)--United States.
Classification: LCC LB1576 .E4255 2020 | DDC 372.6--dc23
LC record available at https://lccn.loc.gov/2019023075

29 28 27 26 25 24 23 22 21 20   1 2 3 4 5 6 7 8 9 10 11 12

We dedicate this book to all teachers who work so hard to bring the light of literacy to children. Stay *Literacy Strong* and carry on.

LITERACY STRONG
ALL YEAR LONG
Powerful Lessons for Grades K–2

Acknowledgments xi
Introduction xiii

1. Starting the Year Literacy Strong 1
   Lesson 1. Phonological Awareness and Phonics: Isolating and Identifying Sounds 8
   Lesson 2. Phonological Awareness and Phonics: Blending and Segmenting 14
   Lesson 3. Phonics: Decoding 19
   Lesson 4. Fluency: Phrasing 27
   Lesson 5. Comprehension: Craft and Structure—Previewing 33
   Lesson 6. Comprehension: Key Ideas and Details—Determining Importance and Summarizing .. 39
   Lesson 7. Comprehension: Key Ideas and Details—Questioning for Close Reading 44
   Lesson 8. Vocabulary: Associating Words 51
   Lesson 9. Vocabulary: Analyzing Words 59
   Lesson 10. Motivation: Motivating Readers 66

2. Beating the Midyear Blahs 75
   Lesson 1. Phonological Awareness and Phonics: Isolating and Identifying Sounds 83
   Lesson 2. Phonological Awareness and Phonics: Blending and Segmenting 90
   Lesson 3. Phonics: Decoding 96
   Lesson 4. Fluency: Phrasing 103
   Lesson 5: Comprehension: Craft and Structure—Previewing 108
   Lesson 6. Comprehension: Key Ideas and Details—Determining Importance and Summarizing .. 116
   Lesson 7. Comprehension: Key Ideas and Details—Questioning for Close Reading 121

    Lesson 8. Vocabulary: Associating Words..........128
    Lesson 9. Vocabulary: Analyzing Words..........134
    Lesson 10. Motivation: Motivating Readers..........144

3. Ending the Year Literacy Strong..........154

    Lesson 1. Phonological Awareness and Phonics: Isolating and Identifying Sounds..........162
    Lesson 2. Phonological Awareness and Phonics: Blending and Segmenting..........168
    Lesson 3. Phonics: Decoding..........174
    Lesson 4. Fluency: Phrasing..........184
    Lesson 5. Comprehension: Craft and Structure—Previewing..........190
    Lesson 6. Comprehension: Key Ideas and Details—Determining Importance and Summarizing..........200
    Lesson 7. Comprehension: Key Ideas and Details—Questioning for Close Reading..........205
    Lesson 8. Vocabulary: Associating Words..........211
    Lesson 9. Vocabulary: Analyzing Words..........219
    Lesson 10. Motivation: Motivating Readers..........227

4. Stopping the Summer Slide..........236

    Lesson 1. Phonological Awareness and Phonics: Isolating and Identifying Sounds..........244
    Lesson 2. Phonological Awareness and Phonics: Blending and Segmenting..........248
    Lesson 3. Phonics: Decoding..........254
    Lesson 4. Fluency: Phrasing..........261
    Lesson 5. Comprehension: Craft and Structure—Previewing..........266
    Lesson 6. Comprehension: Key Ideas and Details—Determining Importance and Summarizing..........274
    Lesson 7. Comprehension: Key Ideas and Details—Questioning for Close Reading..........280
    Lesson 8. Vocabulary: Associating Words..........289
    Lesson 9. Vocabulary: Analyzing Words..........298
    Lesson 10. Motivation: Motivating Readers..........306

Appendix: Rubrics to Assess Student Competencies..........315

    Isolating and Identifying Sounds..........316
    Blending and Segmenting..........317
    Decoding..........318
    Phrasing..........319
    Previewing..........321
    Determining Importance and Summarizing..........323
    Questioning for Close Reading..........325
    Associating Words..........327

  Analyzing Words 329
  Motivating Readers 330

Study Guide 332

References and Resources 339
  Other Suggested Readings 341
  Children's Literature 342
  Children's Literature by Strand 344

About the Authors 345

Acknowledgments

Special thanks to Dr. Janie Hull, and the enduring educators who processed these lessons and allowed me to model in their classrooms. Your love and generosity toward literacy are priceless! Along with these special people in my life, I would like to share my gratitude for my family. I am forever blessed and grateful to my husband, Gregg, our adult children, Nick (Beth), Derek, Jacey (Wayne), and Brooke (Joel), and our two beautiful grandchildren, Evelyn Marie and Wyatt Thomas. Thank you for allowing me to live out my dreams!

—Valerie

Thank you to my "literacy sisters and brothers" from various districts (and publishers) across the country who support my work with spot-on classroom research and expertise, dedication to children, and most of all valued friendships. Also, heartfelt thanks to my children and my supportive husband, Mark, who cheer me on in all my professional endeavors.

—Lori

Thank you to Kathy Rasinski, Jennifer Rasinski, Nancy Padak, Belinda Zimmerman, Gay Fawcett, Chase Young, and Lisa Baum, from whom I have learned so much about early literacy instruction.

—Tim

We are grateful for the talented and tireless staff at ASCD and ILA who work with passion to promote literacy worldwide.

—The *Literacy Strong* Team: Valerie, Lori, & Tim

Introduction

Literacy, which comprises reading, writing, listening, speaking, and language competencies, is at the heart of all learning. Preparing students in the primary grades for academic success means integrating literacy through effective approaches such as interdisciplinary and project- and concept-based learning to motivate and engage them, allowing for an inquisitive stance toward their learning process (Boss & Lamar, 2018; Lanning, 2013; Strobel & van Barneveld, 2009). Incorporating effective brain research connections into learning, acquiring a backward design process (McTighe & Willis, 2019; Wiggins & McTighe, 2011), and keeping literacy as the strong foundation are exactly what is needed to propel learning to higher, stronger ground.

This cohesive, comprehensive literacy experience gives students opportunities to make pertinent connections among learning standards through the various seasons of a school year (beginning of the school year, midyear, end of the school year, and summertime). Much as Earth's seasons are caused by a tilt of its axis while the planet remains pointed in the same direction, school seasons are caused by a tilt of the learner's mindset while the teacher remains focused on student achievement. As we learn to effectively move through the various seasons of a school year, we need to remember to give ample opportunities for students to take in all that each season offers. Farmers would not expect to plant apple seeds during the first season and have instant fruit the next day from the apple tree; the apple seed needs to first take root and grow. "It takes a process to produce a product" (Ellery, 2011, p. 127), and the same is true for our school-based seasons. There are distinct times to plant, water, weed, prune, and harvest knowledge. We must first sow into learners' minds as much seed as is necessary to obtain the kind of harvest needed for the learner to be college- and career-ready. Each season is necessary for the strength, accumulation, and longevity *of learning*. "Practice that is distributed over longer periods of time sustains meaning and consolidates the learnings into long-term storage in a form that will ensure accurate recall and applications in the future" (Sousa, 2011, p. 106). Strong literacy students are able to apply their newfound knowledge throughout the school year as the lessons increase in complexity and are relevant to their developmental needs.

The major goal for *Literacy Strong All Year Long: Powerful Lessons for K–2* (and for the companion volume for teachers of grades 3–5) is to provide educators with ways to effectively keep literacy achievement progressing strongly in their classrooms. This book allows educators to teach literacy strategy lessons that spiral across the entire school year, focusing on reaching various learning styles in today's diverse classrooms. It is our aim to provide lessons that will motivate and engage primary learners to accumulate literacy achievement for long-term retention by enhancing prior learning throughout the school year for different literacy strategy strands (e.g., previewing, questioning for close reading). We have ensured that there are ample opportunities for previous learning to be applied in various situations throughout the seasons of the school year.

We hope that this volume captures our collaborative work as it builds on and extends relevant research on how the brain connects new learning to prior knowledge to strengthen literacy strategies used throughout the year (Caine & Caine, 2013; Jensen & Nickelsen, 2008; National Research Council, 2012; Sousa, 2011; Wolfe, 2010). Current neuroplasticity research on engagement demonstrates how adaptable our brains are, and thus how much capacity we as educators have to unleash student potential and help them acquire a growth mindset (Dweck, 2012; Hildrew, 2018). We must make every effort to layer deeper learning as we assess, plan, implement, assess again, and reflect to maximize the quality of our literacy instruction.

Organization of This Book

Each chapter uses a season of the school year to center instruction with a focus on the English Language Arts Literary Standards (National Governors Association Center for Best Practices and Council of Chief State School Officers, 2010) presented in 40 lessons that are conducive to deeper learning. Each chapter begins with a brief overview of the importance of keeping literacy strong during the specific season of the school year. The remaining portion of the chapter gives educators 10 Literacy Strands in comprehensive literacy lessons for applying strategies aligned to English Language Arts Standards. Each Literacy Strand presented in Chapter 1 spirals throughout the remaining chapters, rising in complexity. This continuum gives educators the opportunity to use students' previous academic vocabulary and learning standards as a springboard. As learners gain knowledge, confidence, and independence over time, the sophistication of the standards also progresses. A comprehensive literacy lesson format (adapted from Ellery & Rosenboom, 2011) guides educators as they gradually release responsibility to students so they can become self-regulated, literacy-strong learners. The interactive lesson format includes engagement strategies such as drama, singing, and gestures (Oczkus, 2009) and encompasses the following features.

Lesson Trailer

The lesson trailers are designed to fulfill the purpose of an action movie or book trailer: they intend to attract educators with the purpose of the lesson and to motivate them to teach the focused literacy lesson in the classroom.

Literacy Enhancer

The literacy enhancer gives an overview of each lesson with a focus on boosting literacy strength in one of the reading component areas of phonological awareness and phonics, fluency, vocabulary, comprehension, and motivation. A literacy strategy is aligned to the highlighted reading component with the focus skill of the strategy noted (e.g., Comprehension: Determining Importance and Summarizing of Key Details and Main Idea).

Key Academic Vocabulary

Key academic vocabulary spirals throughout each Literacy Strand to scaffold lessons across the four seasons. "Vocabulary knowledge develops gradually over time," wrote Marzano and Simms (2013). "Therefore, vocabulary instruction should be thought of as a process—not a singular event" (p. 13). Academic vocabulary needs to be explicitly taught and continuously interwoven in the learning process. When we give students opportunities to apply academic vocabulary to new knowledge, their learning progress becomes seamless (Rasinski & Zutell, 2010).

Preparation

Every great lesson begins with preparation. This focus area of the lesson helps educators answer the question: What is needed to accomplish the lesson with excellence? It is a time to prepare the materials, review the key academic vocabulary, focus on the big ideas and learning objectives, and establish essential questions. Every effort that is made for learning to occur signifies the value placed on establishing an environment that is conducive for learning.

Initiation

This initial phase of instruction develops student interest and motivation by creating an action (e.g., an anticipatory lead-in, hook, or attention-grabber; inquiry-based learning; problem-based learning) that opens the mind of the learner and sets the stage for learning. This focus area of the lesson helps educators answer the question: How can I "hook" my students so they are motivated to learn about lesson content?

Demonstration

This modeling phase allows the teacher to explain clearly and concisely the what, how, and why of a task through explicit demonstration. It sets up the instruction so the teacher can unpack key learning points, with students having a view into the mind of the teacher through think-alouds and real-time examples. This focus area of the lesson helps educators answer the question: What do I need to teach to ensure that students learn?

Collaboration

This section provides instructional-format, interactive, conversational coaching through shared experiences. It allows students to process information and apply accountable talk while responding to and further developing what others share in relationship to their cognitive development from the content. The collaboration phase also allows learners to share text-dependent evidence through apprenticeship learning. This focus area of the lesson helps educators answer the question: How will the learners interact with others and articulate their learning experience?

Application

Real-time practice is the key to this section of the lesson. During this instructional phase, learners can be in guided groups or work independently or with partners to apply their newfound knowledge through approximations and active engagement experiences (e.g., small groups, literacy centers or stations, investigative labs). This focus area of the lesson helps educators answer the question: How do the learners demonstrate their acquired knowledge?

Reflection

Intrapersonal perspective is the focus of this phase of the learning format. Students are provided a time to be self-regulated learners by considering and recording what they have learned and what they still want to learn (e.g., evaluating the feedback from monitoring progress toward a learning goal, learning logs, or written reflection journals). This focus area of the lesson helps educators answer the question: What evidence do the learners share that reflects their active participation in the learning process?

Adaptation and Extension

This section of the lesson provides various ways to adapt and extend learning, allowing flexibility in meeting the diverse instructional levels and needs of learners in today's classrooms. The design of the lesson addresses at least five of the multiple intelligences: visual, verbal, logical, kinesthetic, rhythmic, naturalist, interpersonal, and intrapersonal. This section helps instructors to reach as many of the learning styles and exceptional needs as possible.

Evaluation

Each lesson has "I can . . ." statements and behavior indicators to evaluate the process and product within the lesson. These tools are oriented to reflect what the student knows and still needs to know for intentional instruction as an integral part of the learning cycle, not just the end of the process.

Reproducibles

These resources are designed to allow for collaboration and accountable talk, as well as for interpreting and applying previous learning to new knowledge by relating experiences and acquiring ownership of learning. Chapter 4 features reproducible letters, many of which provide an at-home activity to be used with one or more of the regular reproducibles. We've included notes about what to gather together to send home with each student.

Chapter Overviews

Chapter 1: Starting the Year Literacy Strong. The introduction section of this chapter offers evidence on the importance of getting the school year off to a strong start by teaching literacy routines and setting expectations for students to become stronger readers and writers. Establishing benchmarks for future points of reference to gauge students' learning is addressed. Also described are strategies on how to focus a literacy community on building rapport with students and empowering parents to help lay a solid literacy foundation. These strategy lessons in Chapter 1 are child-centered, interactive, and imaginative and integrate joy into the foundation of the classroom. At the core of Chapter 1 are 10 comprehensive strategy lessons relevant for the beginning of the year that demonstrates the routines, expectations, assessments, and opportunities for collaboration as a literacy community.

Chapter 2: Beating the Midyear Blahs. The introduction section of Chapter 2 highlights the importance of maintaining momentum at the halfway mark or middle months of the school year. This chapter focuses on progressing literacy learning through a time when learning can get stagnant. It offers ways for educators to maintain momentum and monitor expectations that were established at the beginning of the year. This season allows for strengthening the student-teacher-parent (or school to home) relationship because the rapport has been built. The chapter also offers ways to continue evaluating literacy goals and benchmarks by monitoring progress in specific literacy components. Building on the lessons in Chapter 1, this chapter features 10 comprehensive strategy lessons that are relevant in the middle of the year of students' literacy journey. Each lesson spirals from the literacy enhancers (Standards/literacy strategies) featured in Chapter 1.

Chapter 3: Ending the Year Literacy Strong. The introduction highlights the importance of stepping up and finishing not with a slow glide but with a strong climb, giving educators the endurance to stay focused on learning right through the end of the school year. This chapter provides practical ways to be intentional, with appropriate intensity levels that allow literacy goals to be achieved. Also, this chapter reminds educators of the influence that they have acquired as literacy leaders in their classrooms and how to use their influential stance to end the year literacy strong. Ten comprehensive strategy lessons that are relevant to skills acquired by the end of the year highlight the academic vocabulary from previous seasons of the school year found in Chapters 1 and 2.

Chapter 4: Stopping the Summer Slide. The introduction shares the importance of progressing literacy through the summer months. The focus is on continued reinforcement of the literacy strategies from the school year and on reading for pleasure, emphasizing summer reading lists, roles and responsibilities, and continued goal setting as students prepare for their next year's adventure. An extended summer break presents a unique challenge for educators and learners. The 10 comprehensive strategy lessons provide an independent and possibly tutorial learning environment. Each lesson continues to build on the key academic vocabulary within the standards featured in Chapters 1–3.

Literacy Strong All Year Long: Spiraling to Success

We designed the interactive literacy lessons in this book to support you as you guide students throughout the seasons of the school year. When you put literacy at the heart of your classroom, students benefit from a strong foundation and joyfully engage in higher levels of reading and learning. For a quick look at all the lessons in this book, refer to Figure 1, which lists Reading Component Strands, Literacy Strategy Strands, and lesson titles. The chart on the next page will be beneficial as you plan throughout the school year.

FIGURE 1

40 Lessons at a Glance

Reading Component Strand	Literacy Strategy Strand	Chapter 1 Lesson	Chapter 2 Lesson	Chapter 3 Lesson	Chapter 4 Lesson
Phonological awareness and phonics	Isolating and identifying sounds	Need to Know Names	Mingle and Jingle with Vowels	Digraph Hero Teams	I Spy! Capturing Sounds
Phonological awareness and phonics	Blending and segmenting	The Blending Dance	Making Word Smoothies	The Blend Factor	The Sweet Blend of Sounds
Phonics	Decoding	Vowel Changers	Vowel Transformers	Fixated on Prefixes: Divide and Conquer	Working Words Weekly Summer Plan
Fluency	Phrasing	Phrase Scavenger Hunt	Performing Poetry	Text Road Signs: Marking Phrase Boundaries	Weekly Summer Poetry Reading
Comprehension: Craft and Structure	Previewing	Sneak and See 1-2-3	Is It Make-Believe or Real?	We're Going on a Text Trip	Text Trip Travels
Comprehension: Key ideas and details	Determining importance and summarizing	Retell Recipe	Sifting Details	Finding the Topic: It's a Snap!	Home Run with Details
Comprehension: Key ideas and details	Questioning for close reading	The Who, What, Where, When Show	The Question Game	Question the Character	My Question, Your Question!
Vocabulary	Associating words	Up and Down with Opposites!	Meaning Madness Time: What Else Does It Mean?	Shades of Meaning	Describe It in Five!
Vocabulary	Analyzing words	We're Going on a Word Hunt: Nouns and Verbs	Oh, A-Hunting We Will Go: The Path to Plurals	Hunting to Position Prepositions and Verify Verbs	Literary Scrapbooks: From Parts of Speech to a Whole Picture of a Text
Motivation	Motivating readers	Take Off with Reading! Class Book Club	Take Off and Partner Book Talks	Ready, Set, Read!	Splash into Summer Reading!

1

Starting the Year Literacy Strong

Believe you can and you are halfway there.
–Theodore Roosevelt

It is the supreme art of the teacher to awaken joy in creative expression and knowledge.
–Albert Einstein

What is your favorite symbol or sign of the start of school? Maybe it is the aroma of freshly sharpened pencils lined up neatly for crafting creative stories and adventures. Perhaps you love brand-new crayons not yet broken or worn, ready for small hands to grasp and enjoy. Or maybe you can hardly wait to reveal your cozy classroom library, complete with colorful carpet, comfy beanbags, and bins full of wonderful new books that you've collected for your budding readers. Besides creating an inviting learning environment at the beginning of school, classroom management experts Harry Wong and Rosemary Wong (2009) advise teaching the behaviors you expect from your students. They suggest modeling everything from lining up to routines for listening to read-alouds or visiting the classroom library. Ensure success as you set up your classroom, establish routines, and start the year strong with the engaging lessons in this chapter. But first, let's look at some literacy-strong classrooms.

Literacy-Strong Classroom Scenarios

What does a literacy-strong classroom look like at the beginning of the year? The words that come to mind include *child-centered*, *interactive*, *imaginative*, and *joyful*. Here are some classroom stories to inspire you for the first few weeks of school.

Vocabulary: Word Hunt

The students join in as Mr. Fender leads them in a fun and rousing rendition of the familiar chant "We Are Going on a Bear Hunt," with the lyrics replaced to reflect a word hunt. "Can't go over it, can't go under it, gotta read through it," chant the eager hunters as they all point to the word *mink* from the text *A Mink, a Fink, a Skating Rink: What Is a Noun?* by Brian P. Cleary. The class continues to hunt for nouns in other texts as Mr. Fender records their responses on an alphabox. Students sketch drawings of their finds to share. The initial hunt sparks an interest in fearless strategies for figuring out words all year long!

Motivation: Reading Book Club

Miss Jimenez invites her new students to gather on the rug for a read-aloud. She holds up a colorful gift bag and reveals the contents one at a time: toy vehicles, including a car, an airplane, and a train. "We will travel all over the world when we read books even though we are right here in the classroom," she says to entice the class. After brainstorming rules for listening to read-alouds with students, Miss Jimenez passes out class book club tickets. She winks as she invites the students to buckle pretend seatbelts as they "take off" to read their first set of read-aloud books together plus *It's Back to School We Go! First Day Stories from Around the World* by Ellen Jackson and *School Around the World* by Dona Herweck Rice. The class chimes in as Miss Jimenez records the titles of the read-alouds on the class book log. Students share their reactions to the books with text evidence and a thumbs-up for the parts of the text that they enjoyed the most.

Comprehension: The Question Song

Inquiring students chime in to sing verses of "The Question Song" as they listen to their teacher, Mr. Thomas, read aloud from the text *Quentin Quokka's Quick Questions* by Barbara deRubertis. Mr. Thomas holds up a plastic microphone to represent the strategy of questioning throughout reading and asks the class to be on the lookout for questions. Every few pages, he pauses to provide a question prompt and invite partners to pose questions, using their fists as pretend microphones. The class rereads the book for the Read It Three Times Challenge, with each rereading focused on a different question word. Throughout the first reread, students pause to ask a partner questions that begin with *who*. During the second reading, students pose *what* questions throughout. In the final reading, students take turns borrowing the microphone to ask the class a thought-provoking "Why do you think . . . ?" question.

Addressing Beginning-of-Year Challenges

Amid the excitement of the new school year, educators face many competing challenges. Three tasks that teachers need to tackle almost simultaneously are (1) getting to know students and their families and connect with them individually and as a community, (2) gathering and understanding baseline assessment information for each student, and (3) establishing management procedures and routines. In this section are some suggestions for facing these challenges head-on to set the stage for literacy growth.

Questions Teachers Ask to Address Beginning-of-the-Year Challenges

- What are the most essential literacy routines that I need to begin in my classroom?
- What are some ways to successfully train students in literacy routines?
- How do I keep track of student progress?
- How can I actively engage students in lessons?
- How can I establish a rapport with each of my students and their families?
- How do I build a sense of community in my comprehensive literacy classroom?

Essential Strategies for Starting Literacy Strong

1. **Spark the Love of Reading**

   Start the year by showing students how much you love reading. They will be inspired by your enthusiasm when you share one of your favorite books. Primary teacher Amanda Cleary brings in a childhood favorite of hers to read aloud to her students: *Amanda's First Day of School* by Joan E. Goodman. The students enjoy hearing that it was her favorite book as a child and that she has read it over 100 times. You can use read-alouds to calm first-day nervousness. The book *First Day Jitters* by Julie Danneberg is a wonderful choice for this purpose. Sharing titles that you clearly enjoy will inspire your students and set the tone for reading in your classroom, and read-alouds create a positively reinforced environment and a sense of community.

2. **Model Procedures and Literacy Routines for a Well-Run Classroom**

   Every single positive behavior that you want from your students needs to be modeled and taught at the start of school. Students also need to know exactly what is expected of them during classroom literacy routines that include procedures for read-alouds, independent reading, workstations, writers' workshop, and partner reading. Explain, model, and guide routines. Although it may take a bit longer to roll out all the necessary steps by modeling and discussing each one, the payoff is that students actually internalize and use the procedure (McEwan-Adkins, 2012). Spend about 10 minutes each day of the first few weeks of school modeling how to participate in literacy routines (Reutzel & Clark, 2011). You may also want to include photos of students engaged in centers or routines to help your class remember the procedures.

To establish a procedure in your classroom, follow these steps:
- Explain why the procedure is important.
- Demonstrate by role-playing how to perform the procedure properly.
- Invite a student to act out the steps of the procedure in front of the class.
- Guide as the class practices.
- Record the procedure (e.g., for listening to read-alouds) on a chart.
- Refer and return to the chart often to discuss and reflect on how well the class is following the steps.

3. **Make Read-Alouds Interactive**

Use a variety of engagement strategies during read-alouds to actively involve students and improve their reading comprehension.
- *Turn and talk:* Students turn to a partner and take turns responding throughout the read-aloud. To ensure success, provide a sentence stem, such as "My favorite part was____ because____," or "I think____ will happen next because____." Encourage students to use text evidence.
- *Act up:* Pause often and encourage students to use gestures and act out various parts of the reading and vocabulary words.
- *Sketch it:* Provide slates or strips of paper and pause during read-alouds to invite students to sketch what has happened so far in the reading or something that they learned from the text. Encourage students to share their responses with partners and the class.

4. **Grow Independent Readers**

Provide a classroom environment that encourages independent reading at various times throughout the day using a variety of texts. Model how to read independently and build stamina by setting a timer, starting with 5 minutes and eventually building up to 15 minutes. Provide an accessible place for your primary students to stash their personal reading pile of three to five titles, in a box or a bin, on desks, or perhaps in a pack on the back of students' chairs. Donalyn Miller (2009), author of *The Book Whisperer: Awakening the Inner Reader in Every Child*, suggests starting the day with independent reading for 5 to 10 minutes instead of other sorts of warm-up activities.

5. Create a Classroom Library

Set apart an inviting classroom library space that includes at least 10 books per student or 200–300 books (Reutzel & Fawson, 2002). Organize books in baskets or tubs and clearly mark your classroom reading materials by genre, authors, themes, and topics that interest the age group you teach. Display some books with the covers facing out in stands or on shelves. Include a mix of narrative and informational texts. Provide some bins marked by reading levels but don't limit students to their own reading level. Encourage them to keep track of their reading with reading logs. Model by recording class read-alouds on a class reading log.

6. Build a Community with Singing, Poetry, and Chants

Children love the rhythm, rhyme, and repetition that songs, poems, and chants offer. Throughout the first days and weeks of school, display your choice of any poem or song and return to it several times during the day. Use the chants and songs included in the lessons in this book not only to teach the lessons but also to build community with your class. Start a collection of poems, songs, and chants for each student in a notebook so students can return to the familiar favorites for repeated readings.

7. Construct "Getting to Know You" Artistic Projects

Children enjoy sharing information about themselves through artistic expression. Using alliterations, artistic expressions, and even drama can highlight uniqueness while building rapport and unity in the classroom. Try one of these strategies to get to know your students and to build community:

- *Thumbs-up art project:* Set up a thumbprint station where students each make a thumbprint to form a tree or a garden of flowers. Tell students that together they are a team.
- *ABC class name quilt:* Students create an alliteration based on their name and something about themselves on the appropriate ABC puzzle quilt piece to form a class quilt.
- *Character charades:* Students act out their favorite animals, movies, activities, or book characters while the class tries to guess the answer. Once the class has guessed correctly, the student can share why the chosen subject is her favorite, giving the class insight into the student's preferences.

8. Establish Informal and Formative Assessment Procedures

We teach in an assessment-crazed world. The pressure to measure student performance is everywhere. Your school district likely requires tools such as beginning-of-year baseline assessments, ongoing assessments, and formal and informal district, state, and national tests. Planning assessment procedures is part of establishing purposeful literacy routines toward successful instruction.

Determine what type of assessment is best for your classroom needs. Schedule time early in the beginning of the school year to assess. Establish a record-keeping system (e.g., assessment folder, digital file, composition notebook). Throughout the year, you'll also want to keep track of and monitor students' learning progress. The information you gain from these formative assessments is helpful in planning your instruction. One informal assessment method is quick clipboard cruising. By taking quick notes during individual conferences, you can measure how students are doing. Create an on-the-spot running record (Clay, 2000) simply by having individual students read aloud while you note the words they substitute (e.g., saying *home* when the text reads *house*). Record self-corrections as well. Look for patterns and overall comprehension. Ask the following questions when talking to students about the books they are reading (Routman, 2003):

- What are you reading?
- Why did you pick this book?
- Who are the main characters? (fiction)
- What is the problem in the story? (fiction)
- What are your favorite parts, and why?
- What is interesting, and why? (nonfiction)
- What do you want to learn? What are you learning? (nonfiction)

9. Make Parents and Families Partners from the Start

Instead of waiting until a problem arises, call or email parents to say hello. Share one compliment about their child that you can offer based on what you've seen so far. Ask the parents to share something positive about their child that you should know. Set up a videoconference with busy parents who can't make it to the classroom. You can also set up a digital portfolio and send periodic video feeds of their child learning in action. Include a list of popular read-aloud books that parents can use to motivate their child to read:

- *First Day Jitters* by Julie Danneberg
- *Brand-New Pencils, Brand-New Books* by Diane deGroat
- *Amanda's First Day of School* by Joan E. Goodman
- *Wemberly Worried* by Kevin Henkes
- *It's Back to School We Go! First Day Stories from Around the World* by Ellen Jackson
- *It's Time for School, Stinky Face* by Lisa McCourt
- *David Goes to School* by David Shannon

- *Born to Read* by Judy Sierra
- *How Do Dinosaurs Go to School?* by Jane Yolen

Overview of Chapter 1 Lessons

Lesson 1. Phonological Awareness and Phonics: Isolating and Identifying Sounds—Need to Know Names

Lesson 2. Phonological Awareness and Phonics: Blending and Segmenting—The Blending Dance

Lesson 3. Phonics: Decoding—Vowel Changers

Lesson 4. Fluency: Phrasing—Phrase Scavenger Hunt

Lesson 5. Comprehension: Craft and Structure—Previewing—Sneak and See 1-2-3

Lesson 6. Comprehension: Key Ideas and Details—Determining Importance and Summarizing—Retell Recipe

Lesson 7. Comprehension: Key Ideas and Details—Questioning for Close Reading—The Who, What, Where, When Show

Lesson 8. Vocabulary: Associating Words—Up and Down with Opposites!

Lesson 9. Vocabulary: Analyzing Words—We're Going on a Word Hunt: Nouns and Verbs

Lesson 10. Motivation: Motivating Readers—Take Off with Reading! Class Book Club

LESSON 1. PHONOLOGICAL AWARENESS AND PHONICS: ISOLATING AND IDENTIFYING SOUNDS

Title NEED TO KNOW NAMES

Trailer Same sounds sound similar, and alliteration is an alluring way for engaging listeners to recognize and isolate initial phonemes (the smallest unit of sound) in the beginning of a series of words. Alliterative language can have rhythm and become fun tongue twisters. Students practice isolating and identifying sounds as they jump, hop, and reflect, using a mirror to view themselves making initial sounds through this alliteration lesson.

Literacy Enhancer Phonological Awareness and Phonics: Isolating and Identifying Sounds—Initial and Final Consonants, Alliteration

Key Academic Vocabulary

Alliteration: A figure of speech in which a series of words repeat the same initial sound

Isolate: To separate sounds from other sounds in a word

Phoneme: The smallest unit of sound

Learning Objectives

- Isolate and identify initial and final sounds by positioning the mouth, lips, jaw, and tongue to correspond with appropriate single-syllable words.
- Identify the initial sound in a word and pronounce additional words that begin with the same sound to create alliteration.

Essential Questions

- How do you position your mouth for the beginning sound in _____?
- What initial sound do you hear at the beginning of the word _____?
- What other words start with the same sound as the word _____?

STEP 1: PREPARATION

Organize Materials

- Jump rope
- Handheld mirrors
- Multimodal text sets with alliteration
- *Alliteration Picture Cards* reproducible (one copy of each card)
- *Need to Know Names* reproducible (copies or enlarged for display)
- Literacy notebooks

STEP 2: INITIATION

Jingle and Jump with Words

Begin to jump rope while saying or chanting a tongue twister. You can use a book for quick jingle references to highlight alliterations. Ask students to share how the words in the jump-rope jingle connect. Share that you are using alliteration to create rhythm and draw attention to the initial sounds in a series of words that have the same beginning sounds. Continue with a few more tongue twisters and ask students to repeat the alliterations as they jump to the rhythm and beat of the words.

STEP 3: DEMONSTRATION

Using Names for Alliteration

1. Read aloud an alliteration or from an alliteration literature book (e.g., *A, My Name Is . . .* by Alice Lyne). Emphasize the initial sound of each word in the alliteration by slightly changing your voice.
2. Pick up a handheld mirror and create an alliteration using two names that begin with the initial sound of a student in your class. Say the alliteration slowly (e.g., "Nick needs nickels for Nancy's nuts"). Note the position of your mouth as you isolate the beginning sound of each word. Describe the position of your mouth for the initial sound (e.g., "I can see my teeth. I feel like I am smiling a little. My tongue is lifted and touching the top of my mouth").
3. Using the jump rope, repeat the alliteration and jump at each of the words. Say the two names from the alliteration again. Ask if there is anyone in the class whose name also has the same initial sound.
4. Have a student with a name that has the same initial sound be the example alliteration jumper. Ask the student to use the jump rope to jump the two names from the alliteration and then add his name on the third jump (e.g., "Nick, Nancy, Nate").
5. Have the other students stand up and jump any other word they can think of that begins with the same initial sound. Continue with a few more alliterative sentences that you create to emphasize and connect names with students from your class. Have the highlighted students use the mirror to model the initial sound and describe the necessary mouth positions.
6. Create an alliteration anchor chart. Note that alliterative words do not always have the same letter or letters but always have the same isolated initial sound.

STEP 4: COLLABORATION

Have students work in groups to think of storybook or movie characters who have the same initial sound as each name in the group (e.g., Darian = Dorothy from *The Wonderful Wizard of Oz* by L. Frank Baum; Gregg = Grinch from *How the Grinch Stole Christmas* by Dr. Seuss). Have the teams engage in conversational coaching by asking students to create or read an alliteration and discuss the broader concept: "Listen to these names and words. What do they all have in common? How do you position your mouth for the beginning sound in these names and words?"

STEP 5: APPLICATION

Have each student complete the *Need to Know Names* reproducible (Figure 1.1) for a class alliteration name book or word wall. Remind students to use the class anchor chart about alliterations. After they complete the alliteration name book or word wall, have students practice initial sounds using handheld mirrors to see and describe the positioning of their mouth for each word in the set of alliterative words.

STEP 6: REFLECTION

Oral or Written Response

In their literacy notebooks, have students independently create their own alliterations. Ask them to respond to these questions orally or in writing:

- How are all the words in your alliteration alike?
- How do you position your mouth for the initial sound in each of these words?

ADAPTATION AND EXTENSION

- Have students think about how they are like or different from the characters that their names aligned with in step 5 (e.g., "I am Darian. Darian and Dorothy both have the same beginning sounds. I am like Dorothy because we both are courageous"). Use your alliterative sentences to help students notice and isolate the initial and final sounds in words.
- Write a short alliteration poem with students that contains a targeted sound.
- Rewrite a familiar short story by adding alliterations.
- *English Language Learner Suggestion:* Create a sound wall with picture cards organized by various initial sounds associated with words. Or, create an ABC Alliteration class book using the suggested sentence stems. Have students work with partners to think of a name that begins with the same initial sound as the action words highlighted and then have them think of a final word that would make sense and complete the alliteration phrase or sentence:

A = Annie ate an_____.
B = Bob bounces a_____.
C = Carlos cooks_____.
D = Darian draws_____.
E = Elijah eats_____.
F = Frank finds_____.
G = Gabby grows_____.
H = Harper hears_____.
I = Isabel invites_____.
J = Jacey joins_____.
K = Kayla kicks_____.
L = Lori loves_____.
M = Mariah makes_____.

N = Nick notices_____.
O = Opal owns_____.
P = Paul pushes_____.
Q = Quin quits_____.
R = Rachael reads_____.
S = Sarah sings_____.
T = Tim takes_____.
U = Uma ushers_____.
V = Valerie visits_____.
W = Wyatt weighs_____.
X = Xavier examines_____.
Y = Yvonne yells_____.
Z = Zack zips_____.

- *Struggling Reader Suggestion:* Use the *Alliteration Picture Cards* reproducible (Figure 1.2) or objects that all begin with the same initial sounds as anchor images for the alliteration concept. An interactive whiteboard can also be used for students to match the initial and final sounds as they view various picture cards of words with similar sounds.

EVALUATION

"I Can . . ." Statements

- I can identify the initial sound in words.
- I can isolate the initial and final sounds in words.
- I can describe the position of my mouth for a certain sound within a series of words that have the same initial sounds.

BEHAVIOR INDICATORS

- Isolates and identifies initial sounds by positioning the mouth, lips, jaw, and tongue to correspond with appropriate single-syllable words.
- Compares the beginning sounds in words and determines if they make an alliteration.
- Identifies the initial sound in a word and pronounces additional words that begin with the same sound to create a series of words that have the same initial sound to form an alliteration phrase or sentence.

FIGURE 1.1
Need to Know Names

Directions: Write your name on the line provided. Isolate the initial sound in your first name by writing the letter(s) that represent it in the box. This sound, when matched with other words that begin with the same sound, becomes an alliteration. Using the rest of the page, create and write words and images with that same sound. Using your name and two words that begin with the same sound, form a sentence using alliteration and record it below.

Name: _____

Initial sound:

_____

Ch   K   L   Tr   N

My alliteration sentence: _____

_____

_____

_____

_____

Source: Literacy Strong All Year Long: Powerful Lessons for Grades K–2 by Valerie Ellery, Lori Oczkus, and Timothy V. Rasinski. © 2020 ASCD. Readers may duplicate this figure for noncommercial use within their school.

Starting the Year Literacy Strong 13

FIGURE 1.2
Alliteration Picture Cards

Note: These are the words by row: *ball, bat, bounce; car, cat, catch; dance, dirt, dog.*

Source: Literacy Strong All Year Long: Powerful Lessons for Grades K–2 by Valerie Ellery, Lori Oczkus, and Timothy V. Rasinski. © 2020 ASCD. Readers may duplicate this figure for noncommercial use within their school.

LESSON 2. PHONOLOGICAL AWARENESS AND PHONICS: BLENDING AND SEGMENTING

Title THE BLENDING DANCE

Trailer Stomp, stomp! Clap and slide to the side! Reading has rhythm. Blending sounds can represent that rhythm when students learn to combine sounds to form words. Readers practice blending an onset and rimes together as they stomp, hop, clap, and slide through this lesson.

Literacy Enhancer Phonological Awareness and Phonics: Blending and Segmenting

Key Academic Vocabulary

Blending: Combining a sequence of two or more sounds to form a word

Onset: The part of a syllable before the vowel; not all syllables have onsets

Rime: The part of a syllable beginning with the sounded vowel and any consonants that follow

Learning Objectives

- Hear sounds and blend the onset and rimes of single-syllable spoken words together to make meaningful words.
- Substitute onsets and combine with the rime to produce new words.

Essential Questions

- What happens when you blend a sequence of sounds together?
- How can you create new words from an onset and rimes?

STEP 1: PREPARATION

Organize Materials

- Two hula hoops, each a different color
- A stack of index cards, each with an onset (e.g., /b/,/h/, /l/) or rime (e.g., /ike/) written on it
- Small, round plastic bracelets
- Multimodal text set for the topic of study
- *Blending Dance* reproducible (copies or enlarged for display)
- Literacy notebooks

STEP 2: INITIATION

If You're Happy and You Know It

Begin to sing the "If You're Happy and You Know It" song and have students sing along and participate by clapping their hands and making the various body movements. Then, share that you are going to change the words up but keep the same tune. Begin to sing the new version's lyrics (adapted from Yopp & Yopp, 2011), explaining to students what they will be doing (e.g., clapping, stopping) after they hear you segment a word by its sounds (post the new lyrics so they can follow along):

> If you think you know this word, stomp your feet (stomp, stomp).
>
> If you think you know this word, clap your hands (clap, clap).
>
> If you think you know this word, then tell us what you heard.
>
> If you think you know this word, stomp your feet (stomp, stomp) and clap your hands (clap, clap).

Segment the word *bat* by onset and rime: /b/ /at/. Model for students by stomping one foot and saying the onset (/b/). Next, stomp the other foot and say the rime (/at/). Then, clap your hands as you combine the onset and rime into the word (*bat*). Continue with other onset and rime/word family examples.

STEP 3: DEMONSTRATION

So You Think You Can Blend

1. Place two different-colored hula hoops on the floor.
2. For the read-aloud, select a text that focuses on onsets and rimes (e.g., *Ook the Book* by Lissa Rovetch, *Boo to a Goose* by Mem Fox, *Hop on Pop* by Dr. Seuss, *Sheep in a Jeep* by Nancy Shaw).
3. In the read-aloud, each time you get to an onset/rime word, stop and hop in the first hula hoop and say the onset as you stomp your right foot. Next, hop into the other hula hoop and say the rime as you stomp your left foot. Finally, hop out of the hula hoop and slide to the side as you blend the onset and rime, and then clap your hands together to form the word.
4. Place a stack of index cards with a variety of onsets (e.g., /b/, /h/, /l/) inside the first hula hoop. In the second one, place a rime (e.g., /ike/) index card.
5. Hop into the first hula hoop and select an onset card. Produce the sound as you stomp and hop into the second hula hoop holding the onset card. Pick up the rime card and say the rime sound with a stomp.

6. Step out of the second hula hoop and make a dip-and-slide motion as you glide your legs together and blend the onset and rime sounds together. Record the newly formed word on a class chart or place the onset card next to the rime card in a pocket chart and then write the complete word on a new index card.
7. Ask for a student volunteer who would like to hop, stomp, and slide into a word. Have that student come to the hula hoops and ask him or her, "So, do you think you can blend?"
8. Continue to have other students demonstrate blending in front of the class, each time keeping the rime the same but changing out the onset as they blend new words. Add the new words to the class chart.
9. After several students have blended various onset cards to the rime, ask the class, "What do you notice about all these words?" Discuss how you changed the onset to form a completely different word.
10. Revisit a text, noting words that change the onset and have created new words with the rime provided.

STEP 4: COLLABORATION

Conversational Coaching

Engage in conversational coaching by asking students to discuss the following questions with diverse partners:

- How do you blend sounds?
- What pattern do you notice in the words?
- How are these two words similar and different?
- What happens when you change the onset of the word?

STEP 5: APPLICATION

The Blending Dance

Pass out two small, round, plastic bracelets to partners or small groups. Have them use the words from the class chart to practice blending the onset and rime. The students use their fingers to do the blending dance. Have them point to the first small "hoop" (bracelet) and tap their index finger as they say the onset. Then, with their middle finger, have them tap and say the rime in the second bracelet. As they blend the onset and rime, have them glide their fingers together. They can record their newly formed words on the *Blending Dance* reproducible (Figure 1.3).

STEP 6: REFLECTION

Oral and Written Response

In their literacy notebooks, have students independently create their own *Blending Dance* graphic organizer to compile a list of onset and rime words. Have them respond to these essential questions orally or in writing:

- What happens when you blend the sequence of onset and rime sounds?
- How can you create new words from an onset and rimes?

ADAPTATION AND EXTENSION

- Create a word wall with words organized by various word families/rimes.
- Write a short poem with students that contains a targeted rime.
- *English Language Learner Suggestion:* Demonstrate the correct position of the mouth for each onset and rime. Have the students feel the position of their mouth as they form each onset and rime. Have them notice that their mouth changes position only for the onset sound.
- *Struggling Reader Suggestion:* Use an interactive whiteboard for students to match the onset and rimes as they blend new words. Display this chant: "If I know [rime] in [blended word], then I can know [new word that matches rime]." Have students continue by explaining how they can make a new word. Have picture examples with letter cards to match their onsets and rime (e.g., h-at, c-at, b-at; n-ap, m-ap, l-ap; s-ad, m-ad, d-ad).

EVALUATION

"I Can . . ." Statements

- I can blend and segment an onset and a rime to form a word.
- I can identify an onset and the rime in a given word.
- I can generate a new word by changing the onset of a word.

BEHAVIOR INDICATORS

- Listens to a sequence of sounds (onsets and rimes) of single-syllable words and combines them to form the word.
- Identifies the onset and rime in a word.
- Substitutes the onset or rime in a word to form a new word.

FIGURE 1.3
Blending Dance

Step 1: The onset tap	Step 2: The rime tap	Step 3: The blend slide	The word
○	○	 💃	___
Step 1: The onset tap	Step 2: The rime tap	Step 3: The blend slide	The word
○	○	 💃	___
Step 1: The onset tap	Step 2: The rime tap	Step 3: The blend slide	The word
○	○	 💃	___
Step 1: The onset tap	Step 2: The rime tap	Step 3: The blend slide	The word
○	○	 💃	___

Source: Literacy Strong All Year Long: Powerful Lessons for Grades K–2 by Valerie Ellery, Lori Oczkus, and Timothy V. Rasinski. © 2020 ASCD. Readers may duplicate this figure for noncommercial use within their school.

LESSON 3. PHONICS: DECODING

Title VOWEL CHANGERS

Trailer Squid, octopuses, and cuttlefish are among the few animals in the world that can change colors to match their surroundings. Vowels are similar, in that they can change their sounds as they move from one linguistic environment to another. Knowing the five short-vowel sounds and the basic consonant-vowel-consonant (CVC) pattern, students can read and spell a plethora of words that they will practice decoding and encoding according to the context of the text environment.

Literacy Enhancer Phonics: Decoding—Short Vowels and CVC Pattern

Key Academic Vocabulary

Decode: The ability to apply letter-sound relationships to read and pronounce a written word

Encode: The ability to spell words by converting letter-sound relationships into written words

Grapheme: The written symbol (letters) used to represent a phoneme (sounds)

Short vowels: The letters *a, e, i, o, u,* and sometimes *y*; short vowels make a speech sound produced without obstructing the flow of air from the lungs; do not make the sound of the letter name

Vowel: A speech sound produced without obstructing the flow of air from the lungs; the letters *a, e, i, o, u,* and sometimes *y* in written form

Learning Objectives

- Associate the short-vowel sounds with the common spellings (graphemes) for the five major vowels.
- Decode CVC words and distinguish the short-vowel sounds in written one-syllable CVC words.

Essential Questions

- Why is letter-sound correspondence important in reading and writing?
- What other words have the same short vowel as the word _____?

STEP 1: PREPARATION

Organize Materials

- Pictures or media clips of squids, octopuses, or other animals that change colors
- Wikki Stix waxed yarn

- Chart paper
- Bowl of magnetic alphabet letters
- Cans of shaving cream or whipped cream or small buckets of sand
- Multimodal text sets with short-vowel words and CVC pattern words
- *Vowel Picture Cards* reproducible (copies or enlarged for display)
- *Where Is Short Vowel?* reproducible (copies or enlarged for display)
- *If/Then Word Family Chart* reproducible (copies or enlarged for display)
- Literacy notebooks

STEP 2: INITIATION

Environmental Change

Ask students what squid, octopuses, and cuttlefish have in common. Explain that all three of these animals can change their colors to match their surroundings. Display various media clips or pictures of animals that can change their skin tones to match their environment. Invite students to think about ways vowels are like these creatures and share that they are going to find out how. Tell students that the vowels in today's lesson can glide in between two consonants and make a short sound. Some of these vowels even completely change their sound to make a new word according to their surroundings in an oral or written environment.

STEP 3: DEMONSTRATION

Where Is Short Vowel?

1. Introduce the five vowels using the *Vowel Picture Cards* reproducible (Figure 1.4). Begin to sing "Where Is Short Vowel?" from the reproducible in Figure 1.5 using one of the selected vowels. Ask students to listen and think about what most of the words in the song have in common (e.g., short-*a* sound). Display the chosen verse from the song along with the aligned vowel picture card.

2. Use a waxed yarn stick to create a lasso to frame out the short vowels in the verse. Lasso a word that has a CVC pattern and note the pattern in the word. Begin to create a word family list using the featured vowel and final consonant from the lassoed word (e.g., *-at* from *cat*, *-ed* from *bed*, *-it* from *bit*, *-op* from *top*, *-up* from *cup*) as the anchor.

3. Demonstrate how you can change the initial sound to create different words by writing the words *if/then* or using the *If/Then Word Family Chart* reproducible (Figure. 1.6). Point to the word *if* and say, "*If* I know how to read and write the word *fat*, [point to the word *then*] *then* I can read and write the word *hat*." Ask students to turn to a partner and tell how the new word was made.

4. Select a couple of student volunteers to come up and reach into a bowl of pre-selected magnetic alphabet letters. According to the word patterns that you are working with, have students identify the consonant they pull out and continue to add to the *If/Then Word Family Chart* by saying, "*If* I know how to read and write the word _____, *then* I can read and write the word _____."

5. Demonstrate how you can also make new words by keeping the initial and final consonants the same and changing only the vowel in the middle. Select one of the words from the *If/Then Word Family Chart* and model changing the vowel sound to create real words and nonsense words. Start by identifying the vowel in the chosen CVC word from the chart and then point to each of the vowel picture cards and change the vowel sound to correspond to each new word you make. Each time stop to ask students, "Think about the new word. Does this new vowel sound in the middle of the two consonants make a real or nonsense word?"

6. Use one of the newly formed words to substitute in "Where Is Short Vowel?" by rereading the verse of the song and changing an appropriate word to the newly formed word. For example, if you change *cat* to use the short *u* (*cut*), then you would read it like this: "I am a *fat cut*, who naps on a flat mat." Ask students if the sentence makes sense now. Explain how in the context of the sentence, the word *cut* does not make sense. Share how important it is for readers to attend to the surrounding text when decoding words to help them know the correct vowel that makes sense for that environment.

7. Create short-vowel anchor charts with words from the *If/Then Word Family Chart*. You can also use the vowel picture cards or objects for anchor images that all have the same short-vowel sounds.

STEP 4: COLLABORATION

Whipping Up Words and Conversational Coaching

Have students work in groups or with partners to make and break CVC words by changing the letter-sound relationships. Give each team a can of shaving cream or whipped cream or a small bucket of sand to use to write out words. Create a stack of CVC word cards from the class word family lists, omitting one letter on each card. The letter from the word can be the initial consonant, middle vowel, or final consonant. Invite students to spray a small amount of cream or pour some sand on their desks to create a smooth writing surface. Have them select a card from the stack and whip up the word, filling in the missing letter to form a complete CVC word. Have the other team members or partners suggest ways to create a word family from the newly formed word. Have the teams or partners engage in conversational coaching by describing the letter they inserted and why. Have students continue to discuss how they can decode CVC words and make new words from decoded words.

STEP 5: APPLICATION

If/Then Word Family Fun

Have each student complete an *If/Then Word Family Chart* reproducible. Remind them to use the class anchor charts and the words that they created while whipping up words during their small-group time. Have students read through poems and other texts to search and find CVC words that they can practice for continued application of decoding and encoding words.

STEP 6: REFLECTION

Oral or Written Response

In their literacy notebooks, have students independently create word family lists that correspond to words from a text that they are reading. Have students respond to these essential questions orally or in writing:

- Why is letter-sound correspondence important in reading and writing?
- What other words have the same short vowel as the word _____?

ADAPTATION AND EXTENSION

- Have students interact with the various CVC words by doing word sorts. Students can then create a short-vowel word wall with words categorized by short vowels.
- Find various songs about vowels and download them to sing in class (e.g., Jack Hartmann's "Hound Dog").
- Apply resources found online from Timothy Rasinski's work (see "Making and Writing Words": https://www.timrasinski.com/resources.html).
- *English Language Learner Suggestion:* Display pictures of short-vowel words that have the same initial and ending sounds (e.g., *cat, cut; bat, bit*). Have students listen as you say the name of each picture and then slowly segment the CVC sounds within the two pictures you are comparing. Ask, "Do these two pictures have the same meaning?" Explain how they are different and how changing the short-vowel sound in the middle of the word can create a new word. Say the names of the pictures again and have students listen and determine how they are alike (initial and ending sound) and how they are different (middle short-vowel sound).

- *Struggling Reader Suggestion:* Take and display a digital picture of the struggling reader's mouth in each of the short vowel positions for each sound. Note: These pictures can be printed or placed in a digital portfolio. Label each short-vowel photo with the corresponding short-vowel letter. Have the student hear a word and select which mouth photo best represents the position needed for the given word. Use words that have the same initial and final sounds and only a different vowel (e.g., *dog, dig, dug*). Discuss how it was the middle vowel sound that changed in each word presented.

EVALUATION

"I Can . . ." Statements

- I can identify short vowels in single-syllable words.
- I can change short-vowel sounds in single-syllable words to make new words.
- I can read CVC words.

BEHAVIOR INDICATORS

- Associates the short sounds with the common spellings (graphemes) for the five major vowels.
- Decodes regularly spelled, one-syllable CVC words.
- Distinguishes short vowels when reading regularly spelled, one-syllable words.

24　LITERACY STRONG ALL YEAR LONG

FIGURE 1.4
Vowel Picture Cards

 A	 E	 I	 O	 U

Source: Literacy Strong All Year Long: Powerful Lessons for Grades K–2 by Valerie Ellery, Lori Oczkus, and Timothy V. Rasinski. © 2020 ASCD. Readers may duplicate this figure for noncommercial use within their school.

FIGURE 1.5
Where Is Short Vowel?

Directions: Sing to the tune of "Are You Sleeping?"

Short *a*	Where is short *a*? Where is short *a*? Here I am. Here I am. I am in *fat cat*, who naps on a flat mat. ă ă ă, ă ă ă
Short *e*	Where is short *e*? Where is short *e*? Here I am. Here I am. I am in *Jed* and *Ted*, who rest on a red bed. ĕ ĕ ĕ, ĕ ĕ ĕ
Short *i*	Where is short *i*? Where is short *i*? Here I am. Here I am. I am in *Kim* and *Tim*, who sit a bit while Jim swims. ĭ ĭ ĭ, ĭ ĭ ĭ
Short *o*	Where is short *o*? Where is short *o*? Here I am. Here I am. I am in *top cop*, who stops and shops for a pop. ŏ ŏ ŏ, ŏ ŏ ŏ
Short *u*	Where is short *u*? Where is short *u*? Here I am. Here I am. I am in *pug bug*, who chugs a mug and a jug. ŭ ŭ ŭ, ŭ ŭ ŭ

Source: Literacy Strong All Year Long: Powerful Lessons for Grades K–2 by Valerie Ellery, Lori Oczkus, and Timothy V. Rasinski. © 2020 ASCD. Readers may duplicate this figure for noncommercial use within their school.

FIGURE 1.6
If/Then Word Family Chart

If I can read and write	and replace a vowel in the consonant-vowel-consonant pattern	then I can read and write.
Example: $c + a + t = cat$	u	$c + u + t = cut$
___ + ___ + ___ = ___	___	___ + ___ + ___ = ___
___ + ___ + ___ = ___	___	___ + ___ + ___ = ___
___ + ___ + ___ = ___	___	___ + ___ + ___ = ___
___ + ___ + ___ = ___	___	___ + ___ + ___ = ___
___ + ___ + ___ = ___	___	___ + ___ + ___ = ___

Source: Literacy Strong All Year Long: Powerful Lessons for Grades K–2 by Valerie Ellery, Lori Oczkus, and Timothy V. Rasinski. © 2020 ASCD. Readers may duplicate this figure for noncommercial use within their school.

LESSON 4. FLUENCY: PHRASING

Title PHRASE SCAVENGER HUNT

Trailer Scavenger hunts are great fun! During a hunt, children search for specific items in their environment. A critical aspect of reading fluency is the ability to read in meaningful chunks. We often identify nonfluent readers by their word-by-word monotone and staccato reading. In this lesson, students' phrases are put on display so others are made more aware of the importance of phrasing while reading. Students are asked to search for interesting phrases, short sentences, or word chunks from texts in this lesson.

Literacy Enhancer Fluency: Phrasing—Chunking Texts into Meaningful Units and Punctuation

Key Academic Vocabulary

Comma: A punctuation mark used within a sentence to set off meaningful phrases or other meaningful chunks of text

Period: A punctuation mark used at the end of a sentence that is a statement

Phrase: A sequence of two or more words that form a meaningful unit, often preceded and followed by a brief pause when read orally

Punctuation: Marks in writing or printing that are used to separate meaningful elements and make the meaning of the text clear

Sentence: A unit of one or more words that expresses an independent statement, question, request, command, or exclamation

Learning Objectives

- Identify interesting phrases and sentences in texts that students encounter.
- Read phrases and sentences that students collect and are put on display in the classroom.

Essential Questions

- What is a phrase?
- What is a sentence?
- What do phrases and sentences do?
- Why is it important to read in phrases and sentences?

STEP 1: PREPARATION

Organize Materials

- Large magnifying glass
- Multimodal text set for the topic of study
- Chart paper
- *Phrase Scavenger Hunt* reproducible (copies or enlarged for display)
- Literacy notebooks

STEP 2: INITIATION

A-Hunting We Will Go

Hold up a large magnifying glass and share with the students that you are going to go on a scavenger hunt today in search of phrases in the text that help to make for a smooth reading journey. Discuss with students the nature of phrases and sentences. Help students understand that phrases and sentences are important units of meaning that they encounter when they read and that fluent readers read in phrases, whereas less fluent readers tend to read word by word. Use the magnifying glass to point out to students the phrase and sentence units in a text with which they are familiar, such as the Pledge of Allegiance.

STEP 3: DEMONSTRATION

Searching for Sentence Boundaries

1. Use the poem below or find a book that you intend to share with students as a read-aloud. Invite students to go on a listening scavenger hunt, in which they listen for proper phrasing while you read. Read aloud a few pages of the text fluently, exaggerating phrase and sentence boundaries.

   Poem: Begin the School Year Cool

   School, oh school, you are so cool.

   School, oh school, oh school,

   I'd be a fool if I didn't love school.

   Oh school, you are my jewel.

   (With phrase and sentence boundaries added:)

   School, oh school, / you are so cool. //

   School, oh school, oh school, //

   I'd be a fool / if I didn't love school. //

   Oh school, / you are my jewel. //

2. Discuss with students how your reading sounded. Were they able to note the phrase and sentence boundaries as you read?
3. Discuss how breaking the text into phrase and sentence units aided their comprehension of the passage.
4. Read the same passage to students word-by-word and monotonously.
5. Show students how punctuation helps readers break a text into sentences and phrases. Discuss the difference between periods and commas.
6. Discuss how the word-by-word reading affected students' enjoyment and comprehension of the text.

STEP 4: COLLABORATION

Phrase Partners and Conversational Coaching

Have students work in pairs to come up with at least three phrases or short sentences that they are aware of, find interesting, or can find in their reading materials. The pairs can record their phrase choices on the *Phrase Scavenger Hunt* reproducible (Figure 1.7). You can demonstrate some common phrases with which students are already familiar, such as the following:

- Good morning
- Once upon a time
- I pledge allegiance
- Brown bear, brown bear
- What do you see?
- I went walking

After students search for phrases, have them engage in conversational coaching to explain why they felt their selected phrases were interesting. As students call out, write their phrases and sentences on a sheet of chart paper or other classroom display and ask students to write them in their literacy notebooks.

STEP 5: APPLICATION

Rereading for Smooth, Fluent Flow

Over the next several days, invite students to chorally read the phrases and sentences they collected and that are on display in the classroom. Be sure to emphasize to students the importance of reading the phrases and sentences as chunks of text, not word by word. As students become more confident and competent in their reading of the phrases and sentences, invite pairs and individual students to read the display on their own.

STEP 6: REFLECTION

Written Response

After students have practiced reading the display of phrases and sentence over several days, ask them to write in their literacy notebooks about the importance of phrasing in their own reading. As students dictate their responses or write their comments on a sheet of chart paper or other form of classroom display, you may ask them to complete the following sentence stems:

- I think it is important to read in phrases because _____.
- Punctuation is important because _____.
- I think word-by-word reading _____.

ADAPTATION AND EXTENSION

- Over the next several days, continue to point out to students interesting phrases and sentences. Encourage students to find their own phrases and to add these to the classroom display.
- Read and discuss students' dictated responses from Step 6 with the class over several days. Encourage students to offer their own insights.
- Idiomatic expressions are usually in the form of phrases. Explore idiomatic phrases by using Amelia Bedelia books to practice phrasing.
- *English Language Learner Suggestion:* Draw students' attention to challenging words in the phrases they find (e.g., *pledge, allegiance*). Display these words on a word chart and have students keep them in their word journals. Regularly reinforce for them the pronunciation and meaning of these words.
- *Struggling Reader Suggestion:* Make and display a list of 10–20 phrases made up of high-frequency words (see www.timrasinski.com/presentations/fry_600_instant_phrases.pdf). Have students practice reading these chorally two or three times per day (e.g., during small-group instruction, before lunch, after lunch, before the end of the school day).

EVALUATION

"I Can . . ." Statements

- I can identify phrases and sentences when I read.
- I can read a text smoothly in phrases and sentences.
- I can describe what a period does and what I need to do when I encounter a period in a text.

- I can explain what a comma does and what I need to do when I encounter a comma in a text.

BEHAVIOR INDICATORS
- Identifies a phrase in written text.
- Identifies a sentence in written text.
- Provides a reasonable definition of a phrase in written text.
- Provides a reasonable definition of a sentence in written text.
- Identifies a period and its purpose in written text.
- Identifies a comma and its purpose in written text.
- Explains the importance of chunking text into phrases and sentences when reading.

FIGURE 1.7
Phrase Scavenger Hunt

Name: _____ Date: _____

Directions: Search for at least three phrases in your reading material. Record the phrases, where they are located, and why you chose these phrases in the table.

Phrase	Text title and page number	Reason for selection
1.		
2.		
3.		
4.		

Source: Literacy Strong All Year Long: Powerful Lessons for Grades K–2 by Valerie Ellery, Lori Oczkus, and Timothy V. Rasinski. © 2020 ASCD. Readers may duplicate this figure for noncommercial use within their school.

LESSON 5. COMPREHENSION: CRAFT AND STRUCTURE—PREVIEWING

Title SNEAK AND SEE 1-2-3

Trailer Who doesn't love a sneak preview to spark interest and curiosity? Students learn how to use "cover talk" as they explore the title, author, and illustrator and predict the book's contents. This lesson shows students that previewing is as easy as 1-2-3 when they use the information found on the cover of a book.

Literacy Enhancer Comprehension: Craft and Structure—Previewing and Text Cover Features

Key Academic Vocabulary

Author: The person who wrote the book

Back cover: The back of a book that often contains information about the book, author, and illustrator

Book cover: The front of a book that contains the title, author, and illustrator

Illustrator: The person who drew the pictures that go with the book's content

Photographer: The person who took the photos that go with the book's content

Predict: To use information from a text to infer what the text will be about or what a reader might learn from it

Text features: Parts of the text that support the reader in navigating through key characteristics of a text for locating and accessing meaning from the text (e.g., title, headings, photographs, bold words, maps)

Title: The name of the book, which usually tells what it is about or gives clues to the content

Learning Objectives

- Identify the title, author, and illustrator on the covers of a text.
- Evaluate and integrate cover information to begin to predict what the text is about.

Essential Questions

- What is the title of the text? Is there a subtitle?
- How does the title relate to the art on the cover?
- What does an author do? What does an illustrator do?
- How are an author's and an illustrator's jobs different?
- Do some authors illustrate their own books? Why?

STEP 1: PREPARATION

Organize Materials

- Multimodal text set for the topic of study
- *Sneak and See 1-2-3* reproducible (copies or enlarged for display)
- Literacy notebooks

STEP 2: INITIATION

Movie Previews

Ask students if they have ever seen a movie preview. Share examples of movies that your students will be familiar with. Mention the production company or an actor that students might be familiar with (e.g., "I see that this movie is produced by Disney, and I usually like Disney movies"; "I saw the first movie, and this is a sequel"). Ask students to turn and talk as they share movie trailers that they have seen. Say to students, "When you pick up a new book, you're also taking a sneak peek just like a movie preview as you see just enough information on the cover to get excited about the book title and the author who wrote it. Taking a sneak peek of the cover makes me want to see inside. I start to predict what the book may be about!"

STEP 3: DEMONSTRATION

Sneak and See 1-2-3

1. Select a fiction or informational book that has one author and one illustrator listed on the cover along with an illustration and display the cover for all students to see.
2. Tell students that you are going to use the cover to help you figure out what the book is about and other important information using the Sneak and See 1-2-3 technique. Have students repeat the name of the lesson. (*Gesture:* Keep your hand positioned above your eyes like a salute while looking around the cover and say, "Sneak and see." Then, hold up three fingers one at a time and say, "1-2-3.") Tell students that you will be looking for three important pieces of information on the cover of the book.
3. Think aloud as you study the cover art. Say, "I'm sneaking a peek to see what I think this book will be about. I see _____ on the cover, so I think the book will be about _____, but I need to look at the title now to help me out with my prediction."

4. Point to the title and tell students that when you sneak and see, you look at the title and art on the cover for your first step. Read the title aloud. Tell students what you think the book is about based on the title and art. Ask students to repeat the title with you and say "Sneak and See 1, this is the title: _____." (*Gesture:* Point to the title and hold up one finger.)

5. Model how to search to find the author's name on the cover and read the name aloud. Say, "The author is the person who wrote the book. So, let's say, 'Sneak and See 1-2, here is the author's name.'" (*Gesture:* Point to the title and hold up one finger. Then, point to the author's name and hold up two fingers.)

6. Ask students to sneak and see if there is another name on the cover. Read and point to the illustrator's name. Ask students if they like to draw or paint pictures. Tell students that the illustrator is the artist who makes pictures to go with the words in the text. Ask students to join you as you say, "Sneak and See 1-2-3." (*Gesture:* Point to the title and say "title," holding up one finger. Point to the author's name and say "author," holding up two fingers. Point to the illustrator's name and say "illustrator," holding up three fingers.)

7. Turn the book over to the back cover and tell students that sometimes books also have clues on the back cover that help us figure out more about the author, the illustrator, or what the book is about. Read aloud to students any relevant information that may be found on the back cover.

STEP 4: COLLABORATION

Checking for Understanding and Conversational Coaching

As you hold up the book again and point to each of the Sneak and See 1-2-3 parts, encourage students to respond with the word for what you point to (*title, author,* or *illustrator*). Hold up another book or books and ask students to join you in a shared experience as you chant "Sneak and See 1-2-3" and students find, name, and point to the title, author, and illustrator. Call volunteers up to help you identify the three target parts of the cover. Engage in conversational coaching by asking students to discuss the following questions with diverse partners:

- What does "1-2-3" stand for when sneaking a peek at the cover?
- How do the hand gestures help you preview the book?

Throughout the lesson, encourage students to turn and talk to partners to repeat the language and gestures from the lesson.

STEP 5: APPLICATION

Book Study

Distribute books on tables and ask students to work in pairs to study each book cover (front and back) to find the title, author, and illustrator. Ask students to repeat the refrain "Sneak and See 1-2-3." Encourage them to use the words *title*, *author*, and *illustrator* as they point to the information on the covers. Students may work in pairs to copy the information from a cover of a book they select onto the *Sneak and See 1-2-3* reproducible (Figure 1.8). Share with partners and the class.

STEP 6: REFLECTION

Written Response

Ask students to each find a book they have read that's written by an author they know and to copy the name of the author into their literacy notebooks. Provide a list of authors the class knows so students may choose one to reflect on as they respond to text. Have students record in their literacy notebooks their responses to the following question: "Why did you select that author?" Students may write about illustrators, too, if you provide a list of favorite illustrators. Use some of these prompts to help guide student writing:

- I like the author _____ because _____.
- I like the book written by _____ because _____.
- I enjoy books written by _____ because _____.
- My favorite illustrator is _____ because _____.
- Some books illustrated by _____ are _____.
- I like the books illustrated by _____ because _____.

ADAPTATION AND EXTENSION

- Discuss authors who also illustrate their own books (e.g., Eric Carle, Tomie dePaola, Kevin Henkes, Arnold Lobel, Mercer Mayer, Beatrix Potter, Chris Van Allsburg). Reflect on these questions:
    - Why do they illustrate their own books?
    - Do they illustrate books for others, too?
- For a challenge, using cover clues, also discuss the genre or text type that students think the book will be and the reason why the author wrote the text (i.e., to inform, entertain, or persuade).

- *English Language Learner Suggestion:* Provide extra practice by filling a bag with several books. Select student volunteers to come up and grab a book from the bag. Hold up each selected book and have the student and the group identify the title, author, and illustrator and predict what the book might be about. Take turns applying the Sneak and See 1-2-3 method.
- *Struggling Reader Suggestion:* Practice applying the Sneak and See 1-2-3 preview strategy to both fiction and nonfiction texts. Build a two-column chart with a list of ways to make logical predictions using cover clues for both genres.

EVALUATION

"I Can . . ." Statements

- I can identify the title of a book using the book cover.
- I can use the cover art and title to predict what the book is about.
- I can identify the author of a book on the cover.
- I can identify the illustrator or photographer on the book cover.
- I can check the back cover of the book to see what else I can learn about the book or the author.

BEHAVIOR INDICATORS

- Identifies the title on a book cover.
- Applies the term *title* when identifying the title on a book cover.
- Identifies the author's name on a book cover.
- Applies the term *author* when identifying the author's name on a book cover.
- Explains the author's role in writing a book.
- Identifies the illustrator's name on a book cover.
- Explains the illustrator's role in illustrating a book.
- Applies title and cover art when using logic to predict what the text might be about.
- Identifies the back cover.
- Explains the content of the back cover.

FIGURE 1.8
Sneak and See 1-2-3

Directions: Copy the title, author, and illustrator from a book. Illustrate the cover!

Title: _____

Author: _____

Illustrator: _____

I think this book will be about _____ because _____.

Source: Literacy Strong All Year Long: Powerful Lessons for Grades K–2 by Valerie Ellery, Lori Oczkus, and Timothy V. Rasinski. © 2020 ASCD. Readers may duplicate this figure for noncommercial use within their school.

LESSON 6. COMPREHENSION: KEY IDEAS AND DETAILS—DETERMINING IMPORTANCE AND SUMMARIZING

Title RETELL RECIPE

Trailer Yum! It's so good when the ingredients of a recipe come together and the flavor is just perfect! There are so many ingredients that go into creating a retell, and sometimes it can be overwhelming for readers to identify the individual flavors of the story. Readers practice retelling as they prepare this recipe for determining importance and the beginning stages of summarizing what they read.

Literacy Enhancer Comprehension: Key Ideas and Details—Determining Importance and Summarizing and Retelling Sequencing

Key Academic Vocabulary

Information: Gathered knowledge; facts or ideas

Retelling: Recalling in a sequential order what is happening in a text

Sequencing: Placing information in a certain order

Story elements: Parts (ingredients) of a story: characters, setting, events, plot, problem, and solution

Learning Objectives

- Identify the story elements of characters, setting, and events in a story.
- Sequence story elements through a retell of what is read.

Essential Questions

- What is a story element?
- What makes a good retell?
- Why is it important to be able to retell a text?

STEP 1: PREPARATION

Organize Materials

- Cooking utensils
- Ingredients for making a peanut butter and jelly sandwich
- Multimodal text set for the topic of study
- *Retell Recipe* reproducible (copies or enlarged for display)
- Literacy notebooks

STEP 2: INITIATION

Sandwich Sequencing

Make a class list of everything that is needed to make a peanut butter and jelly sandwich. Discuss and chart the steps for making the sandwich. Ask the students, "Does it really matter which step you do first when cooking?" Begin the process of making a sandwich and incorporate transition words in the steps (e.g., *first, second, next, then, finally*). Sing or chant the peanut butter and jelly rhyme from Super Simple Songs at https://www.youtube.com/watch?v=klDHM_sxYxs. Sing or play the rhyme and compare the steps in it with the class's Sandwich Sequencing chart.

STEP 3: DEMONSTRATION

Retell Recipe

1. Think aloud about making the sandwich again and how you used transition words to help you sequence the process. Share how in the sandwich recipe certain ingredients were needed to have it all come together and be yummy. Note that the bottom slice of bread was like the beginning and that the top slice was like the ending.
2. Make the connection to how there are also certain ingredients in a story that help bring flavor to it. Reread a story from a unit you are studying and begin to list the flavorful ingredients found in the story elements (e.g., characters, setting, events, problem, solution).
3. After reading the story, put on an apron and begin to interactively read aloud the *Retell Recipe* reproducible (Figure 1.9). Point out that a retell is in sequential order, like procedural steps for cooking a recipe, so the story elements are the ingredients. Insert the specific story elements from the read-aloud text into the recipe to model a retell. *The Retell Recipe* reproducible can also be used as an anchor chart for future referencing.

STEP 4: COLLABORATION

Conversational Coaching

Engage in conversational coaching by asking students to discuss the following questions with diverse partners:

- What are story elements?
- What makes a good retell?
- Why is it important to be able to retell a text?

STEP 5: APPLICATION

Cooking Up Retells

Have students use the *Retell Recipe* reproducible in groups or individually to practice cooking up a good retell. They can use the retell rubric for narrative text as a taste tester to see how yummy the retell was. Use the following prompting questions as needed:

- Who are the main characters?
- Where does the story begin?
- What are the most important things that happen in the middle of the story?
- Is there a problem in the story?
- How is the problem solved?
- How does the story end?

STEP 6: REFLECTION

Written Response

Have students independently create in their literacy notebooks a retell from a text that they recently heard read aloud or that they independently read, remembering to think about the story elements (ingredients) and the sequential steps to cook up their retells. Here are a few sentence stems to use:

- The characters in the story are _____.
- The character was feeling _____.
- The setting is _____.
- The problem in the story was _____ because _____.
- The problem was solved by _____.

ADAPTATION AND EXTENSION

- Read aloud *Peanut Butter and Jelly: A Play Rhyme*, illustrated by Nadine Bernard Westscott, to discuss the procedure of making a sandwich and highlight transition words.
- Use a hula hoop to represent each of the story elements and have students hop through the hoops as they retell the story.
- Use informational text and model using the text features and text elements (main topic/concept/theme, historical figure, location, motivation, goal, conflict, resolution) in place of the story elements for class and student retells.

- Place a recipe card, a chef's hat, and mixing tools at a literacy station. Have students act out the retelling of a text. The other students can write it all out on a recipe card with transition words and sentence stems provided.
- *English Language Learner Suggestion:* Have students use a tablet to take some pictures or create a sequential list to explain or retell what is happening. They can also use the Explain Everything app, which allows them to explain and visually represent what they want to explain to retell a sequence of events.
- *Struggling Reader Suggestion:* Review the story elements with picture cards for each element (e.g., picture of a person for the character, picture of a house for setting, picture of a lock for the problem, picture of keys for the solution). Cut out sentence strips and have possible illustrations that align with the sentences. Have students place them in order as they retell a text and match the story element cards with the proper parts of their retell.

EVALUATION

"I Can . . ." Statements

- I can identify characters in a story.
- I can describe the setting in a story.
- I can identify the problem and solution in a story.
- I can sequence the order of events of a familiar story through a retell.

BEHAVIOR INDICATORS

- Identifies the characters, setting, and main events in a story.
- Sequences the order of events in which they occur in a story.
- Sequences and relate a series of events in a logical order for a retell.

Starting the Year Literacy Strong   43

FIGURE 1.9
Retell Recipe

Ingredients
Characters (who)
Setting (where)
Main events (what)
Problem (but)
Solution (so)

Directions
1. Gather at least one interesting main character.
2. Place the character into a specific place for the perfect setting.
3. Measure in something the character is doing that is important.
4. Sprinkle in a motivation or goal that the character may have.
5. Allow to steep in questions.
6. Add another dash of an event that is happening with the character.
7. Whisk in a grueling problem.
8. Simmer in ways to solve the problem.
9. Serve up a perfect retell.

Source: Literacy Strong All Year Long: Powerful Lessons for Grades K–2 by Valerie Ellery, Lori Oczkus, and Timothy V. Rasinski. © 2020 ASCD. Readers may duplicate this figure for noncommercial use within their school.

LESSON 7. COMPREHENSION: KEY IDEAS AND DETAILS—QUESTIONING FOR CLOSE READING

Title THE WHO, WHAT, WHERE, WHEN SHOW

Trailer Inquiring minds want to know! Young children are naturally inquisitive, but they often confuse questions with statements when invited to ask a question about a text. A pretend microphone in reading lessons works like magic to help students grasp the concept of question formulation. Help your students internalize how to ask and answer questions about key ideas and details in texts.

Literacy Enhancer Comprehension: Key Ideas and Details—Questioning for Close Reading and Ask and Answer Questions (Who, What, Where, When)

Key Academic Vocabulary

Question: A sentence in interrogative form

What: A question word that asks about the events or things that happened

When: A question word that asks the time of day or year

Where: A question word that asks about the place

Who: A question word that asks about the people or animals in the text

Fiction: The genre that includes different stories that are make-believe; may also include poetry

Informational text: A type of nonfiction text

Nonfiction: The genre that includes factual/real information that is portrayed to answer, explain, or describe

Learning Objectives

- Answer questions about key ideas and details with *who, what, where,* and *when* and using text evidence.
- Ask questions about key ideas and details using *who, what, where,* and *when*.
- Align answers with the corresponding questions.

Essential Questions

- What questions can you ask and answer that start with *who, what, where,* and *when*?
- How do you ask and answer questions with text evidence?
- How can you match an answer with a question that goes with it?

STEP 1: PREPARATION

Organize Materials

- Plastic microphone(s)
- Fiction and nonfiction texts
- *Welcome to the Who, What, Where Show!* reproducible (copies or enlarged for display)
- *Who, What, Where, When Cards* reproducible (copies or enlarged for display)
- Literacy notebooks

STEP 2: INITIATION

Television Show Microphones

Show students a plastic microphone. Ask them if they have seen any television shows where a microphone is used for questioning (e.g., interviews on news or talk shows). In a game show announcer voice, talk into the microphone (or use your fist as a pretend one). Ask a question about a book your class read together recently. Then, tease students by continuing in your announcer voice as you say, "If you get the answer right, you'll win a new car!" Explain that you are just play acting but that they will have a chance to pretend to be on the Who, What, Where Show as they read.

STEP 3: DEMONSTRATION

The Question Song

1. Select a text to read aloud to the class. Show the cover and read the title. Explain to students that good readers use questions to help them understand the text before, during, and after reading. Ask students to brainstorm question words they know and create question anchor charts.
2. Write the three target question words, *who*, *what*, and *where*, on the board. Holding up the read-aloud book, conduct a think-aloud using the cover as you ask and answer the following questions about the text. Invite students to turn and repeat your questions to a partner:
   - Who will be in this book?
   - What will it be about?
   - Where does it take place?
3. *Optional:* Sing the first verse of this song to the tune of "London Bridge":

   The Question Song
   Ask questions before you read,
   Before you read,

Before you read.
Ask questions before you read,
Who, what, and where.

4. Begin reading the text. Pause every few pages to use the microphone as you ask questions about the text. Create questions for *who*, *what*, and *where* that are related to the text. Demonstrate how to reread and then create a question that goes with a specific portion or page of text. Invite students to repeat your questions and answers to a partner. *Optional:* Sing another verse about questioning to the tune of "London Bridge":

    Ask questions during reading,
    During reading,
    During reading.
    Ask questions during reading,
    Who, what, and where.

5. Complete the reading of the text. Create questions for *who*, *what*, and *where* and demonstrate how to reread the text to formulate questions.

6. Invite students to repeat the questions to a partner. *Optional:* Sing a third verse about questioning to the tune of "London Bridge":

    Ask questions after reading,
    After reading,
    After reading.
    Ask questions after reading,
    Who, what, and where.

7. Repeat the entire process using informational text (or fiction if you used informational text for the first example). Add the question word *where* to your demonstrations and lessons.

STEP 4: COLLABORATION

Read It Three Times Challenge and Conversational Coaching

Select a text to read aloud or together (silently) as a class. Prepare the *Welcome to the Who, What, Where Show!* reproducible (Figure 1.10) to use in the lesson. Explain to students that they will reread the text three times, each time focusing on a different question word. Write the word *who* on the board. Pause throughout the reading and invite students to turn to a partner to formulate a question that begins with *who*, then record their responses. Reread the entire book again, form questions that begin with *what*, and record students' responses. Reread the text a third time, encouraging students to indicate when you should pause to ask a *where* question. Encourage students to use text evidence as they answer one another's questions.

Engage students in conversational coaching using the *Who, What, Where, When Cards* reproducible (Figure 1.11). Make sets of the cards and keep them together in an envelope, on tongue depressors, or on key rings. Select a text to read. Try any of the following ways to invite students to ask and answer questions:

- Put every table (or pair) in charge of a different question word.
- Put every table (or pair) in charge of the same question word.
- Pause several times throughout the reading and ask students to create a question for a specific page or sentence using the target question word.
- Offer students the option of free choice and have them select which question to ask.

STEP 5: APPLICATION

Question Jigsaw

Copy and cut apart the *Welcome to the Who, What, Where Show!* reproducible. Give each table one of the questions to record. Students work in teams or pairs to fill in two questions about the text that starts with their target word and then share with the class.

STEP 6: REFLECTION

Written Response

Encourage students to use the question words and write questions in their literacy notebooks. Have them put a star next to their best question and pose it to a partner. Also, students may respond to these essential questions in their literacy notebooks:

- What questions can you ask and answer that start with *who, what, where*, and *when*?
- How do you ask and answer questions with text evidence?
- How can you match an answer with a question that goes with it?

ADAPTATION AND EXTENSION

- Invite students to sit in one large "Question Circle." Review a book that the class has already read, instructing students that they will take turns asking questions about the book. Open the book to a specific page and tell students that they will

carefully pass the microphone and sing "The Question Song" to find out who will make up a question for the page. Whoever is holding the microphone after the first verse creates a question for the page in the book that you are displaying. Partners turn to the person on the right and answer the question.
- *English Language Learner Suggestion:* Share the following read-aloud mentor texts and invite students to ask questions throughout the reading:
  - *Farm Animals* by Daniel Nunn
  - *Quentin Quokka's Quick Questions* by Barbara deRubertis
  - *I Wonder When?* by Mary Elizabeth Salzmann
  - *Swirl by Swirl: Spirals in Nature* by Joyce Sidman

- *Struggling Reader Suggestion*: Guide students who are having difficulty formulating questions by providing question stems on the *Who, What, Where, When Cards* reproducible. Repeat the process as you sing the other two verses of the song and students take turns asking questions about the text. Students can also sit in several circles around the room and all sing at the same time, pausing between verses to take turns asking questions.

EVALUATION

"I Can . . ." Statements

- I can answer a question that starts with *who, what, where,* or *when.*
- I can give text evidence when I answer a question.
- I can ask a question that starts with *who, what, where,* or *when.*

BEHAVIOR INDICATORS

- Asks questions about key ideas and details using the question words *who, what, where,* and *when.*
- Answers questions using complete sentences.
- Answers questions about key ideas and details using the question words *who, what, where,* and *when* with text evidence.

Starting the Year Literacy Strong   49

FIGURE 1.10

Welcome to the Who, What, Where Show!

Who?

Who _____
_____

Who _____
_____

What?

What _____
_____

What _____
_____

Where?

Where _____
_____

Where _____
_____

Source: Literacy Strong All Year Long: Powerful Lessons for Grades K–2 by Valerie Ellery, Lori Oczkus, and Timothy V. Rasinski. © 2020 ASCD. Readers may duplicate this figure for noncommercial use within their school.

FIGURE 1.11

Who, What, Where, When Cards

Directions: Cut the cards apart. Hold up a card when you want to ask a question. Optional: Put the cards in an envelope in your notebook, on craft sticks, or punch holes and hold together on key rings or with yarn.

Source: Literacy Strong All Year Long: Powerful Lessons for Grades K–2 by Valerie Ellery, Lori Oczkus, and Timothy V. Rasinski. © 2020 ASCD. Readers may duplicate this figure for noncommercial use within their school.

LESSON 8. VOCABULARY: ASSOCIATING WORDS

Title UP AND DOWN WITH OPPOSITES!

Trailer Children experience opposites early in their lives. Picture a two-year-old stomping and shouting "No!" while Mom or Dad is saying yes. However, the concept of opposites is a bit tricky to explain in words to students. Definitions include words such as *different, opposing,* and *related*. An effective way to teach students about opposites is to share examples and then guide them to generalize about the concept.

Literacy Enhancer Vocabulary: Associating Words and Antonyms

Key Academic Vocabulary

Adjective: A word that describes a noun (a person, place, or thing)

Antonym: A word that has an opposite meaning of another word

Noun: A person, place, or thing

Opposite: Two words or concepts that are in some way related but distinctly different in meaning from each other

Verb: An action word

Learning Objectives

- Identify, match, and name opposites (antonyms) of frequently occurring verbs to demonstrate understanding.
- Identify, match, and name opposites (antonyms) of frequently occurring adjectives to demonstrate understanding.

Essential Questions

- How do opposite verbs relate to each other and to the topic?
- How do opposite adjectives relate to each other and to the topic?
- Why do we need to learn about opposites?

STEP 1: PREPARATION

Organize Materials

- Two cups, each a different color (e.g., red, blue)
- Index cards or sticky notes
- Multimodal text set with antonyms
- *Opposite Verbs Cards* reproducible (copies or enlarged for display)
- *Opposite Adjectives Cards* reproducible (copies or enlarged for display)
- Literacy notebooks

STEP 2: INITIATION

Opposites All Around

Hold up two cups and tell students that one has cold water in it and the other has hot water. Ask students to share how the two cups are different. Next, turn off the lights and then turn them back on. Invite students to discuss what they know about opposites. Ask students to list pairs (or draw pictures; e.g., sad face, smiley face) of words that are opposites and record them on a chart. Share that students will explore how opposite verbs and adjectives relate to each other.

STEP 3: DEMONSTRATION

Read-Alouds: Acting Out and Charting Opposites

1. Read aloud from one or more picture books about opposites. Write a list of opposite pairs collected from the reading on the board or a chart. Explain that learning about opposites helps expand our vocabulary because it can help clarify what a word means and does not mean. Here are some suggested opposite books:
   - *The Foot Book* by Dr. Seuss
   - *Olivia's Opposites* by Ian Falconer
   - *Exactly the Opposite* by Tana Hoban
   - *Opposites* by Sandra Boynton
   - *What's Up, Duck? A Book of Opposites* by Tad Hills

2. Tell students that they are going to act out some pairs of verbs, also called action words, that are opposites. Ask students to pay close attention so they can tell what the two words have in common and how they are different. Write each of these opposite word pairs on separate index cards or sticky notes: *walk/run, stand/sit, stop/go, sleep/wake,* and *float/sink.* Here's a list of common opposite verbs to use in your lessons:
   - *give/take*
   - *work/play*
   - *walk/run*
   - *stand/sit*
   - *stop/go*
   - *sleep/wake*
   - *float/sink*
   - *smile/frown*
   - *catch/throw*
   - *fall/rise*
   - *push/pull*
   - *buy/sell*
   - *enter/exit*
   - *break/fix*
   - *love/hate*
   - *lose/find*
   - *lend/borrow*
   - *grow/shrink*
   - *lock/unlock*
   - *enter/exit*
   - *win/lose*
   - *come/go*
   - *arrive/leave*

3. Invite two students to stand in front of the class and give them cards with one of the opposite word pairs. Have one of the volunteers act out one of the words on the card while the other volunteer acts out its opposite. Ask the rest of the class to guess the two words. Put the cards on the chart or board side by side. Discuss how the two words are related and how they are different. Repeat the process, allowing different students to act out the word pairs. Invite students to sing one of these opposite songs to the tune of "London Bridge":

   Opposites Are Different

   Opposites are different,

   Different, different.

   Opposites are different,

   Like *stop* and *go*.

   (Act out the words *stop* and *go* in the last line and then replace them with other opposite pairs of verbs.)

   We Are Opposites

   I walk and you run,

   You run, you run.

   I walk and you run,

   We are opposites!

   (Point to yourself and your partner and act out the words while singing. Then, substitute other opposite pairs of verbs for *walk* and *run*.)

4. Repeat the lesson to introduce frequently occurring adjectives. Explain to students that describing words are called *adjectives*. Try singing and acting out pairs of adjectives with the "Opposites Are Different" song. Here's a list of common opposite adjectives to use in your lessons:

   - bad/good
   - better/worse
   - cold/hot
   - dark/light
   - gentle/rough
   - fat/skinny
   - old/young
   - small/large
   - shallow/deep
   - cool/warm
   - correct/wrong
   - dead/alive
   - dangerous/safe
   - hard/easy
   - hard/soft
   - heavy/light
   - rough/smooth
   - big/little
   - dirty/clean
   - dry/wet
   - empty/full
   - good/bad
   - left/right
   - long/short
   - loud/quiet
   - rich/poor
   - sweet/sour
   - whole/part

- *top/bottom*
- *mean/nice*
- *brave/afraid*
- *huge/tiny*
- *funny/serious*
- *quiet/loud*
- *wise/foolish*
- *best/worst*
- *interesting/dull*
- *bright/dull*

STEP 4: COLLABORATION

What's Your Opposites Story and Conversational Coaching

Read aloud a page or two from a familiar children's story. Underline or point to the adjectives in the text and explain that these are the describing words. Reread the story by substituting opposites for the adjectives and invite students to raise their hands to signal when you are using an opposite. Pause often for students to engage in conversational coaching by inviting them to turn and talk to a partner about the substituted words. Here's a version of *Goldilocks and the Three Bears* with opposite adjectives:

> Once upon a time, there lived three bears who went for a walk because their porridge was too <u>cold</u>. While they were out walking, a <u>big</u> girl named Goldilocks knocked on their door. When nobody answered, she entered the <u>occupied</u> house. She was <u>full</u>, so she tried Papa Bear's porridge, but it was too <u>cold</u>. Next, she tried Mama Bear's porridge, but it was too <u>hot</u>. Then, she tried Baby Bear's porridge, and it was just <u>wrong</u>.

Write the original words and their opposites on the board from your read-aloud. *Optional:* Use the same or another familiar text and substitute the verbs with opposites. Use your software to create a grid (perhaps 6 × 4) that works best for your students.

STEP 5: APPLICATION

Flap Book of Opposites

Students work on creating a flap book of opposites by folding a standard sheet of paper in half vertically—so it's long and skinny, like a hot dog bun. Turn the flap book sideways so the fold is at the top. Write one word on the outside flap and then write the corresponding opposite on the inside. Illustrate and use to quiz partners. *Optional:* Students can cut apart the *Opposite Verbs Cards* reproducible (Figure 1.12) or the *Opposite Adjectives Cards* (Figure 1.13) reproducible and glue the cards onto their flap books, one word on the outside and its opposite on the inside.

Classic Partner Card Games

Have students practice using opposites by playing any of the following games using the *Opposite Verbs Cards* or *Opposite Adjectives Cards* reproducible or using the *Blank*

Opposites Cards reproducible (Figure 1.4) to create their own cards. Be sure to model and monitor while students play before putting the game in a partner station. When possible, students should use phrases such as "My word is _____. It means _____. The opposite of my word is _____."

- *Go Fish* card game: The dealer mixes up the cards and gives each player six cards. The remaining cards are placed face down in a stack the middle of the table. Players hold their cards fanned out in their hands. In turns, each player tries to match one of the cards in his hands by asking another player for the opposite card. If the other player has it, then the asker receives the match and wins the pair. If the other player doesn't have it, then the asker draws another card from the pile, and the next player takes a turn. The player with the most pairs at the end of the game is the winner.
- *Concentration* game: Partners mix up the cards and place the cards face down between them. In turns, each student flips over two cards to see if they match. If they don't, the flipper turns the cards back over, and the partner takes a turn. If a match is made, the student puts the match face up in front of herself and takes another turn. Partners continue until all the matches are made. The one with the most matches wins. *Optional:* Play to beat the clock rather than the partner. Use an egg timer. See how fast the two partners can make matches by taking turns. The matching cards are displayed and shared.
- *Race the clock:* Students take turns dumping the cards, mixing them up, and matching them into pairs. Each student works to beat his best time, not a partner's time. *Optional:* Have students work as a team to beat the clock.

STEP 6: REFLECTION

Written Response

Have students independently write and illustrate their favorite opposite pairs in their literacy notebooks and respond to this essential question: Why do we need to learn about opposites?

ADAPTATION AND EXTENSION

- Write opposite word pairs on separate index cards or sticky notes, one word each. Make enough cards for each student to hold one word from a pair of opposites. Mix up the cards and pass them out. If you have an uneven number of students, assign one student to two cards. Have students illustrate the word on their card. Next, play music to signal students to walk slowly around the room. When the music stops, they teach the student(s) nearest them their word.

Students continue until they find a student with the matching opposite. Then, the pair works together to write a two- or three-sentence story using their opposites. Pairs take turns acting out their opposite sentences.

- *English Language Learner Suggestion:* Play charades with opposite word or picture cards. A student draws a word and acts it out. The group guesses the word and its opposite.
- *Struggling Reader Suggestion:* Brainstorm and list opposites on a chart. Students select one opposite pair to sketch. Assemble all the students' opposite pairs into a class book.

EVALUATION

"I Can . . ." Statements

- I can identify the meanings of verbs that are opposites.
- I can match verbs to their opposites.
- I can name the opposite of a verb.
- I can identify the meanings of adjectives that are opposites.
- I can match adjectives to their opposites.
- I can name the opposite of an adjective.

BEHAVIOR INDICATORS

- Identifies the meaning of each word in a pair of verbs that are opposites.
- Matches a common verb to its opposite.
- Names the opposite of a given verb.
- Identifies the meaning of each word in a pair of adjectives that are opposites.
- Matches a common adjective to its opposite.
- Names the opposite of a given adjective.

FIGURE 1.12
Opposite Verbs Cards

stop	go	sleep	wake
lose	find	come	leave
walk	run	win	lose
stand	sit	push	pull
fall	rise	float	sink
enter	exit	smile	frown

Source: Literacy Strong All Year Long: Powerful Lessons for Grades K–2 by Valerie Ellery, Lori Oczkus, and Timothy V. Rasinski. © 2020 ASCD. Readers may duplicate this figure for noncommercial use within their school.

FIGURE 1.13
Opposite Adjectives Cards

good	bad	dry	wet
hot	cold	long	short
top	bottom	thick	thin
heavy	light	smooth	rough
dirty	clean	loud	quiet
dark	light	big	small

Source: Literacy Strong All Year Long: Powerful Lessons for Grades K–2 by Valerie Ellery, Lori Oczkus, and Timothy V. Rasinski. © 2020 ASCD. Readers may duplicate this figure for noncommercial use within their school.

LESSON 9. VOCABULARY: ANALYZING WORDS

Title WE'RE GOING ON A WORD HUNT: NOUNS AND VERBS

Trailer Oh, a-hunting we will go! There is something about going on a pursuit that intrigues us. Before haphazardly venturing out for a hunt, you must ask what or who you are hunting and what the hunted can do. Students also must answer these questions when they are hunting for meaning in a text. Join your students on an adventurous word hunt for nouns and verbs!

Literacy Enhancer Vocabulary: Analyzing Words—Parts of Speech: Nouns and Verbs

Key Academic Vocabulary Vocabulary from a previous lesson has been marked with an asterisk (*).

> *Common noun:* A nonspecific type of noun that names any regular, ordinary person, animal, place, thing, or idea
>
> *Noun:* A part of speech that is a type of naming word that represents a person, animal, place, thing, idea, or concept; usually followed by a verb; there are more nouns in the English language than any other words
>
> *Parts of speech:* Categories of words used in English grammar (e.g., nouns, verbs, adverbs, adjectives, prepositions)
>
> *Proper noun:* A specific type of noun that names a particular person, animal, place, thing, or idea and begins with a capital letter
>
> *Verb:* A part of speech that is a type of word that demonstrates an action (physical or mental) or tells what the subject (noun) of a simple sentence is doing; without a verb, a sentence would not exist

Learning Objectives

- Identify and categorize frequently occurring nouns and verbs orally and in writing.
- Identify and use various parts of speech (nouns and verbs) in writing and speaking.

Essential Questions

- How can you identify various types of nouns and verbs?
- How do you use common nouns and verbs correctly when you speak and write?

STEP 1: PREPARATION

Organize Materials

- Cameras or handheld devices with cameras

- Multimodal text set for the topic of study with a focus on nouns and verbs
- *Alphaboxing Nouns* reproducible (copies or enlarged for display)
- *Alphaboxing Verbs* reproducible (copies or enlarged for display)
- Literacy notebooks

STEP 2: INITIATION

Going on a Word Hunt

Wear a tour guide hat or cup your hand on your forehead to appear like you are searching for something on a hunt. Select a noun and chant to the tune of "We're Going on a Bear Hunt." Have students repeat each line after you:

> **We're Going on a Word Hunt**
>
> We're going on a word hunt!
>
> I'm not afraid!
>
> Are you?
>
> Not me!
>
> Got a real good friend [Hug a partner] by my side.
>
> Oh! Oh!
>
> What do you see?
>
> Oh, look! It's a word!
>
> Can't go over it.
>
> Can't go under it.
>
> Can't go through it.
>
> Got to just say it!
>
> Got to just read it!
>
> Got to just write it!
>
> Oh! Oh!
>
> I know the word.
>
> It has [description of the noun].
>
> It has [another description of the noun].
>
> It has [another description of the noun].
>
> It's a [the type of noun: person, animal, place, thing, or idea].
>
> It's a [the word]!

Repeat the verse with a different noun. After several verses, explain to students that they are going to be examining parts of speech. Students will also analyze these words to bring meaning to what they read. *Note:* In a follow-up lesson, change the chant from nouns to verbs. Change "It has" to "It can" and give descriptions by using synonyms of the verb. End the chant with "The word is _____!"

STEP 3: DEMONSTRATION

Read-Alouds and Charting Nouns and Verbs

1. Read aloud from one or more picture books about nouns. Create an anchor chart for nouns and write any common or proper nouns collected from the reading. Explain how learning about parts of speech, such as nouns or verbs, helps to structure our sentences and expand our vocabulary. Here are a few suggested noun and verb books:
   - *A Mink, a Fink, a Skating Rink: What Is a Noun?* by Brian P. Cleary
   - *To Root, to Toot, to Parachute: What Is a Verb?* by Brian P. Cleary
   - *Add It, Dip It, Fix It: A Book of Verbs* by R. M. Schneider

2. Revisit the anchor chart from the read-aloud and examine the difference between a common noun and a proper noun. Model how all these words can answer the question "What is it?" or "Who is it?" by showing something from around the room and asking, "What is this?" Have students respond with the object's name and remind them that the name is a noun. Continue pointing to several things around the room. Revisit the anchor chart from the read-aloud, point to a word, and ask, "What is it?" If there is a person on the list, point and ask, "Who is it?"

3. Have students turn and talk about the difference between the *who* and *what* of questions that were asked. Discuss how all these words are called nouns: The ones that answer the *what* are common nouns given to objects, animals, things, and even ideas, and the ones that answer the *who* are proper nouns (i.e., names) given to people.

4. Repeat the lesson to introduce verbs using an anchor chart of verbs. Ask students questions such as "What does it do?" "What can it do?" and "What action does it make?"

STEP 4: COLLABORATION

Capturing Images and Conversational Coaching

Assign groups or partners to go on a hunt for different types of nouns (i.e., people, animals, places, things, ideas) or verbs. Using a still or video camera, have students explore the room or outside to take pictures of various nouns and verbs to use as their prizes from the hunt. *Optional:* Have students write and illustrate some of the words from the read-aloud anchor chart on index cards or construction paper. Students can also use various apps to create collages or clip art programs for their noun or verb images.

Have students engage in conversational coaching by identifying words as nouns and saying what types of nouns they are. Have them use the questions for nouns (What is this? What is that? Who is this?). After addressing nouns, have students ask the questions for verbs (What does it do? What can it do? What action does it make?). Display the hunted prize collection of nouns or verbs on a word wall titled "Oh, A-Hunting We Will Go!"

STEP 5: APPLICATION

Alphaboxing with Nouns and Verbs (adapted concept from Ellery, 2014, and Hoyt, 2009). Have students practice vocabulary words by hunting for nouns or verbs and filling out either the *Alphaboxing Nouns* reproducible (Figure 1.14) or the *Alphaboxing Verbs* reproducible (Figure 1.15). Invite students to organize words from the anchor chart or the word wall according to the beginning letter in the captured noun or verb. If a noun or verb is not available for a particular alphabox, have students go on another hunt for one that best completes the missing letter.

STEP 6: REFLECTION

Oral and Written Response

Have students ask the questions (What is this? Who is that? What does it do? What action does it make?) and identify words as nouns or verbs based on the appropriate question. In their literacy notebooks, have students record and sort nouns and verbs from a text. Students can also select several nouns and verbs from the class word wall and create a poem or story. If focusing on verbs, students can use the words to make a paper action chain using the verbs in the order they appeared in the story. Students can then revisit the chain to retell the story's events in sequential order.

ADAPTATION AND EXTENSION

- Read Cleary's *A Mink, a Fink, a Skating Rink: What Is a Noun?* Use the pattern of the book to create a Mad Libs–style poem using nouns or verbs.
- Have students practice identifying parts of speech using online games such as these to enhance their language development: "The Grammar Gorillas: Beginner" (nouns and verbs only; www.funbrain.com/grammar/index.html), "Ice Cream Talk: Nouns and Verbs" (www.abcya.com/nouns_and_verbs.htm),

"Picture the Verb" (www.turtlediary.com/kindergarten-games/ela-games/picture-the-verb.html).

- *English Language Learner Suggestion:* Create gestures to represent types of nouns. Show images of a variety of nouns and have students demonstrate the types of noun by a gesture:
    - *Person:* Point to yourself.
    - *Animal:* Hold up your hands to mimic a begging dog.
    - *Place:* Sweep your arms out wide.
    - *Thing:* Pick up a small object.
    - *Idea:* Point to your brain.
- *Struggling Reader Suggestion:* Play a form of charades where the students have a chance to act out the meaning of a part of speech to form a visual image. For nouns, have students act out a noun from a text while the other students try to guess what or who is being acted out. For verbs, have students randomly select a verb and act it out for their partner. The partner guesses the word and then uses it in a sentence or locates it in a text.

EVALUATION

"I Can . . ." Statements

- I can identify a noun.
- I can identify a verb.
- I can explain the function of a noun and a verb.
- I can categorize nouns and verbs.
- I can use frequently occurring nouns and verbs to communicate properly in my writing.

BEHAVIOR INDICATORS

- Demonstrates the ability to identify nouns.
- Demonstrates the ability to identify verbs.
- Demonstrates the difference between a noun and a verb.
- Uses singular nouns with matching verbs in basic sentences.

FIGURE 1.14
Alphaboxing Nouns

Directions: Complete each box with an image or word that begins with that letter and is a noun. Choose one noun for the XYZ box.

Noun: A part of speech that is a naming word that can answer questions that identify a **person, animal, place, thing,** or **idea.** For example, What is it? What is this? What is that? Who is it? Who is this? Who is that?

A	B	C	D	
E	F	G	H	
I	J	K	L	
M	N	O	P	
Q	R	S	T	
U	V	W	XYZ	

Source: Literacy Strong All Year Long: Powerful Lessons for Grades K–2 by Valerie Ellery, Lori Oczkus, and Timothy V. Rasinski. © 2020 ASCD. Readers may duplicate this figure for noncommercial use within their school.

FIGURE 1.15
Alphaboxing Verbs

Directions: Complete each box with an image or word that begins with that letter and is a verb. Choose one verb for the XYZ box.

Verb: A word that demonstrates an **action (physical or mental) or state of being**. The word tells what a noun is doing by answering questions. For example, What is [the noun] doing? What is he or she doing? What are they doing? What action is taking place?

write 	listen 	speak 

A	B	C	D
E	F	G	H
I	J	K	L
M	N	O	P
Q	R	S	T
U	V	W	XYZ

Source: Literacy Strong All Year Long: Powerful Lessons for Grades K–2 by Valerie Ellery, Lori Oczkus, and Timothy V. Rasinski. © 2020 ASCD. Readers may duplicate this figure for noncommercial use within their school.

LESSON 10. MOTIVATION: MOTIVATING READERS

Title TAKE OFF WITH READING! CLASS BOOK CLUB

Trailer Children enjoy participating in clubs for the sense of community and belonging that they provide. The entire class will enjoy taking off with books as they travel together to other lands, times, and worlds. Students learn to keep track of the class read-alouds with the Class Book Club Reading Log reproducible. Keeping a book log motivates students to read and comprehend a wide variety of interesting fiction and informational texts all year long.

Literacy Enhancer Motivation: Motivating Readers—Text Features, Book Logs, Predicting, Summarizing

Key Academic Vocabulary Vocabulary from a previous lesson has been marked with an asterisk (*).

Author*: The person who wrote the book

Predict*: To use information from a text to infer what the text will be about or what one might learn from it

Summarize: To tell what has happened in the text by sharing important points and details

Title*: The name of the text; tells what it is about or gives clues to the content

Learning Objectives

- Identify titles of books read by the class.
- Keep an individual book log by listing books read and evaluate each text by giving reasons.
- Identify at least three different types of books (e.g., fairy tales, poetry books, nonfiction).
- Examine discussion rules of taking turns talking and looking at one another.

Essential Questions

- What are some types of books that the class has read?
- What makes you like or dislike a book?
- What are some different types of books that you have read?

STEP 1: PREPARATION

Organize Materials

- Fiction or informational books
- *Optional:* Paper bag with a toy vehicle in it

- *Take Off with Reading Book Club Tickets* reproducible (copies or enlarged for display)
- *My Reading Log* reproducible (copies or enlarged for display)
- Literacy notebooks

STEP 2: INITIATION

Take Off! Invitation to Join the Club

Ask students if they've ever belonged to a club. Remind them that this category can include sports, scouting, or their own made-up club. Share a quick story about one you were in as a child. Tell students that sometimes children and adults belong to book clubs for which they all read the same book and discuss it together. Share with students that this year they are all going to be part of a special club, the class book club, and that the class is going to read lots of different kinds of wonderful books together.

Ask students if they enjoy going on trips or traveling by car, airplane, or boat. Tell them that the class book club is going to travel all over the world—and the universe in their imaginations—as they read books. Hold up a few books as examples, display the covers, and share where the books will take the students (e.g., the zoo, outer space, a magical land in a fairy tale). Hand out tickets from the *Take Off with Reading Book Club Tickets* reproducible (Figure 1.16) to each student. *Optional:* Bring in a paper bag with a few books in it and a toy airplane, car, or spaceship. Pull them out as props when you discuss the class book club.

STEP 3: DEMONSTRATION

Read Aloud and Record on the Log

1. Select a fiction or informational book and display the cover for all students to see.
2. Ask students to pretend to buckle their seat belts as the class book club prepares to take off in an imaginary vehicle (e.g., airplane, spaceship, bus, car). Tell students that the book club is headed on a special trip through the book. Countdown to read time: "3, 2, 1, read!" *Optional:* Collect students' book club tickets before the journey.
3. Think aloud as you study text features (i.e., title, cover art, author's and illustrator's names). Invite students to share what they think the text will be about. Talk about what type of book it is (e.g., story book, adventure, animal). Chant the "I Like Books" chant once to students:

I like _____ [type of story, such as nonfiction, adventure, or animal] books. Yes, I do!

I like _____ [type of story again] books. How about *you*?

4. Read the text aloud to students, stopping at least once in the middle to discuss what has happened so far. Use the sentence stem "So far" and model how to summarize. Invite student partners to also give their summaries using the same sentence stem. Before reading any further, pause to model how to predict what will happen next in the text and say, "I think _____ will happen next because _____." (If you're using a nonfiction text, say, "I think we will learn _____ next because _____.") Invite partners to share their predictions using the same frame.
5. After reading, have students share their favorite parts using the frame "My favorite part was because _____." Share your favorite part and reason as well.
6. Tell students that the class book club is going to keep track of the books the class reads. Display the *Class Book Club Reading Log* reproducible (Figure 1.17) and think aloud as you fill in each part of the log for the read-aloud book. Invite students to help you rate the book and give reasons for their thinking. *Optional:* Invite students to use a gesture to go with each of the ratings (see chart on the next page).

STEP 4: COLLABORATION

Logging, Chanting, and Conversational Coaching

After reading another book to the class, distribute the *Class Book Club Reading Log* reproducible to each student. After you model how to fill out the class log for this book, have students complete their logs with the same information. Students can keep their logs on construction paper, in file folders, or as a digital portfolio log. Collect a stack of books to show the class. Make sure to include fiction, nonfiction, poetry, and a variety of genres. Ask students to name the kinds of books they like. (Accept any response, including long books, short books, big books, and pretty books.) As you hold up each title and show the cover, invite the class to chant the "I Like Books" chant with you as you whet their reading appetites with an interesting smattering of books (e.g., fairy tales, adventure, mystery, humor, poetry, nonfiction). Have partners engage in conversational coaching about these essential questions:

- Why do you like or dislike the book?
- What features of the book supported your interest?

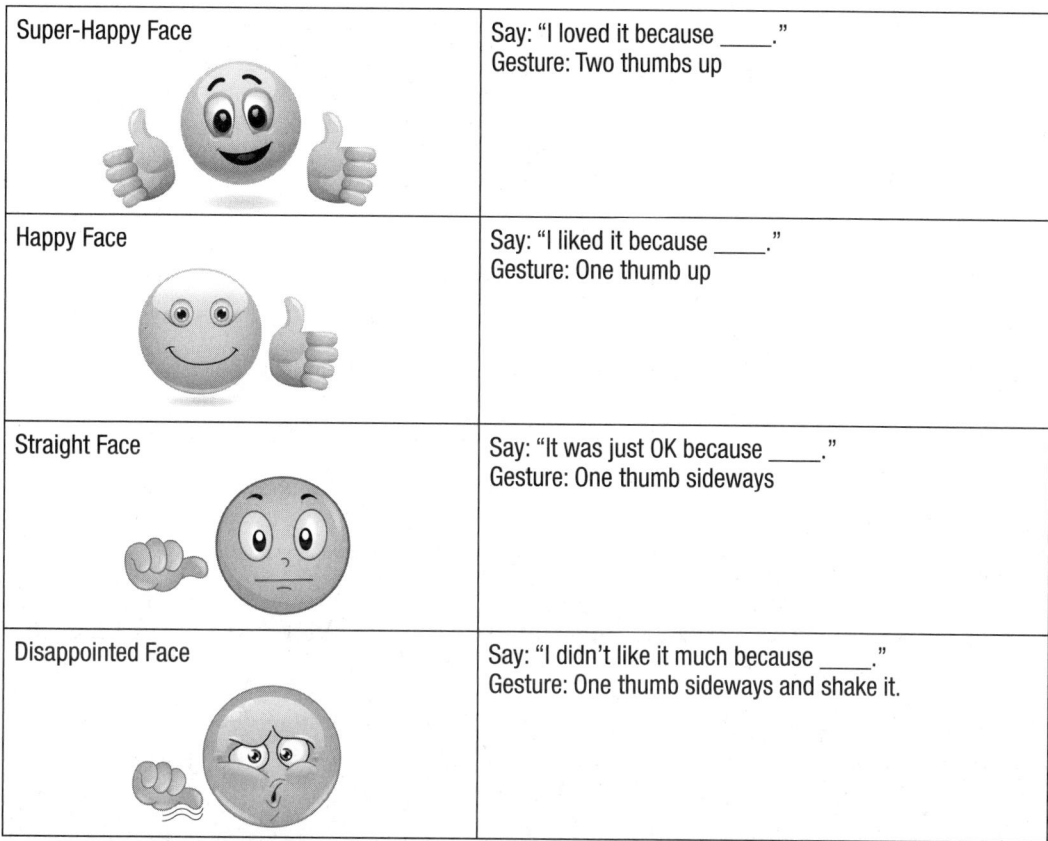

Source: Literacy Strong All Year Long: Powerful Lessons for Grades 3-5 by Lori Oczkus, Valerie Ellery, and Timothy V. Rasinski. Copyright © 2018 ASCD. Readers may duplicate this figure for noncommercial use within their school.

Invite students to share their favorite types of books and then chant their favorite genre in the "I Like Books" chant.

STEP 5: APPLICATION

Share a Rating: Partner Practice with Books

Distribute books for partners to read and discuss. The books may be familiar or new to students. Ask them to practice sharing the title, author, and personal rating with their partner. Make sure students give reasons for their ratings. Encourage students to use the following discussion frames to discuss the books:

- The title of this book is _____.
- The author is _____.
- I [loved it/liked it/thought it was just OK/didn't like it] because _____.

Work with students either as a class or in small groups as they complete their *My Reading Log* reproducible (Figure 1.18) with the book they just shared with their partner. Tell students that book club members will write down the books they've read to help keep track of their reading and to be able to reflect on a variety of books read over time.

STEP 6: REFLECTION

Written Response

Have students record their responses to the following prompts in their literacy books:

- The book _____ was written by _____.
- I [loved it/liked it/thought it was just OK/didn't like it] because _____.
- I like [genre or type] books because _____.

Have students put a star next to their favorite book and write about it using the prompts above.

ADAPTATION AND EXTENSION

- Pair students with cross-age buddies in an upper grade level to read together for 20–30 minutes every week, all year long. The buddies also may keep an additional copy of the *My Reading Log* reproducible with their names on it to record the books they read together. The older student can help the younger student fill out the form.
- *English Language Learner Suggestion:* Invite students to bring a book to circle time to participate in a small-group circle chant. Ask them to turn to a partner and share the title and author of their book. Then, invite students to listen while each child in the circle takes a turn chanting the "I Like Books" chant. Chanting the final line ("How about *you*?") the student points to the next person to continue. When everyone has had a turn, invite partners to tell each other why their book is their favorite by showing some evidence or an example from the text.
- *Struggling Reader Suggestion:* Meet in a small group and invite students to share one book log entry. Encourage them to act out a favorite scene from the book and tell why they selected it.

EVALUATION

"I Can . . ." Statements

- I can tell the author of a book.
- I can tell the title of a book.
- I can identify different types of books.
- I can rate a book and give reasons to support my opinion.
- I can record the date, title, author, and my rating on my book log.

BEHAVIOR INDICATORS

- Identifies the title of a book on the cover.
- Identifies the author's name on a book cover.
- Identifies different types of books.
- Rates a book and gives at least one reason for the rating using the text.
- Records the title, author, and personal rating on a book log.
- Consistently maintains a book log to keep track of independent reading.

FIGURE 1.16
Take Off with Reading Book Club Tickets

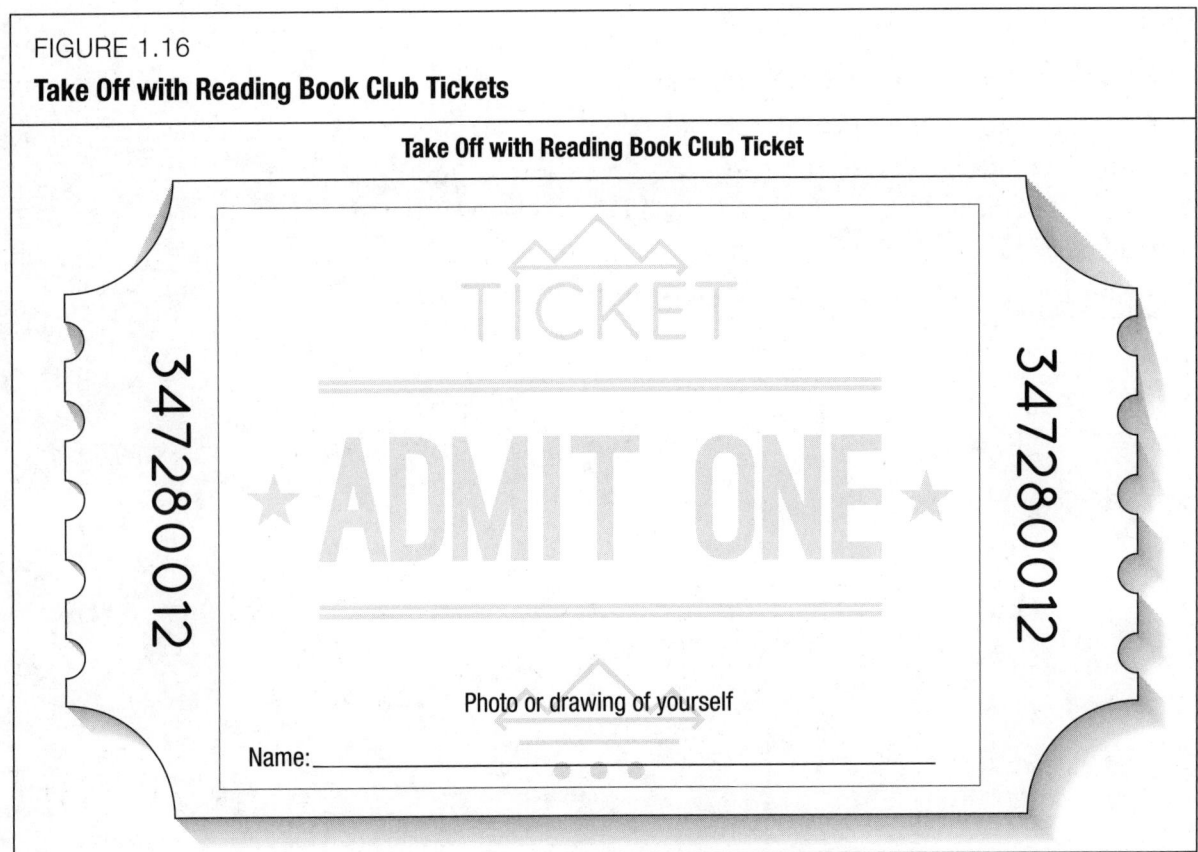

Source: Literacy Strong All Year Long: Powerful Lessons for Grades K–2 by Valerie Ellery, Lori Oczkus, and Timothy V. Rasinski. © 2020 ASCD. Readers may duplicate this figure for noncommercial use within their school.

FIGURE 1.17
Class Book Club Reading Log

Date	Title (Draw the cover)	Author and Illustrator	Rating (Circle one)
		Author: Illustrator:	4 = Great 3 = Good 2 = Just OK 1 = Didn't like it
		Author: Illustrator:	4 = Great 3 = Good 2 = Just OK 1 = Didn't like it
		Author: Illustrator:	4 = Great 3 = Good 2 = Just OK 1 = Didn't like it
		Author: Illustrator:	4 = Great 3 = Good 2 = Just OK 1 = Didn't like it

Source: Literacy Strong All Year Long: Powerful Lessons for Grades K–2 by Valerie Ellery, Lori Oczkus, and Timothy V. Rasinski. © 2020 ASCD. Readers may duplicate this figure for noncommercial use within their school.

FIGURE 1.18
My Reading Log

Date	Title (Draw the cover)	Author and Illustrator	Rating (Circle one)
		Author: Illustrator:	4 = Great 3 = Good 2 = Just OK 1 = Didn't like it
		Author: Illustrator:	4 = Great 3 = Good 2 = Just OK 1 = Didn't like it
		Author: Illustrator:	4 = Great 3 = Good 2 = Just OK 1 = Didn't like it
		Author: Illustrator:	4 = Great 3 = Good 2 = Just OK 1 = Didn't like it

Source: Literacy Strong All Year Long: Powerful Lessons for Grades K–2 by Valerie Ellery, Lori Oczkus, and Timothy V. Rasinski. © 2020 ASCD. Readers may duplicate this figure for noncommercial use within their school.

~2

Beating the Midyear Blahs

If a child can't learn the way we teach,
maybe we should teach the way they learn.
—Ignacio Estrada

The greatest sign of success for a teacher . . . is to be able to say,
"The children are now working as if I did not exist."
—Maria Montessori

Staying motivated and literacy strong is especially important during the middle months of the academic calendar. Just like a marathon runner passing the halfway point in a race, we can view our position at the middle of the school year with a sense of satisfaction from reaching the halfway point *and* a realization of the enormous effort needed to reach the finish line. Sometimes, depending on where you live and teach, the weather dramatically affects the classroom mood with a seemingly endless string of rainy, snowy, cold days. The good news about the middle of the school year is that there is still plenty of time for your students to grow academically. We often notice spikes in student maturity levels, and sometimes reading and writing jump to new heights as well. Assessing progress and targeting the ongoing needs of students, especially struggling readers, becomes a priority at this critical juncture in the school year (Hiebert & Taylor, 1994; Torgesen, 2004).

So, how do we maintain momentum, stay focused, and remain literacy strong in the middle of the school year? Here are some great ways to beat the midyear blahs, energize your students, yield positive results, and bring joy to the classroom.

Literacy-Strong Classroom Scenarios

What does a literacy strong classroom look like in the middle of the school year? Here are some short classroom stories for inspiration.

Motivation: Take Off and Partner Talk!

The students in Mrs. Chan's class settle into their positions on the rug to "take off and partner talk" as they listen to the reading of the delightful story *The Cat with Seven Names* by Tony Johnston. The students place their partner bookmarks on their laps as they lean in to listen to the tale. Before reading, Mrs. Chan directs the class to the bookmark to review the before-reading prompts for fiction: "When I look at the cover and title, I can use both prompts to help me predict. The cat reminds me of my friend's cat because it's so plump. The title is making me think the story will explain why the cat has so many names."

Next, Mrs. Chan flips through a few of the pages, showing the art. She asks students to take turns with their partners and share, using the sentence stem "I think this is about _____" or "This reminds me of _____." "I think the cat is a stray because it is begging to come in the door," predicts Javier. "I think we will find out the cat's names," pipes up Sam.

The students eagerly listen as Mrs. Chan reads the story of the gray cat who visits each neighbor only to receive a new name from each one. During the reading, she pauses to invite students to share reasons why the first character (a librarian) named the cat Stuart Little. The read-aloud continues as the students enthusiastically engage in their partner conversations, using their bookmarks as guides. Later in the classroom library and partner reading center, students use the same bookmark prompts to discuss their independent reading books in pairs. Their reading comprehension soars!

Associating Words: Meaning Madness Time

Giggles abound as the six students at the small guided reading group table listen to Mr. Abbot read aloud the first few pages of *Amelia Bedelia* by Peggy Parish. He records on a chart one of the multiple-meaning words, or homophones, that the maid in the story confuses. Mr. Abbot writes the word *draw* on the board and underneath it places a large sticky note with a drawing of a person drawing and another sticky note with a drawing of a person closing some drapes. Mr. Abbot invites the students to sketch in the air and then pretend to close drapes. He explains: "Amelia Bedelia books are loaded with these sorts of fun words, like *draw*, that can mean two things. She almost always gets things mixed up. We call these words homophones, which are words that sound the same but have different meanings."

The students read the rest of the book silently as the teacher rotates around the table to coach each child. After the reading, he provides two sticky notes. Each child selects one word with two meanings and sketches an image illustrating each meaning on separate sticky notes. Four of the students pick the same example of a homophone in a phrase from the book: "dress the chicken." The students giggle again as they sketch a chicken in jeans, a dress, and even a hat, along with another drawing of a chicken on a plate with stuffing. Meaning madness time makes learning words fun and keeps momentum moving forward!

Comprehension: Is It Make-Believe or Real?

As Miss Campbell holds up each book title from a pile, students sing verses of the "Fiction or Nonfiction Song" (to the tune of "London Bridge"):

> Is it pretend, or is it real?
>
> Is it real?
>
> Is it real?
>
> Is it pretend, or is it real?
>
> Fiction or nonfiction?

Students hold up either their fiction card or their nonfiction card to show their understanding of which type of book is on display at a given moment. Miss Campbell records the book titles on either the "Fiction" or "Nonfiction" side of a two-column chart. She slows the process down for a read-aloud of one of the titles. She displays the book *Ice Bear: In the Steps of the Polar Bear* by Nicola Davies. Students hesitate as they choose which card to show. Miss Campbell asks students to tell the student next to them their reasons for their choices. "The pictures are drawings, so I think it's fiction," shares Ben, and Nadia agrees with a nod. As Miss Campbell reads the facts about polar bears, some students change their minds as they hold up their nonfiction cards.

Next, Miss Campbell invites pairs to share their thoughts about the genre. Later in the morning, students write in their literacy notebooks their responses as they fill in the sentence stem "I like the nonfiction book written by _____ because _____." Nadia writes, "I like the nonfiction book *Ice Bear* written by Nicola Davies because I learned that tiny ice crystals help clean dirt off the bear's fur."

Questions Teacher Ask to Address Midyear Challenges

- What are some ways to continue to inspire my students to read more texts and to read more rigorous texts?
- What are some strategies that will encourage my students to work collaboratively?
- How do I help students become more independent readers?
- What are some formative assessment strategies that I can use to show growth and adjust instruction to meet students' needs?
- What can I do to ensure that all my students learn the expected literacy standards?
- How can I actively engage students in lessons?
- How can I continue to maintain a strong rapport with each of my students and their families?

Educators face many competing challenges in the middle of the school year. In this section are some suggestions for facing these challenges head-on to set the stage for maximum literacy growth.

Addressing Midyear Challenges
Essential Moments for Maintaining Momentum

1. Inspire Students to Read with Funny Books

A whopping 70 percent of students ages 6–17 say they enjoy and prefer reading books that make them laugh (Scholastic, 2015). What does this mean for the classroom? If we read aloud from humorous texts, our students will be inspired to read them on their own. Host a read-aloud/laugh-around and invite students to each share a funny poem, story, or joke book while sitting in a circle. Record video or audio (with permission) of students sharing their titles and post on the class or school website. Take what Miller (2009) calls "shelfies" (i.e., photos of students with their funny books) and compile them into a class album. Stock up on silly and outrageous books for read-alouds and the classroom library. Of course, you can rely on kid favorites, such as the Junie B. Jones series by Barbara Park, anything by Dr. Seuss, and the Captain Underpants series by Dav Pilkey. Try some of these to see if they tickle your students' funny bones:

- *I Wanna Iguana* by Karen Kaufman Orloff
- *How I Became a Pirate* by Melinda Long
- *Never Ride Your Elephant to School* by Doug Johnson

- *Monkey and Duck Quack Up!* by Jennifer Hamburg
- *Polar Bear's Underwear* by Tupera
- *Don't Let the Pigeon Drive the Bus!* by Mo Willems

2. Focus on Fluency

As you read aloud to your students, remember to chat with them about the content of the text. Also, share how you embedded fluency in your reading. Help students recognize that you changed your voice when becoming a different character in the reading by using prosodic functions, such as pitch, tone, and stresses (Ellery, 2014). Help students notice where you became louder or softer, or faster or slower, in your reading. Then, discuss how your fluency made the reading more interesting and understandable. Be sure also to point out to students that before you read to them, you rehearsed the book so you'd be able to read with fluency. This is an important message for students as they reread to gain momentum. Whenever they are to read something orally for an audience, they should rehearse the text in advance (repeated readings).

3. Teach Close Reading with Poems

Invite students to reread poems to partners or chorally as a class. Encourage rereading poems for fluency and understanding. Keep a notebook of poems so students can return to them to reread many times. Make copies of poems for students to mark up with crayons or highlighters as they reread for close reading lessons. Reread to ask questions, circle interesting words, underline main ideas and details, and put stars or smiley faces next to favorite words or parts (Rasinski & Oczkus, 2015a, 2015b, 2015c).

4. Try Short, One-Minute Assessments

Use informal, quick-check assessments at least once a month for all students and every two weeks for struggling readers. The assessments will give you ongoing information about the reading strategies that your students are using, their comprehension, and their fluency. Be sure to then use the information you've gathered to guide your conferences with students and to help you decide what to focus on in your lessons.

Have individual students read for one minute while you mark the substitutions and omissions that each student makes. Also, note how many words the student reads and how fluently in just one minute. Reread the text aloud to the child. After this, remove the passage and ask the child to retell the story. Note the child's responses. Did the student tell what was read in order, including main ideas and details? To find more tips, try *3-Minute Reading Assessments: Word Recognition, Fluency, and Comprehension: Grades 1–4* (Rasinski & Padak, 2005).

5. Boost Reading with Big Buddies and Beam Reading

When younger and older children read together, they both benefit (Topping, 1995). Have your students read once a week with a buddy class of upper-grade students. For a 20–30-minute period, follow a simple protocol in which the older student reads aloud to the younger one first. A flashlight or laser pen can be used for beam reading to allow tracking and to demonstrate reading rate (Ellery, 2014). The older buddy should select a title that the younger buddy will enjoy, and the older buddy needs to practice reading the text fluently before reading it to the younger buddy. If there is time, the younger student may select a brief text to read aloud to the older student.

6. Teach Informational Text Features with a Text Feature Wall

Informational text features serve as road markers that guide readers through nonfiction texts. Over a few weeks, teach your students about informational text features by building a text feature wall or chart. Divide a large chart or chart paper into sections and label them with text features, such as headings, table of contents, visuals, maps, bold words, captions, and glossary. As you read informational texts with students, teach lessons on each of the features. Either make copies of texts and cut out text features to glue or tape onto the text feature wall or cut apart kids' weekly newspapers or magazines as examples (Kelley & Clausen-Grace, 2008; Oczkus, 2014).

7. Cover and Retell with a Partner

Younger children experience challenges when retelling and summarizing. They need to practice without the stress of having to write, too. Try the strategy "Read, Cover, Remember, Retell" (Hoyt, 2002, p. 58). Students work in pairs and take turns reading a page at a time. Each student covers the text just read with a hand, tries to remember the material, and summarizes or retells without looking. The student may peek just once. Both partners continue taking turns reading, covering, and retelling the material. When you use this strategy in a center or workstation, be sure to model and coach often so students continue to improve in their retellings.

8. Celebrate Wonderful Words Everywhere!

Vocabulary is a strong predictor of reading success. Teaching vocabulary improves reading comprehension for native speakers and second-language students alike (Beck, Perfetti, & McKeown, 1982; Carlo et al., 2004). Students can study words by sorting, illustrating, and playing games such as Concentration. Here are some word walls and charts to display in your primary room:

- An alphabetical word wall that features a space for each letter (at least 8½-by-11-inch) for adding student names and high-frequency words

- Charts of synonyms for the word *said*
- Charts of synonyms for the feeling words *happy* and *sad*
- Charts of words for common adjectives and verbs (See the "Shades of Meaning" lesson in Chapter 3)

9. Lucky Listeners

Ask students to practice reading a book, a poem, or other reading material at school. Then, have them take the text home to reread again to at least three "Lucky Listeners" (Rasinski & Griffith, 2011). The dog, a baby, and Grandma all count!

10. Try These Suggested Read-Alouds
- *Ice Bear: In the Steps of the Polar Bear* by Nicola Davies
- *Monkey and Duck Quack Up!* by Jennifer Hamburg
- *Never Ride Your Elephant to School* by Doug Johnson
- *The Cat with Seven Names* by Tony Johnston
- *How I Became a Pirate* by Melinda Long
- *I Wanna Iguana* by Karen Kaufman Orloff
- *The Adventures of Captain Underpants* by Dav Pilkey
- *Polar Bear's Underwear* by Tupera
- *Don't Let the Pigeon Drive the Bus!* by Mo Willems
- Amelia Bedelia books by Peggy Parish
- Junie B. Jones books by Barbara Park
- Dr. Seuss books

11. Midyear Word Ladder

Start with a word that means "to advance forward."

Progress	Take away three letters to make a word that means "to squeeze or hold closely."
Press	Change one letter to make a type of clothing.
Dress	Take away the first letter and change the last letter to make a word that describes what you do when you are tired.
Rest	Change one letter to make a word that means the opposite of *worst*.
Best	Change one letter to make a piece of clothing that goes around your waist and holds up your pants.
Belt	Change one letter to make a metal object that rings when struck.
Bell	Change the vowel to make the beak or mouth part of a duck.
Bill	Change one letter to make a shape that medicines come in.
Pill	Change the last letter to make a heap of wood, clothes, or other things.

Pile   Change one letter to make a distance of 5,280 feet.

Mile   Add two of the same letter to make a word that means "between the beginning and the end."

Middle   Now, fill in the blanks below with appropriate words from the word ladder:

Now that we are in the _____ of the school year, it is important that we not _____ but continue to do our _____ to make _____ toward becoming good readers.

Overview of Chapter 2 Lessons

Lesson 1. Phonological Awareness and Phonics: Isolating and Identifying Sounds—Mingle and Jingle with Vowels

Lesson 2. Phonological Awareness and Phonics: Blending and Segmenting—Making Word Smoothies

Lesson 3. Phonics: Decoding—Vowel Transformers

Lesson 4. Fluency: Phrasing—Performing Poetry

Lesson 5: Comprehension: Craft and Structure—Previewing—Is It Make-Believe or Real?

Lesson 6. Comprehension: Key Ideas and Details—Determining Importance and Summarizing—Sifting Details

Lesson 7. Comprehension: Key Ideas and Details—Questioning for Close Reading—The Question Game

Lesson 8. Vocabulary: Associating Words—Meaning Madness Time: What Else Does It Mean?

Lesson 9. Vocabulary: Analyzing Words—Oh, A-Hunting We Will Go: The Path to Plurals

Lesson 10. Motivation: Motivating Readers—Take Off and Partner Book Talks

LESSON 1. PHONOLOGICAL AWARENESS AND PHONICS: ISOLATING AND IDENTIFYING SOUNDS

Title MINGLE AND JINGLE WITH VOWELS

Trailer A-E-I-O-U, and vowels were their name-o! There's a short vowel here and a long vowel there. Everywhere vowels are heard, A-E-I-O-U! That's right: Every word has a vowel in it. Readers practice isolating and identifying vowel sounds as they mingle and jingle through this vowel lesson.

Literacy Enhancer Phonological Awareness and Phonics: Isolating and Identifying Sounds—Short and Long Vowels

Key Academic Vocabulary Vocabulary from a previous lesson is marked with an asterisk (*).

Alliteration*: A figure of speech in which a series of words repeat the same initial sound

Isolate*: To separate sounds from other sounds in a word

Long vowel: A speech sound produced without obstructing the flow of air from the lungs; the letters *a, e, i, o, u,* and sometimes *y;* long vowels make the same sound as the letter name

Phoneme*: The smallest unit of sound

Short vowel*: A speech sound produced without obstructing the flow of air from the lungs; the letters *a, e, i, o, u,* and sometimes *y;* short vowels do not make the sound of the letter name

Learning Objectives

- Isolate and identify vowel sounds by positioning the mouth, lips, jaw, and tongue to correspond with appropriate short and long vowels in single-syllable words.
- Distinguish long- from short-vowel sounds in spoken single-syllable words.

Essential Questions

- How do you position your mouth for the short vowel _____ in the word _____?
- How do you position your mouth for the long vowel _____ in the word _____?
- What vowel sound is in the word _____?
- What other words have the same vowel sound as the word _____?

STEP 1: PREPARATION

Organize Materials

- Handheld mirrors
- Multimodal text sets with a variety of single-syllable words with short or long vowels
- *Vowel Picture Cards* two-page reproducible (one copy of each card)
- *Vowel Mouth Position* posters (take pictures of the mouth position of short and long vowel sounds to display)

STEP 2: INITIATION

Let's Sing "A-E-I-O-U"

Begin to sing the "A-E-I-O-U" jingle to the tune of "Bingo":

There was a word that had a vowel, and A-E-I-O-U was its name-o.

A-E-I-O-U,

A-E-I-O-U,

A-E-I-O-U,

And vowel was its name-o!

Share a word such as *bat* and begin to sing the verse:

There was a word that had a short *a* vowel, and /ă/ was its name-o.

/ă/-/ă/-/ă/-/ă/-/ă/,

/ă/-/ă/-/ă/-/ă/-/ă/,

/ă/-/ă/-/ă/-/ă/-/ă/,

And short *a* was its name-o! With an /ă/-/ă/ here

And an /ă/-/ă/ there, Here an /ă/,

There an /ă/, Everywhere an /ă/-/ă/!

Continue with other short- and long-vowel words as you scaffold the various vowel sounds over time.

STEP 3: DEMONSTRATION

Positioning Vowels

1. Say three words with the same initial and final sounds but different vowel sounds (e.g., *dig, dog, dug*). You can also use words with the same initial sound

but different vowel and ending sounds (e.g., *rake, ride, rope*). Remind students how these three words make up an alliteration because they all have the same initial sound.

2. Use a handheld mirror to isolate the vowel sound in each word and describe the position of your mouth for that particular vowel in the sample word.
3. Read aloud from a text that has multiple uses of the vowel sound you are highlighting. Isolate and identify the vowel sound in a word by demonstrating how to position your mouth for the vowel sound and how to make the specific vowel sound.
4. Create anchor charts for the vowel you are studying. Make sure to note the position of the mouth for each vowel. Use the two-page *Vowel Picture Cards* reproducible (Figure 2.1) or objects that have the vowel sounds as anchor images for each vowel.

STEP 4: COLLABORATION

Mingle and Jingle and Conversational Coaching

Distribute a vowel image card to each student. Play some music and have students walk around and exchange their card with another student's while saying, "I have the /____/ vowel sound." Have students continue mingling and exchanging their vowel picture cards until you stop the music. When the music stops, have each student find the closest partner and take turns singing the "A-E-I-O-U" jingle with the right sound: (e.g., "With an /ă/-/ă/ here and an /ă/-/ă/ there, here an /ă/, there an /ă/, everywhere an /ă/-/ă/, and short *a* was its name-o!"). Have the partners engage in conversational coaching: "How do you position your mouth for the short *a* vowel sound?" Restart the music and have students continue to mingle and jingle for a few more rounds.

STEP 5: APPLICATION

Sorting Vowels

At a center or literacy station for word work, have students sort items or picture cards into appropriate vowel categories. Remind them to use the class vowel anchor charts as they reflect on the characteristics of each vowel sound and the positioning of their mouth for each sound.

STEP 6: REFLECTION

Oral or Written Response

Have students independently demonstrate the sound that each vowel makes. Have them respond to the essential questions orally or through written response in their literacy notebooks:

- How do you position your mouth for the short vowel in the word _____?
- What vowel sound is in the word _____?
- What other words have the same vowel sound as the word _____?

ADAPTATION/EXTENSION

- Teach students hand cues for each vowel sound. You can use the alphabetic American Sign Language sign or create your own hand cues and make a visual chart of them by using the free Whiteboard Lite: Collaborative Drawing app (play.google.com/store/apps/details?id=greengar.white.board.lite &hl=en).
- Use a vowel-mapping app like VowelViz (itunes.apple.com/us/app/vowelviz/id740035896?mt=8) that allows students to view the vowel production in real time.
- *English Language Learner Suggestion:* Save prerecorded vowel sounds to a digital portfolio on a computer. Display the *Vowel Mouth Position* poster. Place a mirror so that students can see the position of their mouth. Have the students listen to the prerecorded sound and then record themselves making the various vowel sounds as an anchor chart for their digital portfolio.
- *Struggling Reader Suggestion:* Have students take turns selecting a small object from ones you've provided. Have them identify how they position their mouth for the vowel sounds as they say the name of the object as well as the initial and final sounds. They can check the position of their mouth against the *Vowel Mouth Position* poster and sort the objects according the vowel sounds.

EVALUATION

"I Can . . ." Statements

- I can identify the short-vowel sound in single-syllable words.
- I can identify the long-vowel sound in single-syllable words.
- I can produce the vowel sound in single-syllable words.
- I can tell the difference between short- and long-vowel sounds in single-syllable words.

BEHAVIOR INDICATORS

- Isolates and identifies short-vowel sounds by positioning the mouth, lips, jaw, and tongue to correspond with appropriate short vowels in single-syllable words.
- Isolates and identifies long-vowel sounds by positioning the mouth, lips, jaw, and tongue to correspond with appropriate long vowels in single-syllable words.
- Distinguishes long- from short-vowel sounds in spoken single-syllable words when reading regularly spelled, one-syllable words.

FIGURE 2.1
Vowel Picture Cards

Short Vowels

Note: These are the words by row: *apple, bat, cat; bed, egg, pen; igloo, pig, pin; clock, octopus, ostrich; bug, jug, umbrella.*

(continued)

Source: Literacy Strong All Year Long: Powerful Lessons for Grades K–2 by Valerie Ellery, Lori Oczkus, and Timothy V. Rasinski. © 2020 ASCD. Readers may duplicate this figure for noncommercial use within their school.

Long Vowels

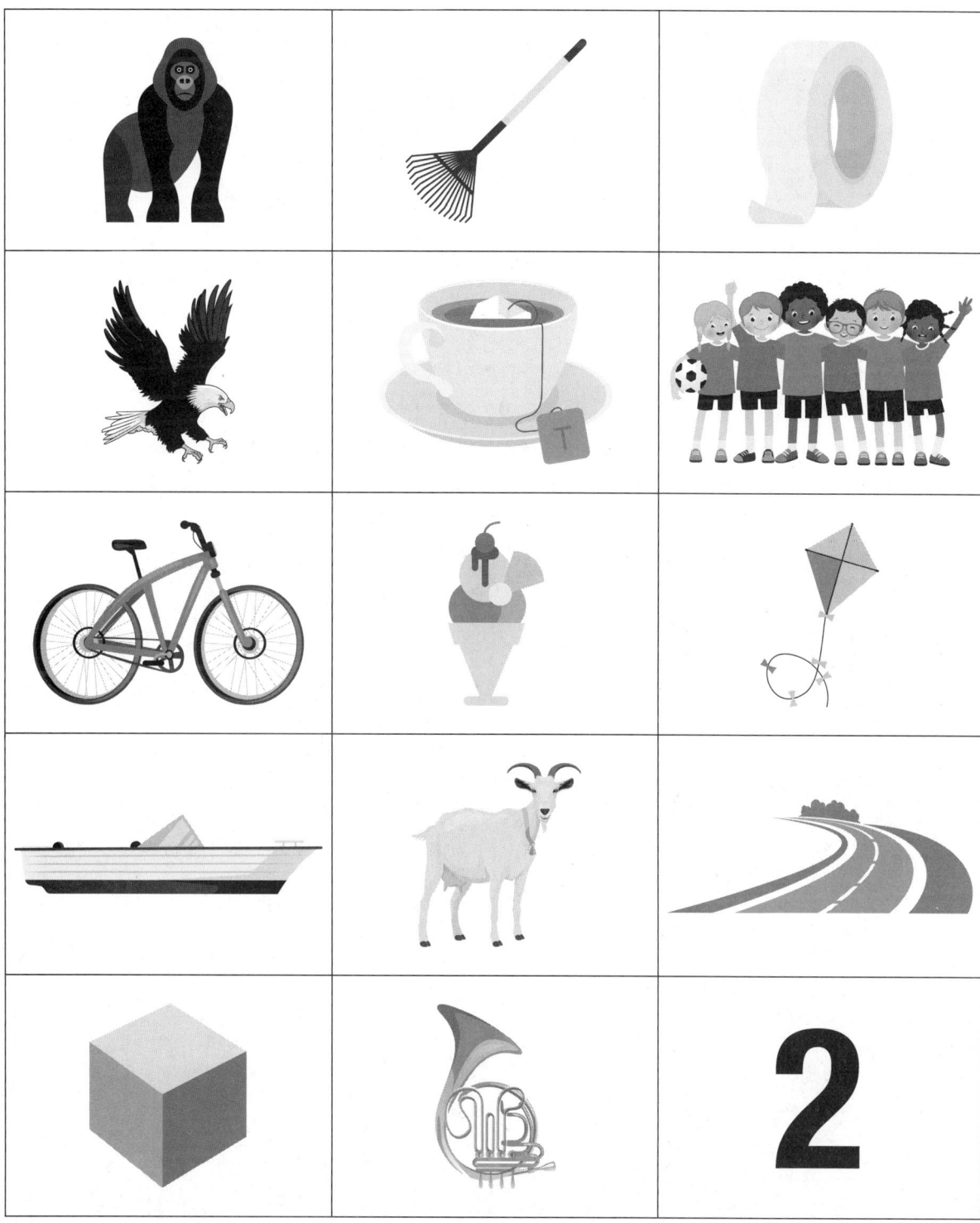

Note: These are the words by row: *ape, rake, tape; eagle, tea, team; bike, ice cream, kite; boat, goat, road; cube, tuba, two.*

Source: Literacy Strong All Year Long: Powerful Lessons for Grades K–2 by Valerie Ellery, Lori Oczkus, and Timothy V. Rasinski. © 2020 ASCD. Readers may duplicate this figure for noncommercial use within their school.

LESSON 2. PHONOLOGICAL AWARENESS AND PHONICS: BLENDING AND SEGMENTING

Title MAKING WORD SMOOTHIES

Trailer Refreshingly smooth and packed with a blend of wonderful ingredients! Word smoothies are a healthy blend of sounds and syllables. Help readers whip up the perfect word by segmenting just the right ingredients and then blending them together to form a smooth read of words.

Literacy Enhancer Phonological Awareness and Phonics: Blending and Segmenting—Whole-Part-Whole and Syllables

Key Academic Vocabulary Vocabulary from a previous lesson is marked with an asterisk (*).

Blending*: Combining a sequence of two or more sounds to form a word

Onset*: The part of a syllable before the vowel; not all syllables have onsets

Rime*: The part of a syllable beginning with the sounded vowel and any consonants that follow

Segmenting: Breaking a word by phonemes (sounds) and syllables

Syllable: A part of a word that contains only one sounded vowel; words can be made up of one or more syllables

Learning Objectives

- Orally produce single-syllable words by segmenting and blending sounds (phonemes).
- Segment single-syllable words into their complete sequence of individual sounds (phonemes).

Essential Questions

- How can you blend and segment sounds in spoken words?
- How many parts do you hear in the word _____?

STEP 1: PREPARATION

Organize Materials

- Blender
- Fresh fruit (e.g., bananas, strawberries, peaches)
- Liquid (e.g., milk, water, fruit juice)
- Cups
- Knife for slicing the fruit

- hula hoop
- Multimodal text set for the topic of study
- *Making Word Smoothies* reproducible (copies or enlarged for display)
- Literacy notebooks

STEP 2: INITIATION

Making a Fruit Smoothie

Gather ingredients and prepare an area for demonstrating how to make smoothies. Ask students for ideas on how to make a great smoothie and chart their responses. Show some of the fresh fruit that you gathered to make a smoothie today. Hold up a piece of fruit (e.g., banana) and explain that it is a whole fruit and that when eaten by itself you taste only its flavor. However, when you blend it with other fruit, all the flavors come together to make one smooth, refreshing taste. Almost like drinking a delicious dessert!

Explain that you could place whole fruit into the blender, but that some fruits need to be cut into smaller chunks to blend more easily. Slice the fruit and put into the blender. Add liquid (e.g., milk, water, fruit juice) as the other main part of a good smoothie. Start the blender. As it begins to "digest" the contents, turn to a higher speed to hasten the process. Compare these steps with the class chart on how to make a smoothie. Share that the students are going to compare making a smoothie with reading. Pour and enjoy.

STEP 3: DEMONSTRATION

Making a Word Smoothie

1. Select several single-syllable and onset/rime words from the class read-aloud.
2. Hold up a bracelet and remind students how we can use two of them to blend sounds. Review the *Blending Dance* reproducible from Chapter 1 with the onset/rime words and how we can hop, stomp, slide, and clap to form a word.
3. Hold up one bracelet and explain how it will be a symbolic representation of a blender in making a word smoothie.
4. Revisit the class chart on how to make a smoothie. Share that you are going to use that same concept to make a word smoothie. Here's a sample chart:

Fruit Smoothie	Word Smoothie
Fruit represents the whole.	Words represent the whole.
The fruit is cut into parts.	The word is segmented into sound parts.

Fruit Smoothie	Word Smoothie
A variety of fruit goes in the blender.	A variety of sounds goes in the "blender."
Liquid is added for a smoother blend.	Context is added for a smoother read.
The blender speed rises as it begins to "digest" the content by cutting and blending the contents.	Reading speed rises as the reader begins to "digest" the content by segmenting and blending sounds in words.

5. Revisit the selected text, noting words that have just one syllable. Think aloud about the words you selected and why they are one-syllable long (e.g., "All words have syllables, which can be a letter or a combination of letters that we combine/voice together. I know that every syllable must contain a vowel. The words I chose from the text are all one-syllable words, and they each have a vowel."). Model a few examples.
6. Inside the bracelet (substituting as the blender), place a "basket of fruit" (construction paper patterns, plastic, or real). Place a letter with "sound slashes" (e.g., /f/) on each fruit to represent each sound in the selected word (e.g., by using permanent marker and paper taped onto the fruit). *Optional:* In advance, you can number the sounds in the order in which they form the word.
7. Select a piece of fruit with a letter/sound on it. Say its sound and place the fruit inside the bracelet. Each time you add a piece of fruit (letter) to the bracelet, record the new word smoothie ingredient on the interactive whiteboard with a plus sign. This will make a math sentence for adding together the letters in the blender.
8. Continue until all the sounds for the word have been placed inside the bracelet. Remind students to only produce the sound of each letter on the fruit, not the letters' names. Have students begin to blend the sounds by saying slowly each sound of the fruit in order. Gradually go faster and faster, as if you are turning up the speed of the blender until the word is fully blended in a smooth fashion.
9. Revisit the text and place the selected word back into context for a smooth read.

STEP 4: COLLABORATION

Conversational Coaching

Engage in conversational coaching by asking students to discuss the following questions with different partners:

- How many sounds do you hear in the word _____?
- What are the sounds you hear in the word _____?
- What is the difference between _____ (word) and _____ (word)?

Have students discuss the steps for making a word smoothie.

STEP 5: APPLICATION

Blending the Word

Using the *Making Word Smoothies* reproducible (Figure 2.2), have students work in groups or individually to select single-syllable words to segment and blend. Remind them to use the class chart on how to make a smoothie as they think about blending and segmenting the words. Have students practice breaking each word apart by its individual sounds and then blending the sounds back together as the whole word to demonstrate the whole-part-whole concept of a word.

STEP 6: REFLECTION

Oral or Written Response

Have students select five one-syllable words from a text that they are reading and record them as a "math sentence" in their literacy notebooks. Ask students to respond to the essential questions orally or in writing:

- How can you blend and segment sounds in spoken words?
- What does the whole-part-whole concept of a word mean to you?

ADAPTATION/EXTENSION

- Use the online Syllable Dictionary (www.howmanysyllables.com) as a reference for finding out how many syllables are in a word and how to pronounce a word.
- *English Language Learner Suggestion:* Distribute clay and have students roll the clay in a long log shape. Say a word slowly pronouncing each sound individually. Then, have students repeat the sounds and break off a small piece of the clay to represent each one. Next, have students pick up the first piece of clay, say its sound again, and blend by pinching the vowel sound to the initial sound. Continue the process until the word is blended back to original state.
- *Struggling Reader Suggestion:* Substitute fruit with two or three blocks to blend phonemes. Each block should be a different color that represents a specific sound. Have students push one block forward and say the sound it represents. Slowly move each block to touch the next one as the sounds are being voiced. Once all blocks are lined up, have students say the complete word aloud.

EVALUATION

"I Can . . ." Statements

- I can identify and blend the syllables in a word.
- I can identify and segment the syllables in a word.
- I can blend and segment onsets and rimes in single-syllable spoken words.

BEHAVIOR INDICATORS

- Orally produces single-syllable words by segmenting and blending sounds.
- Distinguishes the sounds in spoken single-syllable words.
- Identifies the vowels in single-syllable words.

FIGURE 2.2
Making Word Smoothies

Directions: In each box, write the letter/sound that you want to blend to make a word. Then, in the blender, write the word that you whipped together.

Source: Literacy Strong All Year Long: Powerful Lessons for Grades K–2 by Valerie Ellery, Lori Oczkus, and Timothy V. Rasinski. © 2020 ASCD. Readers may duplicate this figure for noncommercial use within their school.

LESSON 3. PHONICS: DECODING

Title VOWEL TRANSFORMERS

Trailer In the world of words, there are a few letters that can change everything! They are known to transform one word into an entirely new word. Although there are only five of them, they are mighty—so mighty that a word cannot be a word without one of them. They are known as the vowel transformers! Students practice decoding words as they associate, distinguish, and ultimately transform words with short and long vowels.

Literacy Enhancer Phonics: Decoding—Short and Long Vowels—Silent *e*

Key Academic Vocabulary Vocabulary from a previous lesson is marked with an asterisk (*).

Decode*: The ability to apply letter-sound relationships to read and pronounce a written word

Grapheme*: The written symbol (letters) used to represent a phoneme (sounds)

Long vowels: The letters *a, e, i, o, u,* and sometimes *y*; long vowels make a speech sound produced without obstructing the flow of air from the lungs; make the same sound as the letter name

Short vowels*: The letters *a, e, i, o, u,* and sometimes *y*; short vowels make a speech sound produced without obstructing the flow of air from the lungs; do not make the sound of the letter name

Syllable*: A basic unit of spoken language containing a vowel sound

Vowel*: A speech sound produced without obstructing the flow of air from the lungs; the letters *a, e, i, o, u,* and sometimes *y* in written form

Learning Objectives

- Distinguish long- from short-vowel sounds in written one-syllable words.
- Identify final-*e* and common vowel team conventions for representing long-vowel sounds.

Essential Questions

- How will recognizing the difference between short and long vowels help me read and write words?
- What happens to many words when an *e* is placed at the end of it?

STEP 1: PREPARATION

Organize Materials

- Box with lid
- Markers to write on the box
- Sample vowel objects, pictures, or word cards, including a cap, a cup, and a cape
- Toys that transform, pictures of transforming toys, or a video clip of a transforming toy
- Sticky notes
- Index cards
- Multimodal text sets for the topic of study
- *Two Brothers* reproducible (copies or enlarged for display)
- *Vowel Transformers T-Chart* reproducible (copies or enlarged for display)
- Literacy notebooks

STEP 2: INITIATION

Transforming Words

In advance of the lesson, decorate a lidded box with vowels and the label "Vowel Transformers." Place a few items in the box that can be transformed by vowels to make new items (e.g., *cap → cup*, *bag → bug*). These items can be real, toys, or picture cards.

In the classroom, display various transforming toys or pictures of them and ask students what makes these items transformers. Explain that transformers are given that name because they can change some of their parts to form something different. Show students the "Vowel Transformers" box. For example, hold up a cup, place it inside the box, close the lid, and say aloud, "Vowel transformers can be more than meets the eye." Open the box and pull out the cap. Ask students, "What transformed the cup into a cap?" Discuss their responses. Display the words *cup* and *cap*. Highlight how the vowel was transformed from a short *u* into a short *a* to create a new word. Share that students are going to continue to transform single-syllable words with vowels.

STEP 3: DEMONSTRATION

Special Transformer

1. Review how every word has a vowel in it. Remind students that the English language has many vowel sounds that can be formed from just five vowels. These sounds can be the short vowels that change to match their surroundings.

Explain that there are other vowels that can transform a word to sound completely different from the short-vowel word. They are called the long vowels, and when read aloud, these long vowels say their letter name (i.e., ā, ē, ī, ō, ū), as in the word *cake*. You can hear the letter *a* make its own letter name as a sound.

2. Hold up the cap. Place it back in the "Vowel Transformers" box and pull out a cape. Ask students to share what they notice about the vowel sounds in these words. Write the words and highlight the difference in their spellings. Place a sticky note over the *e* in *cape*. Read the short-vowel word again. Lift the sticky note and read the long-vowel version. Point out that *cap* is a consonant-vowel-consonant (CVC) word and that adding an *e* at the end of *cap* changes it to a consonant-vowel-consonant + silent *e* (CVC*e*) word. The change from a short-vowel sound to a long-vowel sound transforms the word into a new one, *cap* to *cape*.

3. Read aloud books that have several CVC and CVC*e* words in them or read the *Two Brothers* reproducible (Figure 2.3) to highlight CVC and CVC*e* words. Reread the poem while completing the *Vowel Transformers T-Chart* reproducible (Figure 2.4). Discuss how when *e* is added to the end of words, the *e* is silent and the other vowel is transformed into a long-vowel sound that says its letter name. Share that not all CVC and CVC*e* words can be transformed into words that make sense (e.g., *bike*, *trike*) and that most words that end with *e* transform the other vowel in the word to a long-vowel sound. Here's a sample chart:

Transforming Words		Non-Transforming Words	
Short Vowel (CVC)	Long Vowel (CVC*e*)	Short Vowel (CVC)	Long Vowel (CVC*e*)
hop	hope	get	bike
hug	huge	has	decide
Nat	Nate	his	inside
not	note	pup	trike
rid	ride		
scrap	scrape		

STEP 4: COLLABORATION

Hop to Hope and Conversational Coaching

Distribute to half the class one index card per student featuring a CVC word that can transform into a new word by adding *e* at the end. Give the other students a small sticky note with lowercase *e* written on it. Play music and have students hop around the room until the music stops. Then, have each CVC student and closest silent-*e* student become partners. Say to them, "Now that you have *hopped* to a partner, I *hope* you can use the silent *e* as a vowel transformer and create a new word." Invite the partners to engage in conversational coaching by asking them to transform their CVC word into a CVC*e* word by linking arms and saying the newly formed word. Then have the partners share how their two words differ in meaning.

   Here are some sample CVC words for the index cards:
- *a_e:* at, can, cap, fad, hat, mad, man, mat, pal, pan, plan, rag, rat, rip, Sam, scrap, stag, tap, van, wag
- *e_e:* pet
- *i_e:* bit, dim, din, fin, hid, kit, pin, rid, rip, shin, sit, slid, slim, spin, strip, Tim, twin, whit
- *o_e:* cod, cop, dot, glob, hop, mop, nod, not, rob, rod, rot, slop, ton, wok
- *u_e:* cub, cut, dud, hug, tub, us

STEP 5: APPLICATION

Searching for the Silent E

Place a copy of the *Vowel Transformers T-Chart* reproducible at a word workstation. Invite teams, partners, or individual students to use multimodal texts to search for words to sort. On individual index cards, have students write CVC*e* words that can be transformed into short-vowel words by deleting the silent *e* at the end of the words. Have students vertically fold the end of each index card toward the word until it covers up the letter *e* to create a flap card. Ask partners to create sentences using each word in context and then compare how the word was used in the chosen text.

STEP 6: REFLECTION

Oral or Written Response

Ask students to select words from the *Vowel Transformers T-Chart* and write a sentence using each word in an appropriate context. Challenge them to connect the sentences together to create a story using as many of the words on the chart as they can. In their literacy notebooks, have students independently create their own alliterations. Have students respond to these essential questions orally or in writing:

- How do you determine the difference between short and long vowels in words?
- What happens to a word when an *e* is placed at the end of it?

ADAPTATION/EXTENSION

- Create a vowel word wall with words categorized by short and long vowels. Use a completed *Vowel Transformers T-Chart* reproducible to populate your word wall.
- Use a variety of poetry to teach vowels. Use professional resources that have vowel lessons designed around poetry, like *Learning Through Poetry: Long Vowels* by Mary Jo Fresch and David L. Harrison (2013).
- *English Language Learner Suggestion:* Have the students interact with online vowel games for hearing the sounds and visual engagement. Examples include LearningGamesforKids.com's games that focus on short vowels (www.learninggamesforkids.com/spelling_games/short-vowel-games/all-short-vowels/short-vowel-game.html) and PBS's Word Transformer: Word Party for *r*-controlled words (pbskids.org/electriccompany/games/wordtransformer).
- *Struggling Reader Suggestion:* Select two colored index cards and a stack of white index cards. On one colored index card, write the letter *e* to represent the silent *e* that can transform a short-vowel word to a long-vowel word. Write out five short-vowel words on the other colored index cards. If needed, have a picture to illustrate each word. Have students read the short-vowel word card and use it in a sentence. Then place the silent *e* card next to the word. Have students write the new "transformed" word on a blank white index card, say the long-vowel name, and use it in a sentence. Here are some sample words for short-vowel cards:
    - *a = mad, can, cap, tap, wag*
    - *i = kit, fin, win, bit, pin*
    - *o = pop, top, mop, tot, rob*

EVALUATION

"I Can . . ." Statements

- I can decode the short and long vowels in words.
- I can sort CVC and CVC*e* words.
- I can read long-vowel words with a silent *e* at the end.

BEHAVIOR INDICATORS

- Associates the long and short sounds with the common spellings (graphemes) for the five major vowels.
- Identifies final-*e* and common vowel team conventions for representing long-vowel sounds.
- Distinguishes long and short vowels when reading regularly spelled one-syllable words.

FIGURE 2.3
Two Brothers: Nat and Nate

Nate wants to ride his bike.
He hops on it. It is not a trike.
The bike is huge, and he falls down.
He gets a scrape and has a frown.

Nat hopes to cheer Nate up.
He wants to rid his frown with a pup.
Nate decides to scrap the ride.
He hugs the pup and goes inside.

Source: Literacy Strong All Year Long: Powerful Lessons for Grades K–2 by Valerie Ellery, Lori Oczkus, and Timothy V. Rasinski. © 2020 ASCD. Readers may duplicate this figure for noncommercial use within their school.

FIGURE 2.4
Vowel Transformers T-Chart

Name: _____

Directions: Read the text and search for words that have the CVC or CVC*e* pattern that can be transformed by adding or deleting the *e* at the end. Write them on the chart in the correct "Transforming Words" column. If a word cannot be transformed from CVC to CVC*e* or from CVC*e* to CVC, write it in the correct "Non-Transforming Words" column.

Transforming Words		Non-Transforming Words	
Short-Vowel Words (CVC)	**Long-Vowel Words (CVC*e*)**	**Short-Vowel Words (CVC)**	**Long-Vowel Words (CVC*e*)**

Source: Literacy Strong All Year Long: Powerful Lessons for Grades K–2 by Valerie Ellery, Lori Oczkus, and Timothy V. Rasinski. © 2020 ASCD. Readers may duplicate this figure for noncommercial use within their school.

LESSON 4. FLUENCY: PHRASING

Title PERFORMING POETRY

Trailer It's showtime! One of the best ways to develop fluency is to have students rehearse and perform poetry. Poems are short texts that can easily be chunked into sentences and phrases that reflect the rhythm of the poem. When students are given opportunities to perform poetry, they have an authentic purpose for developing fluency.

Literacy Enhancer Fluency: Phrasing—Chunking Texts into Meaningful Units

Key Academic Vocabulary Vocabulary from a previous lesson is marked with an asterisk (*).

Comma*: A punctuation mark used within a sentence to set off meaningful phrases or other meaningful chunks of text

Period*: A punctuation mark used at the end of a sentence that is a statement

Phrase*: A sequence of two or more words that form a meaningful unit, often preceded and followed by a brief pause when read orally

Poem: A text in verse form that is often characterized by alliteration, assonance, rhyme, or rhythm to express meaning

Punctuation*: Marks in writing or printing that are used to separate meaningful elements and make the meaning of the text clear

Sentence*: A unit of one or more words that expresses an independent statement, question, request, command, or exclamation

Learning Objectives

- Explore opportunities to read, rehearse, and perform poetry for young children.
- Identify and read interesting phrases and sentences in poems that students rehearse and perform.

Essential Questions

- What is a poem?
- What are common features found in poetry for young children?
- Why is it important to rehearse and read poems in phrases and sentences?

STEP 1: PREPARATION

Organize Materials

- Collections of poetry for primary students
- Chart paper

- *Performing Poetry* reproducible (copies or enlarged for display)
- Literacy notebooks

STEP 2: INITIATION

Perform a Poem

Find a poem, rhyme, or song that is familiar to most of your students (e.g., "Hickory Dickory Dock," "Jack and Jill"). Put the text on display on chart paper in your classroom. Discuss with students the nature of poetry versus informational and narrative texts. Begin to "perform" the poem with proper phrasing and expressions. Help students see that the rhyme and rhythm often found in poetry help the reader break the poem into meaningful phrases and sentences.

STEP 3: DEMONSTRATION

Mark the Phrases

1. Read the poem on display in your classroom aloud, with good expression and volume. Emphasize the importance of breaking the poem into appropriate phrasal units.
2. Read the poem aloud a second time. As you read, insert slash marks at the appropriate phrase and sentence boundaries. Discuss with students the nature of these slash marks and how they mark units of meaning and points at which the reader should briefly pause.
3. Invite students to read the poem two more times with you, noting and emphasizing the phrase boundaries as you read.
4. Display a second copy of the poem that does not contain the phrase markings. Ask students to read the poem with you, making sure that they phrase the poem into appropriate phrasal units.

STEP 4: COLLABORATION

Poetry Partners

Distribute a copy of the poem and the *Performing Poetry* reproducible (Figure 2.5) to each student. Have students refer to the guidelines for performing poetry to check their rehearsal. Next, have them work in pairs or groups of three. Ask students to spend five minutes continuing to rehearse the poem, exploring various ways that it can be performed by two or three students (e.g., alternating lines, choral reading).

After several minutes of rehearsal, invite the groups of students to perform the poem for the class. Discuss how each group may have used a different form of performance but that the need to read with appropriate phrasing and rhythm was essential for a meaningful and enjoyable performance. Ask individual students in the audience to comment on what they particularly liked about each group performance. You may wish to invite students to snap their fingers in appreciation after each performance, as in a poetry coffeehouse.

STEP 5: APPLICATION

Make It a Poetry Slam!

Over the next several days, assign new poems to pairs or small groups of students. Allow students time during the school day to rehearse their assigned poem with their group members. As students rehearse, coach and give formative feedback to individual group members, remembering to focus your comments on fluent and expressive reading of the phrases within the poem.

At the end of the school day or on the following day, allow student groups to perform the poems that they have been rehearsing. Set the stage for the performances by placing stools at the front of the room and inviting parent and teacher guests to be part of the audience. Encourage positive responses from the audience after each performance, focusing particularly on students' expressive reading in phrases.

Assigning poetry to students and having them rehearse and perform their assigned poems can become a regular classroom routine in which students rehearse and perform poetry over several weeks.

STEP 6: REFLECTION

Oral Response

After students perform their assigned poems, invite classmates and others in the audience to make specific, positive comments about the performances. Be sure to emphasize the importance of expressive phrasing that reflects the rhythm of the poem.

Written Response

After they've engaged in several poetry performances, ask students to write personal responses in their literacy notebooks about the experience. Have students comment on what they had to focus on to achieve a performance that an audience would find meaningful and enjoyable. You may ask them to complete the following sentence stems:

- I like to read poems because _____.
- To perform a poem for an audience, it is important to _____.
- The part I like best about reading and performing poetry is _____.

ADAPTATION/EXTENSION

- Over several weeks, introduce students to the poetry of different poets (e.g., David Harrison, Brod Bagert, Bruce Lansky, Shel Silverstein). Engage students in discussions about their favorite poets.
- Have students break poems into multiple parts so they can be performed by groups of two to four students.
- *English Language Learner Suggestion:* Identify and display on a word chart difficult words from the poems that students read. Practice these words with students regularly, remind students of their meaning, and encourage students to use these words in their own oral and written language.
- *Struggling Reader Suggestion:* Engage in additional repeated reading of the poems with your struggling readers. Continue to display and read poems that were introduced in previous days. Be sure to remind students to track the words in each poem visually even if they have the poem memorized. It is only reading if the reader sees the words while reciting them.

EVALUATION

"I Can . . ." Statements

- I can read a poem with good expression and phrasing.
- I can identify the features that are common in poetry for children.
- I can rehearse a poem.
- I can perform a poem for an audience.
- I can be a good audience member when listening to poetry.
- I can tell what makes for a good reading of a poem.

BEHAVIOR INDICATORS

- Independently engages in rehearsal of a poem.
- Performs a poem with good fluency and phrasing.
- Identifies common features found in poetry for children.
- Listens attentively as an audience member when poetry is being read aloud.
- Provides positive and constructive feedback when listening to a classmate read a poem.

FIGURE 2.5
Performing Poetry

Directions: Review the Performing Poetry Guidelines. Read the sample poem below or another poem. Insert appropriate phrase and sentence boundaries. Remember to use slash marks to mark units of meaning within the poem and places for pausing as a reader. Reread for phrasing with expression and volume and then perform the poetry for a partner or the class.

Performing Poetry Guidelines
- Make eye contact.
- Capture your audience's attention by looking into their eyes.
- Project your voice. Speak loud and clear so you can be heard.
- Use facial expressions. Make appropriate expressions to demonstrate emotions.
- Apply gestures. Use appropriate hand and body movements to perform the poem.

Winter Is More Than Cold

Winter is here it's time for the cold,
But play it smart and be a bit bold.
Grab a book to have and hold.
Read a book. It's as precious as gold!

Source: Literacy Strong All Year Long: Powerful Lessons for Grades K–2 by Valerie Ellery, Lori Oczkus, and Timothy V. Rasinski. © 2020 ASCD. Readers may duplicate this figure for noncommercial use within their school.

LESSON 5: COMPREHENSION: CRAFT AND STRUCTURE—PREVIEWING

Title Is It Make-Believe or Real?

Trailer Fairy tales, cartoon characters, and superheroes frolic in the active imaginations of children. Distinguishing between what's real and what's make-believe can present challenges for young students who often float in and out of the world of pretend. Explore child-centered options to help students identify fiction and nonfiction in fun and active ways!

Literacy Enhancer Comprehension: Craft and Structure—Previewing

Key Academic Vocabulary Vocabulary from a previous lesson is marked with an asterisk (*).

Author*: The person who wrote the book

Back cover*: The back side of a book that often contains information about the book and its author and illustrator

Book cover*: The front of a book that contains the title, author, and illustrator

Fiction*: The genre that includes stories that are make-believe; may also include poetry

Illustrator*: The person who drew the pictures or illustrations that go with the book's content

Informational text*: A type of nonfiction text

Nonfiction*: The genre that includes factual, real information that is portrayed to answer, explain, or describe

Photographer*: The person who took the photos that go with the book's content

Predict*: To use information from a text to infer what the text will be about or what a reader might learn from it

Text features*: Parts of the text that support the reader in navigating through key characteristics of a text for locating and accessing meaning from the text (e.g., title, headings, photographs, bold words, maps)

Title*: The name of the book, which usually tells what it is about or gives clues to the content

Learning Objectives

- Recognize common types of fiction texts.
- Recognize different types of nonfiction texts.

- Categorize books and texts into fiction or nonfiction categories.
- Use the term *informational text*, with *nonfiction* as a synonym.

Essential Questions

- What are the characteristics of a fiction text?
- What are the characteristics of a nonfiction text?
- How can you tell if a text is fiction or nonfiction?
- What are some examples of fiction texts?
- What are some examples of nonfiction texts?

STEP 1: PREPARATION

Organize Materials

- Chart paper for a two-column chart
- *Is It Make-Believe or Real?* reproducible (one copy)
- *Fiction or Nonfiction Song* reproducible (copies or enlarged for display)
- *Fiction/Nonfiction Organizer* reproducible (copies or enlarged for display)
- Literacy notebooks

STEP 2: INITIATION

Is It Make-Believe or Real?

Ask students if they enjoy pretending. Share a pretend activity that you engaged in as a child (e.g., your backyard was a swamp and the tree a pirate ship). Invite partners to briefly share their pretend games and scenarios with each other. Ask, "Was your game real or make-believe?" Ask students if they enjoy reading make-believe books or watching make-believe shows on television. Tell students to think about the "real" or "true" shows or books they know. Share a few examples of your own. Tell students that today they will consider what kinds of books are fiction, or make-believe, and what kinds of books are nonfiction, or real.

STEP 3: DEMONSTRATION

Making a Fiction/Nonfiction Chart

1. Make a chart and divide it into two columns: Fiction and Nonfiction. Define *fiction* as make-believe and *nonfiction* as real. Tell students that they are going to look at books and texts and decide whether they are either fiction or nonfiction. (Fill in the chart as you teach the lesson.)

Here's a sample chart:

Fiction	Nonfiction
Is it make-believe? • Is not real/made up • Uses the language of stories • Is read to enjoy • Is read from beginning to end • Contains illustrations • Is organized by setting, characters, events, and sometimes problems • Sometimes has a theme or teaches us a lesson, such as friendship, courage, or honesty	Is it real? • Contains real/true information • Uses the language of facts • Is read to learn • Allows for skipping around from one piece of information to another when reading • Sometimes has illustrations or photographs • Includes text features such as table of contents, headings, glossary, labels, graphs, photographs, and illustrations

2. Share with students the image of the wizard from the *Is It Make-Believe or Real?* reproducible (Figure 2.6). Think aloud as you share whether you think the character is make-believe or real and tell why. Tape the wizard onto the make-believe side of the chart.

3. Share with students the picture of the newspaper from the *Is It Make-Believe or Real?* reproducible. Think aloud about this picture and invite students to tell you if it belongs on the make-believe side of the chart or the real side. *Optional:* Sing the first three verses of the "Fiction or Nonfiction Song" (see reproducible in Figure 2.7) and invite the class to sing with you.

4. Gather a stack of picture books, poetry books, and magazines, covering both fiction and nonfiction. Hold up the first fiction book and begin to preview the text features. Show the cover and read the title. Read a page or two aloud. Flip through the rest of the book and ask, "Based on the text features, is it make-believe or real?" Have students turn to partners and share. Hold up another fiction book and ask students if it is make-believe or real. Flip through the book, making some of the other points about fiction to add to the chart. *Optional:* Sing verses 1 and 2 from the "Fiction or Nonfiction Song."

5. Share a few of the nonfiction books. Discuss the covers and then flip through the books. Ask students what makes them different from the fiction texts you showed. Complete the chart by adding points about nonfiction texts. *Optional:* Sing verses 3 and 4 from the "Fiction or Nonfiction Song."

STEP 4: COLLABORATION

Conversational Coaching

Engage in conversational coaching by asking students to discuss the following question with diverse partners: "Which book is fiction or nonfiction, and why?" Have students add the titles of the books on the class chart in the appropriate column. *Optional:* As you show book covers, have students hold up either the wizard image or the newspaper image, using different-colored craft sticks or straws to represent the images unless you choose to provide them for each student. Invite partners to discuss, then debrief with the class.

STEP 5: APPLICATION

Categorize and Shop

Provide students with copies of publishers' book catalogs (e.g., Scholastic). Give students the two-column *Fiction/Nonfiction Organizer* reproducible. Ask students to cut out book covers from the catalogs, sort them according to type of book, and paste them in the appropriate column. Students can also find books in the classroom library and write the cover information on the *Fiction or Nonfiction Organizer* (Figure 2.8) reproducible.

STEP 6: REFLECTION

Written Response

Invite students to select one fiction title and one nonfiction title and think of one or two reasons why they enjoy each book. Use some of these starters and have students respond in their literacy notebooks. Ask students to consider if they usually prefer fiction or nonfiction or if they like both the same and to tell why, using these sentence stems:

- I like the fiction book called and written by _____ because _____.
- Another reason I like this book is _____.
- I like the nonfiction book called _____ and written by _____ because _____.
- Another reason I like this book is _____.

ADAPTATION/EXTENSION

- Challenge students to study informational texts and decide if the author wrote the book to answer a question, to explain something, or to persuade the reader.
- Try the ReadWriteThink.org lesson plan called "Comparing Fiction and Nonfiction with Little Red Riding Hood Text Sets" (www.readwritethink.org/classroom-resources/lesson-plans/comparing-fiction-nonfiction-with-889.html).

- *English Language Learner Suggestion:* Place a variety of fiction and nonfiction books in a bag. Invite students to take turns reaching in to randomly grab one of the books. Students in the group indicate whether the book is fiction or nonfiction by holding up either their wizard or newspaper cards. Invite students to read the books and share their favorite parts. *Optional:* Tape each card to a tongue depressor.
- *Struggling Reader Suggestion:* Post signs that say *fiction* and *nonfiction* or *wizard* and *newspaper* on opposite sides of the room. Hold up books one at a time and read the title and first page. Students indicate which genre it is by walking to the correct sign. They turn to a partner and share why they think the book falls under that genre.

EVALUATION

"I Can . . ." Statements

- I can identify a fiction text.
- I can identify a nonfiction text.
- I can sort fiction and nonfiction books into separate piles.
- I can give one reason why a book is fiction or nonfiction.
- I can give two or three reasons why a book is fiction or nonfiction.

BEHAVIOR INDICATORS

- Identifies fiction books using a wide range of examples.
- Gives one reason why a book is fiction.
- Shares two or more reasons why a book is fiction.
- Identifies nonfiction books using a wide range of examples.
- Gives one reason why a book is nonfiction.
- Shares two or more reasons why a book is nonfiction.
- Names several types of fiction texts (e.g., poems, Readers Theater scripts, adventure stories, mysteries).
- Names several types of nonfiction texts (e.g., how-to, explanations).
- Sorts a stack of books into fiction and nonfiction.

FIGURE 2.6
Is It Make-Believe or Real?

Source: Literacy Strong All Year Long: Powerful Lessons for Grades K–2 by Valerie Ellery, Lori Oczkus, and Timothy V. Rasinski. © 2020 ASCD. Readers may duplicate this figure for noncommercial use within their school.

FIGURE 2.7
Fiction or Nonfiction Song

Sing to the tune of "London Bridge"

Is it pretend, or is it real?
Is it real? Is it real?
Is it pretend, or is it real?
Fiction or nonfiction.

Fiction books are made-up stories,
made-up stories, made-up stories.
Fiction books are made-up stories
that are not true.

Information books are nonfiction,
are nonfiction, are nonfiction.
Information books are nonfiction,
they're about topics
like birds that are blue.

When we read nonfiction,
nonfiction, nonfiction,
When we read nonfiction,
we learn about real things
both old and new.

Source: Literacy Strong All Year Long: Powerful Lessons for Grades K–2 by Valerie Ellery, Lori Oczkus, and Timothy V. Rasinski. © 2020 ASCD. Readers may duplicate this figure for noncommercial use within their school.

FIGURE 2.8
Fiction or Nonfiction Organizer

 Fiction	 Nonfiction

Source: Literacy Strong All Year Long: Powerful Lessons for Grades K–2 by Valerie Ellery, Lori Oczkus, and Timothy V. Rasinski. © 2020 ASCD. Readers may duplicate this figure for noncommercial use within their school.

LESSON 6. COMPREHENSION: KEY IDEAS AND DETAILS—DETERMINING IMPORTANCE AND SUMMARIZING

Title SIFTING DETAILS

Trailer Interesting or important? How can readers identify what is important versus what is just interesting in a text? The answer can be found in the concept of a sieve. Readers learn how to sift through information to locate key details in a text to bring meaning to what they are reading.

Literacy Enhancer Comprehension: Key Ideas and Details—Determining Importance and Summarizing

Key Academic Vocabulary Vocabulary from a previous lesson is marked with an asterisk (*).

Essential: Absolutely necessary for the meaning and purpose

Information*: Gathered knowledge; facts or ideas

Key detail: An important feature, fact, or item that supports the overall meaning

Retelling*: Recalling in a sequential order what is happening in a text

Sequencing*: Placing information in a certain order

Sift: To filter and examine what is most important

Story elements*: Parts (ingredients) of a story: characters, setting, events, plot, problem, and solution

Learning Objectives

- Identify interesting and informational facts in a text.
- Determine what details are essential for overall meaning.

Essential Questions

- What is an essential detail?
- How can you tell the difference between an important fact and an interesting detail?

STEP 1: PREPARATION

Organize Materials

- Variety of sieves, sifters, or colanders
- Bucket of sand with small and large stones
- Multimodal text set for the topic of study

- *Sifting the Details* reproducible (copies)
- Literacy notebooks

STEP 2: INITIATION

Separating with a Sieve

Hold up a sieve or colander and ask students its purpose (e.g., cooking, building sand castles, digging for gold, filtering different types of building materials). Explain how even archaeologists use sieves to sift through the soil to recover artifacts. Demonstrate how to filter through a sieve using a bucket of sand with some stones in it. Highlight how this instrument has a mesh or perforated bottom to help separate elements. It also can be used for characterizing the particle-size distribution from big to small. Tell the students, "In today's lesson, we are going to use buckets and sieves as representations to sift out important details in a text we are reading."

STEP 3: DEMONSTRATION

Sifting Details

1. Prior to meeting with students, select a few big stones and write some key details from a selected text on them. Place the stones in a bucket of sand. You can also have a few smaller stones to represent interesting information from the text.
2. Remind students that we have been learning that retells help us sequence the story elements and recall important information in a text. Hold up the bucket and share that the contents in the bucket represent all the information found within this particular text. Based on the unit of study, select a text and read aloud, noting along the way certain key details (e.g., characters, setting) that would probably be on some of the bigger stones in the bucket.
3. Ask questions as you are reading and thinking aloud (e.g., "What is happening?" "Who is affected?" "Why is the author introducing this idea?"). It is important to note that in any piece of text, the author gives us many interesting ideas, but it is our job as reader to filter to a few key details and gather deeper meaning.
4. After reading, sift the contents of the bucket using a sieve. Demonstrate that only the stones are now left in the colander and that some are bigger than others. Note that the larger stones represent the meaningful ideas to build comprehension of what is read. Give a building analogy, noting that cornerstones are the solid structural foundation. The cornerstones allow for all other construction to rise and develop from them. Hold up a large stone and read the detail that you previously wrote on it. Share how the information is important in the

text and serves as a major part in developing understanding. Hold up a smaller stone and note that the information on it is just interesting, reminding students that the smaller stones represent minor details covering fewer specifics and are not necessary to comprehend the text.

STEP 4: COLLABORATION

Conversational Coaching

Engage in conversational coaching by asking students to discuss the following questions with diverse partners:

- What essential information helps make the author's point of view?
- How do you distinguish interesting information from important information?

Have groups complete an *Interesting Information Versus Important Information* chart. Review the group's collaboration charts and create a class anchor chart. Here's a sample chart:

Interesting Information	Important Information
• Is a minor detail • Can be omitted and meaning would still be clear • Is not important for the overall meaning • Contains secondary points and general information • Supports the key details • Is not necessary to remember when comprehending the text	*May include some of the interesting information features plus the following:* • Is a major detail • Can't be omitted without losing crucial understanding • Is essential for overall meaning • Contains primary points and specific information • Supports the main topic • Necessary for clear and complete understanding of the text

STEP 5: APPLICATION

Finding Important Details

Have students work in groups or individually on the *Sifting the Details* reproducible (Figure 2.9) to determine details from a text or topic. Remind them to use the class anchor chart as they determine what information will be placed on a stone to represent the foundation of key details to support the overall meaning.

STEP 6: REFLECTION

Written Response

In their literacy notebooks, have students independently write about the difference between interesting and important information. Have them record a couple examples from a text that they recently heard read aloud or that they independently read.

ADAPTATION/EXTENSION

- Bring in a play microphone and have students become reporters by using the heading or other text features and asking a reporter's questions (i.e., who, what, when, where, why) to help determine key details in the text.
- Students can become detectives and search for signal or transition terms in the text that support the key details (e.g., *first, second, another, besides, in addition, also*).
- Create a scavenger hunt with sticky notes to locate key details in a text. Use sticky notes in different colors, one color for the important details and another color for the interesting details.
- Create a song or rap that identifies the key details in a text or use the "Five Elements of a Story" video/rap (www.flocabulary.com/fivethings) that creatively covers the five main elements of a story.
- *English Language Learner Suggestion:* Create stones with images on them to represent each of the story elements (e.,g., character = person, setting = house, problem = lock, solution = key).
- *Struggling Reader Suggestion:* Use two colors of highlighters, one to highlight major details and another to highlight interesting minor details that support the major details.

EVALUATION

"I Can . . ." Statements

- I can identify key details using essential elements in a text.
- I can differentiate important/key details from just interesting information in the text.
- I can answer questions using specific details from the text.

BEHAVIOR INDICATORS

- Identifies key details in a text.
- Determines what is interesting and what is important.
- Asks and answers questions about key details in a text: who, what, where, when, and why.

FIGURE 2.9
Sifting the Details

Five Essential Elements

Stone 1 = _____

Stone 2 = _____

Stone 3 = _____

Stone 4 = _____

Stone 5 = _____

Narrative Text
Stone 1 = Characters
Stone 2 = Setting
Stone 3 = Main events
Stone 4 = Problem
Stone 5 = Solution

Informational Text
(These elements are not in all informational texts, such as descriptive texts.)
1 = Main topic/concept/theme
2 = Location
3 = Main events
4 = Conflict
5 = Resolution

Source: Literacy Strong All Year Long: Powerful Lessons for Grades K–2 by Valerie Ellery, Lori Oczkus, and Timothy V. Rasinski. © 2020 ASCD. Readers may duplicate this figure for noncommercial use within their school.

LESSON 7. COMPREHENSION: KEY IDEAS AND DETAILS—QUESTIONING FOR CLOSE READING

Title THE QUESTION GAME

Trailer On the popular television game show *Jeopardy!*, contestants are shown the answer to a question first as they try to guess the question that goes with it. This lesson includes lots of engaging options to help students internalize how to ask and answer questions about key ideas and details in the texts they read.

Literacy Enhancer Comprehension: Key Ideas and Details—Questioning for Close Reading: Forming Questions

Key Academic Vocabulary Vocabulary from a previous lesson is marked with an asterisk (*).

Answer clues: General knowledge information from a text that aligns with *who, what, when, where,* or *why* questions

Question*: A sentence in interrogative form

What*: A question word that asks about the events or things that happened

When*: A question word that asks the time of day or year

Where*: A question word that asks about the place

Who*: A question word that asks about the people or animals in the text

Why: A question word that asks for a reason

Learning Objectives

- Answer questions about key ideas and details with *who, what, when, where, where,* or *why* and use text evidence.
- Ask questions about key ideas and details using *who, what, when, where,* or *why* that aligns with answer clues given.
- Align and answer clues with the corresponding questions.

Essential Questions

- What questions can I ask and answer that start with *who, what, where, when,* and *why*?
- How do I ask questions that align with answer clues from the text?

STEP 1: PREPARATION

Organize Materials

- Plastic microphone(s)
- Fiction and nonfiction texts

- Construction paper
- Markers in different colors
- Paper
- Multimodal text set for the topic of study
- *What's My Question? Game Flap Book* reproducible (copies or enlarged for display)
- *Question-and-Answer Match Cards* reproducible (copies or enlarged for display)
- Literacy notebooks

STEP 2: INITIATION

What's My Question?

Tell students that they are going to play a new game called the What's My Question? Game, where they know the answer and have to figure out the question, like on the television game show *Jeopardy!* Write on the board a food you ate for breakfast, such as cereal. Then, ask students to guess the question. Guide the students to ask, "What did you eat for breakfast?" Repeat with other foods you've eaten at meals lately. Ask a student to give the name of a family member without identifying who it is (relationship). Write the name on the board. Then, ask the other students to create a corresponding question, such as "Who is your big brother?" Tell students that you are going to show them how to play the same question game with books.

STEP 3: DEMONSTRATION

Questioning with a Familiar Story

1. Select a familiar fiction story to read aloud to the class, such as *Goldilocks and the Three Bears* or *The Three Billy Goats Gruff*. Every few pages, write an answer on the board and have students guess the question (e.g., *A:* Porridge, *Q:* What did Goldilocks eat? *A:* Too hot, *Q:* Why did the bears go for a walk? *A:* Baby Bear's chair, *Q:* What did Goldilocks break?). *Optional:* Write each answer on the board and invite students to chant, "What's my question?" before sharing the corresponding question. You may wish to use a plastic microphone as you question.

2. Conduct a think-aloud as you form three questions about the text you just read aloud. Write the questions on separate sticky notes and post them on the board. Next, write the answers to the questions on separate sticky notes and post them on the board out of order. Then, match the answers and questions by placing them across from each other. Share how you support your answers with text evidence from the illustrations, the text, or both to justify your reasoning.

Here's an example:

Answers	Questions
Goldilocks	Who is the main character?
Porridge	What did the bears intend to eat for breakfast?
In Baby Bear's bed	Where was Goldilocks when the bears came home?

3. Mix up the questions and the answers. Read one of the answers and model how to read an answer and decide which question goes with it.
4. Display another text that the class has read recently. Start with facts or events from the story and show how to write a question to correspond with each answer or idea from the reading. Repeat the activity in item 2 by writing answers and questions on separate sticky notes and placing them in columns on the board. Then, mix them up and invite students to help you match them. *Optional:* Repeat the lesson another day with an informational text. Use text features such as headings and bold words to form your answers and questions.

STEP 4: COLLABORATION

Question/Answer Walk and Conversational Coaching

Continue using the same questions and answers as in your demonstration. Write the three answers separately on three large pieces of construction paper in one color and write the three questions separately on large pieces of construction paper in another color. Invite six student volunteers to come to the front of the room and hold the papers. Have the students holding the answers stand on one side of the room and the students holding the questions on the other. Call on one of the students holding an answer. Ask the class to help figure out which question matches that answer by sharing with a partner first and then discussing as a class. The student with the answer walks to stand with the student holding the corresponding question. Continue until all the answers and questions are matched.

Invite small groups to engage in conversational coaching to practice asking and answering questions using the *What's My Question? Game Flap Book* reproducible (Figure 2.10). Have students look through the reading material together to create answers and questions. Coach students as they share text evidence for their answers. *Optional:* Add a fourth flap for a question that begins with *when*.

STEP 5: APPLICATION

Games and More

- *Partner Q&A:* Invite students to work in pairs to complete the *What's My Question? Game Flap Book* reproducible as they choose a familiar text and take turns creating answers and guessing questions.
- *Concentration match:* Write questions and answers on separate cards and place them in a pocket chart. Have students turn over two cards at a time to try to match each question and its answer and justify why they match. Continue until all questions and answers are matched and justified.
- *Facts and questions:* Work with students in small groups using an informational text. Invite students to write facts they've learned from the text on separate sticky notes and place them on a chart or board. Point to and read one of the facts. Create a question to go with the fact. Here's an example:
  - *Fact:* Stickleback fish have spines on their backs.
  - *Question:* What do stickleback fish have on their backs?

STEP 6: REFLECTION

Written Response

Encourage students to write questions in their literacy notebooks using the question words. Have students put a star next to their best question and pose the question to a partner. Students can use these questions to create their own set of question-and-answer match cards using the reproducible in Figure 2.11. Also, students may respond to these essential questions in their literacy notebooks:

- What questions can I ask and answer that start with *who, what, where, when,* and *why*?
- How do I ask questions that align with answer clues from the text?

ADAPTATION/EXTENSION

- Read aloud texts that promote questioning, such as the Lift-the-Flap Questions and Answers series books by Katie Daynes or Scholastic's Question and Answer series books.
- As a class and in teams, invite students to create question-and-answer books about informational text topics such as the solar system, dinosaurs, and plants.
- *English Language Learner Suggestion:* Work with students in a small group to write together answers and questions for informational text. Use text features such as headings and bold words to form your answers and questions.

- *Struggling Reader Suggestion:* Try teaching questioning by using a favorite book series such as Henry and Mudge by Cynthia Rylant. When students are familiar with the characters and the author's style, it is easier for them to formulate questions.

EVALUATION

"I Can . . ." Statements

- I can answer a question that starts with *who, what, when, where,* or *why*.
- I can give text evidence when I answer a question.
- I can ask a question that starts with *who, what, when, where,* or *why*.
- I can align answers and questions on a specific topic.

BEHAVIOR INDICATORS

- Answers questions about key ideas and details using the question words *who, what, when, where,* and *why* with text evidence.
- Answers questions using complete sentences to demonstrate understanding of key details in a text.
- Asks questions about key ideas and details using the question words *who, what, when, where,* and *why* that align with answer clues given.

FIGURE 2.10
What's My Question? Game Flap Book

Directions:

1. Fold a sheet of paper in half, turning and folding three times. When you unfold it, the creases will show eight sections.

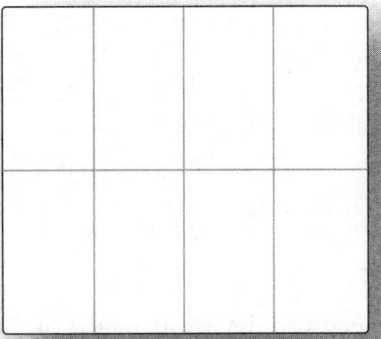

2. Holding the paper like a hotdog bun, cut along three creases (dotted in diagram) from the edge to the midpoint crease.

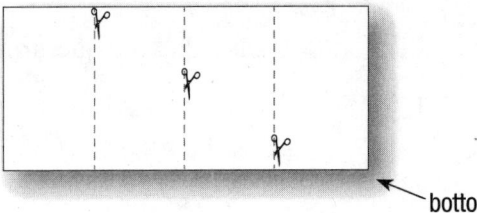

← bottom of the "bun"

3. On the inside of the bun, on the uncut side, write one question in each (folded) section.

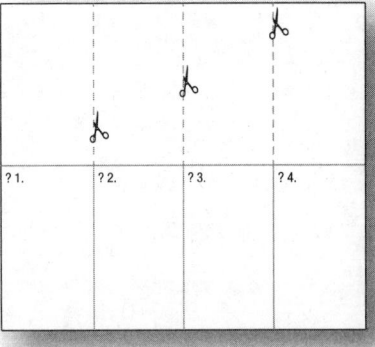

4. On the cut side of the bun, write the answer on the OUTSIDE of each flap, ensuring that the flap covers the corresponding question.

5. Trade game flaps with a partner. Take turns reading the answers, guessing the questions, and opening the flaps to see the questions.

Source: Literacy Strong All Year Long: Powerful Lessons for Grades K–2 by Valerie Ellery, Lori Oczkus, and Timothy V. Rasinski. © 2020 ASCD. Readers may duplicate this figure for noncommercial use within their school.

FIGURE 2.11
Question-and-Answer Match Cards

Directions: Write questions and answers in the corresponding boxes. Cut the cards apart, flip them over, and mix them up. Take turns making matches until all the questions and answers are paired.

Question:	Answer:
Who _____ _____ ?	_____ _____ _____
Question:	Answer:
What _____ _____ ?	_____ _____ _____
Question:	Answer:
Where _____ _____ ?	_____ _____ _____

Source: Literacy Strong All Year Long: Powerful Lessons for Grades K–2 by Valerie Ellery, Lori Oczkus, and Timothy V. Rasinski. © 2020 ASCD. Readers may duplicate this figure for noncommercial use within their school.

LESSON 8. VOCABULARY: ASSOCIATING WORDS

Title MEANING MADNESS TIME: WHAT ELSE DOES IT MEAN?

Trailer Primary students absolutely love wordplay! Words that carry multiple meanings but are spelled the same, such as *duck*, *fly*, and *row*, are part of the meaning madness. Students learn the concept of multiple-meaning words and will gain a strong understanding of these sometimes tricky words by hearing lots of examples. Whether you call them homographs, homonyms, or multiple-meaning words, your students will call them fun!

Literacy Enhancer Vocabulary: Associating Words—Homographs and Homonyms

Key Academic Vocabulary Vocabulary from a previous lesson is marked with an asterisk (*).

Adjective*: A word that describes a noun (a person, place, or thing)

Antonym*: A word that has an opposite meaning of another word

Homograph: A word that has more than one meaning

Homonym: Another name for a homograph

Noun*: A person, place, or thing

Opposite*: Two words or concepts that are in some way related but distinctly different in meaning from each other

Verb*: An action word

Learning Objectives

- Identify words that have two different meanings.
- Explain two meanings for the same word.
- Demonstrate understanding of multiple-meaning words by drawing, acting, and writing sentences.

Essential Questions

- What are homographs (homonyms), or multiple-meaning words?
- What are some examples of multiple-meaning words?
- How can you show that you understand multiple-meaning words?

STEP 1: PREPARATION

Organize Materials

- Chart paper
- Plastic baseball bat

- Toy animal bat
- Multimodal text set with homonyms
- *Meaning Madness Cards* reproducible (copies or enlarged for display)
- *My Meaning Madness Words* reproducible (copies or enlarged for display)
- Literacy notebooks

STEP 2: INITIATION

Meaning Madness Bats

Write the word *bat* on chart paper. Hold up a plastic baseball bat and say, "We hit a ball with a bat." Point to the word *bat* and ask the class to chant, "Meaning madness time! What else can *bat* mean?" While holding the baseball bat in one hand, hold up a toy animal bat in the other hand. Say, "A bat hunts at night." Ask the class to tell you what they know about animal bats and what they notice about the spelling of the word and its meaning. Write the two *bat* sentences on the chart and either sketch drawings of each bat or use the *Meaning Madness Cards* reproducible (Figure 2.12). Ask students to turn and discuss the two meanings of the word *bat*.

STEP 3: DEMONSTRATION

Homograph Read-Alouds

1. Read aloud a picture book that features homographs. Ask students to listen to the read-aloud and listen for words that are interesting. Are there any words that make the book humorous or funny? After reading the book, invite students to help you list the homographs. Explain that a homograph is a word that has two different meanings. Here are some suggested books featuring homographs:
    - *The Dove: Funny Homograph Riddles* by Marvin Terban
    - The Amelia Bedelia series books by Peggy Parish
    - *Zoola Palooza: A Book of Homographs* by Gene Barretta
2. Ask students to discuss the homograph words they learned from the read-aloud: "What did you notice about the words?" (The same word can have multiple meanings.) Repeat with several examples, each time holding a pretend object in each hand. Invite the class to "hold" one of the two different meanings of the word in each of their hands, too. Ask the class to chant while snapping their fingers: "Meaning madness time! What else can (word) mean?" Create a chart as you read for students to reference. Invite them to sketch the different word meanings on the chart. Here are some common homographs:

back	fly	roll	spring
ball	left	rose	stick
bank	light	row	tie
bark	march	ruler	trip
bat	park	saw	watch
bow	pen	seal	wave
fall	play	ship	
fan	ring	sink	

STEP 4: COLLABORATION

Meaning Madness Time Riddles and Conversational Coaching

Make up riddles for the pairs of words on the chart. Encourage students to turn to their partner and answer the riddle or sketch on paper. Have pairs share their responses through conversational coaching. Here are some examples of riddles for the same homograph:

- I am a creature that hunts at night. I love to eat mice. What am I?
- You use this to hit the ball when you play baseball. What is it?

Act Up!

Give each table a Meaning Madness Card to act out while the rest of the class guesses the word.

STEP 5: APPLICATION

My Meaning Madness Words

Have students work independently to write sentences and sketch drawings to go with the words on the Meaning Madness Cards as well as any other homographs that the class has learned (e.g., "The bat landed on my new bat"). Students then record their responses on the *My Meaning Madness Words* reproducible (Figure 2.13).

STEP 6: REFLECTION

Written Response

Have students write and illustrate their favorite homograph pairs in their literacy books. Have students respond to these essential questions:

- What are homographs (homonyms), or multiple-meaning words?
- What are some examples of multiple-meaning words?
- How can you show that you understand multiple-meaning words?

ADAPTATION/EXTENSION

- Pair students and ask them to illustrate homographs in any of the Amelia Bedelia books using the *My Meaning Madness Words* reproducible. Combine students' illustrations for a book about Amelia Bedelia's words or make an Amelia Bedelia dictionary and put the words in alphabetical order.
- *English Language Learner Suggestion:* Have students use markers or paint to create symbols or doodles for multiple-meaning words.
- *Struggling Reader Suggestion:* Have partners cut apart a *Meaning Madness Cards* reproducible and then mix up the cards. Each student takes a turn drawing a card and acting out the word while the partner tries to guess it.

EVALUATION

"I Can . . ." Statements

- I can give a definition of a multiple-meaning word.
- I can explain two meanings for the same word.
- I can write sentences, draw, or act out my understanding of two different meanings of a word.

BEHAVIOR INDICATORS

- Provides the definition of a multiple-meaning word.
- Explains two meanings for the same word.
- Provides sentences, drawings, or dramatizations for two different meanings of a word.

FIGURE 2.12
Meaning Madness Cards

bark	bark	bat	bat
duck	duck	fly	fly
rose	rose	seal	seal
sink	sink	wave	wave

Source: Literacy Strong All Year Long: Powerful Lessons for Grades K–2 by Valerie Ellery, Lori Oczkus, and Timothy V. Rasinski. © 2020 ASCD. Readers may duplicate this figure for noncommercial use within their school.

FIGURE 2.13
My Meaning Madness Words

Write the word: _____

What does it mean? _____ **or** _____

Draw a picture.	Draw a picture.
Write a sentence and underline the word.	Write a sentence and underline the word.

Write the word: _____

What does it mean? _____ **or** _____

Draw a picture.	Draw a picture.
Write a sentence and underline the word.	Write a sentence and underline the word.

Source: Literacy Strong All Year Long: Powerful Lessons for Grades K–2 by Valerie Ellery, Lori Oczkus, and Timothy V. Rasinski. © 2020 ASCD. Readers may duplicate this figure for noncommercial use within their school.

LESSON 9. VOCABULARY: ANALYZING WORDS

Title OH, A-HUNTING WE WILL GO: THE PATH TO PLURALS

Trailer Trails, clues, and tracks can lead you on a path to find what you are searching for when you're hunting. Good hunters know how to follow a lead and trace it to a find. Proficient readers can also follow clues in a text as they analyze words and capture meaning. Go on an adventurous hunt for nouns and learn to multiply your newfound words through plurals!

Literacy Enhancer Vocabulary: Analyzing Words—Parts of Speech: Plural Nouns, Irregular Nouns, Subject-Verb Agreement

Key Academic Vocabulary Vocabulary from a previous lesson is marked with an asterisk (*).

Common noun*: A nonspecific type of noun that names any regular, ordinary person, animal, place, thing, or idea

Irregular plural noun: A type of a noun that changes its spelling in the plural form in ways other than what is normal by adding *-s* or *-es* to the end of the noun; can end in a variety of ways, with no consistent pattern (e.g., *foot → feet, man → men, mouse → mice, person → people*)

Noun*: A part of speech that is a type of naming word that represents a person, animal, place, thing, idea, or concept; usually followed by a verb; most common type of word in the English language

Parts of speech*: Categories of words used in English grammar (e.g., nouns, verbs, adverbs, adjectives, prepositions)

Plural: A form of a word that conveys quantity (more than one)

Proper noun*: A type of noun that names a specific person, animal, place, thing, or idea and begins with a capital letter

Verb*: A part of speech that is a type of word that demonstrates an action (physical or mental); tells what the subject (noun) of a simple sentence is doing; necessary to form a sentence

Learning Objectives

- Form regular plural nouns orally by adding /s/ or /es/ (e.g., *dog → dogs, wish → wishes*).
- Explore and apply singular and plural nouns with matching verbs in basic sentences (e.g., "He hops," "We hop").

- Form and use frequently occurring irregular plural nouns (e.g., *children*, *feet*, *fish*, *mice*, *teeth*).

Essential Questions

- What happens to a noun when you make it plural?
- How do you tell the difference between singular and plural nouns?
- What can you do to help understand how nouns and verbs agree?
- How can you identify various irregular plural nouns?

STEP 1: PREPARATION

Organize Materials

- Items or pictures for a noun scavenger hunt
- Magnifying glasses
- Bug catcher nets
- Bags
- Cameras (optional)
- Two different-colored hula hoop
- Index cards or sticky notes
- Two different-colored markers
- Multimodal text set for the topic of study with a focus on irregular nouns
- *Who or What Am I? Clue Cards* reproducible (copies or enlarged for display)
- *Pluralizing Nouns Guide* reproducible (copies or enlarged for display)
- *Oh, A-Hunting I Will Go for Nouns* reproducible (copies or enlarged for display)
- Literacy notebooks

STEP 2: INITIATION

Capturing Words

Set up a scavenger hunt experience by placing hidden treasures (e.g., specific noun items or pictures) around the room. They can be related to a specific topic or theme you are studying. Begin to chant or sing this song:

> **Oh, A-Hunting We Will Go**
>
> Oh, a-hunting we will go, a-hunting we will go!
>
> We'll catch a person, animal, place, or thing,
>
> Put it in a bag, and begin to sing.
>
> Oh, a-hunting we will go!

Ask students to think about the kind of words they will be hunting today based on the verse, and review any nouns from the anchor chart in the "We're Going on a Word Hunt: Nouns and Verbs" lesson in Chapter 1.

Remind students that good hunters will make sure they are prepared for their adventures with the necessary supplies for a successful hunt. Give each team a magnifying glass or net, a bag, and one of the cards from the *Who or What Am I? Clue Cards* reproducible (Figure 2.14) or create your own clue cards to align with nouns around the room. Students can also use a camera if available. Explain that they will read their clue cards and begin to follow the trail to capture their word prize. Set a timer for five minutes and say, "Let the hunt begin!" When the time is up, have students keep their prize hidden in their bag and place the bags on display. Share that students are going to use these "finds" to discover more about nouns and verbs and how they work together in sentences to make sense of what we say and to bring meaning to what we read.

STEP 3: DEMONSTRATION

Making Plurals

1. Place two hula hoops in the front of the room. Stand in the first hoop and say a singular noun that represents a person, animal, place, or thing (e.g., *girl*, *dog*, *school*, *bus*) found in the *Who or What Am I? Clue Cards* reproducible (e.g., "I can be called a princess. I am a small female. Who am I?"). Use the noun in a simple sentence (e.g., "The *girl* reads") and then record the word with a marker on an index card or sticky note. Ask, "What is the girl doing?" Review that the person in this sentence is the noun and that the action in the sentence is the verb.

2. Put the index card or sticky note on the floor inside the first hoop. Hop into the second hoop, say the plural form of the word in the first hoop (e.g., *girls*), and use it in a sentence (e.g., "The *girls* read"). Ask, "What is different about this word from the one in the first hoop?" Discuss how they hear an /s/ or /es/ sound in the second word. Ask, "What does adding *-s* or *-es* do to a word? Does adding an *-s* or *-es* change the word's meaning?" Pick up the index card or sticky note from the first hoop and record the plural form of the word by adding the letter(s) to the word with a different-colored marker. Then, put the index card or sticky note on the floor inside the second hoop. Continue hopping in the hoops to demonstrate examples of the noun categories.

3. Read the "Jump or Jingle" poem aloud or watch the video of the poem by Nursery Rhymes TV (www.youtube.com/watch?v=PqHTOl1R0T0). Point out that all the animals are plural nouns with an action verb. Have students review some

of the animal nouns by jumping in the first hula hoop and removing the plural to make the singular noun and then jumping in the second hoop for the plural noun. Discuss what letters changed to make the noun plural. *Optional:* Begin to chart only the regular singular nouns changing to the plural pattern. Demonstrate how with subject-verb agreement, a singular subject takes a "plural" verb and a plural subject takes a "singular" verb (e.g., *frog jumps* vs. *frogs jump*). Here are the verbs shown and sung in the video in order: *jump, hump, wiggle, jiggle, hop, clop, slide, glide, creep, leap, bounce, pounce, stalk,* and *walk*. You can also add a fox to the poem to practice the *-es* plural.

4. Explain how most nouns follow the path for plurals by adding *-s* or *-es* to the end of the word. However, just like in everyday life, words can declare their individuality and go down different paths. These paths can change nouns into words that are completely different from the original ones (e.g., *foot → feet, person → people*). Share that it is in our best interest as readers to examine a few of these frequently occurring irregular nouns and learn to accept them in the world of words. Replay the "Jump or Jiggle" video and record the two nouns that have a different way of becoming plural (i.e., *mice, deer*). Share how these words are irregular and don't conform to the same pattern as most other words. You can also add a wolf to the poem to practice the *-ves* irregular plural.

5. Read aloud from one or more picture books about nouns. Write a list of nouns collected from the reading on the board or a chart. Explain how learning about parts of speech such as nouns helps to structure our sentences and expand our vocabulary. Here are some suggested singular and plural noun books that feature both regular and irregular plurals:
   - *1 Hunter* by Pat Hutchins
   - *If You Were a Noun* by Michael Dahl
   - *One Fish Two Fish Red Fish Blue Fish* by Dr. Seuss
   - *Your Foot's on My Feet! and Other Tricky Nouns* by Marvin Terban
   - *Feet and Puppies, Thieves and Guppies: What Are Irregular Plurals?* by Brian P. Cleary

6. Create an anchor chart for guidelines on how to make a noun plural, or display the *Pluralizing Nouns Guide* reproducible (Figure 2.15) for future reference.

STEP 4: COLLABORATION

Pluralizing Nouns and Conversational Coaching

Have the class try to guess the nouns in the bags. Have each team read or explain the clues they had that sent them on a path to discover their noun. Give the class a chance to guess the noun before having the team pull the item or picture out of the bag. Next, have one team member hop into the first hoop and repeat the singular noun. Then, have the student hop into the second hoop and share the plural form of the noun. Record finds on a class T-chart, with one column titled "Singular Nouns" and the other titled "Regular Plural Nouns."

Before the next team's turn, have students engage in conversational coaching by identifying the word as a noun, the type of noun it is, and how you change it to make it mean more than one. After addressing the noun, have students ask the questions for verbs (e.g., "What does it do?" "What can it do?" "What action can it make?"). Continue until all the hunting teams have had a chance to share and record their nouns.

STEP 5: APPLICATION

Oh, A-Hunting I Will Go for Nouns

At a work center, place the hula hoop, bags of nouns, and clue cards for students to practice working with a variety of nouns and their plurals. Have partners or individual students complete the *Oh, A-Hunting I Will Go for Nouns* (Figure 2.16) reproducible as they hunt for nouns and trace the context clues to determine the type of noun, whether it is plural, and how it can become plural if it is singular. Students can also select several nouns from the reproducible to demonstrate their plural form in a seasonal paragraph, poem, or story.

STEP 6: REFLECTION

Oral or Written Response

Have students record and sort plural nouns orally or in written form in their literacy notebooks from what they are reading. Invite them to select several irregular plural nouns and complete these sentences:

- When I have only one of these, I have a _____.
- When I have more than one _____, I have _____ because _____.
- Have students respond to these essential questions:
    - What happens to a noun when you make it plural?
    - How do you tell the difference between singular and plural nouns?
    - What are different ways to form a plural noun?

ADAPTATION/EXTENSION

- Revisit the nouns and verbs alphaboxes from the "We're Going on a Word Hunt: Nouns and Verbs" lesson in Chapter 1 and create noun and verb word cards.

Have students match up the cards to make a noun + verb alliteration. Ask students to put the two words into a sentence and discuss if it is realistic or nonsense. If it's nonsense (e.g., *apples* + *ate*), then students can edit the sentence to make sense (e.g., "I *ate* two *apples* today").
- Give a team a stick or ruler to pretend that it's a baton used in a relay race. Call out a singular form of a noun or verb and have the team spell the word in the plural form. One student says the first letter in the word and passes the baton to the next student on the team, who says the second letter and passes the baton to the next team member. Continue around until the word is spelled completely. If a student misses a letter, he is out and the team must restart the race.
- Create a matching card game and have students look for a singular word to match with its plural form. Once the match is made, invite students to use each word properly in a sentence. You could also download an app on a tablet (e.g., Plurality by Zorten Software; http://www.zorten.com/plurality) as a memory game for irregular plural nouns.
- *English Language Learner Suggestion:* Have students view online video clips about irregular and plural nouns and verbs and have them practice orally pronouncing the examples and describing their learning process with a partner. Here are some possible videos to use:
    - "Singular & Plural Nouns" by Turtlediary.com: http://www.turtlediary.com/kids-videos/singular-plural-nouns-g3.html
    - "Fun Learning Song for Kids—More Than One" by DJC Kids: www.youtube.com/watch?v= j6yjcZkj5UY
    - "Parts of Speech: Common & Proper Nouns, Learning English Grammar for Children" by Kids Educational Games: www.youtube.com/watch?v=7xr-xSf94r8
    - "Irregular Verbs Song, Max the Cat, Part 1:" www.youtube.com/watch?v=Ov2v50af7bo (source unknown)
- *Struggling Reader Suggestion:* Write several plural and singular noun stems on cards and have students work with partners to complete them. *Optional:* Have predetermined nouns for students to match to complete the stems. Here are some example stems for this exercise:
    - a _____; many _____
    - 1 _____; 6 _____
    - an _____; some _____
    - one _____; lots of _____

EVALUATION

"I Can . . ." Statements

- I can say words that mean one or more than one.
- I can change a regular noun to make it plural.
- I can use singular and plural nouns with matching verbs in basic sentences.
- I can demonstrate how a verb relates to the noun.
- I can use frequently occurring nouns and verbs to communicate properly in my writing.

BEHAVIOR INDICATORS

- Transforms a regular noun into its plural form.
- Uses singular nouns with matching verbs in basic sentences.
- Identifies frequently occurring irregular plural nouns in basic sentences.

FIGURE 2.14
Who or What Am I? Clue Cards

I can be called a princess. I am a small female. Who am I? 	I work outside. I teach sports. Who am I? 
I can fly. I live in a nest. What am I? 	I have fur. I like to run around on a wheel. What am I? 
I help students learn. Both teachers and students work at me. What am I? 	I am outdoors. I have a swing. What am I? 
I hold paper together. I can clamp paper. What am I? 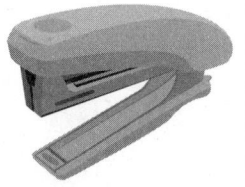	I have hands. I have numbers and tell time. What am I? 

Answers: person, person, animal, animal, place, place, thing, thing

Source: Literacy Strong All Year Long: Powerful Lessons for Grades K–2 by Valerie Ellery, Lori Oczkus, and Timothy V. Rasinski. © 2020 ASCD. Readers may duplicate this figure for noncommercial use within their school.

FIGURE 2.15
Pluralizing Nouns Guide

Regular Nouns Plural Forms: Adding -s or -es

Most singular nouns form the plural by adding -s:
- ball → balls
- boy → boys
- dog → dogs
- hat → hats

dog · dogs

A singular noun ending in s, x, z, ch, or sh makes the plural by adding -es:
- bus → buses
- coach → coaches
- dish → dishes
- fox → foxes

fox · foxes

Regular Nouns Plural Forms: Dropping -y and Adding -ies

A singular noun ending in -y and preceded by a consonant makes the plural by dropping the y and adding -ies:
- baby → babies
- candy → candies
- fly → flies
- puppy → puppies

Note: For nouns ending in -y and preceded by a vowel, just add an -s:
- boy → boys

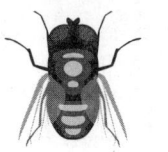

fly · flies

Regular Nouns Plural Forms: Dropping -f or -fe and Adding -ves

Some singular nouns ending in -f make the plural by dropping the -f and adding -ves:
- half → halves
- knife → knives
- leaf → leaves
- wolf → wolves

Note: For some nouns ending in -f or -fe, just add an -s:
- belief → beliefs

leaf · leaves

Irregular Nouns Plural Forms

Some singular nouns make the plural by changing the word itself without a real pattern:
- child → children
- foot → feet
- man → men
- person → people
- tooth → teeth

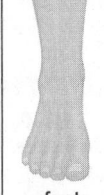
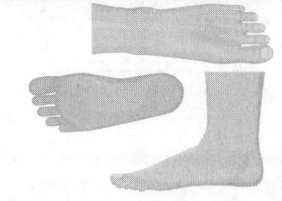

foot · feet

Source: Literacy Strong All Year Long: Powerful Lessons for Grades K–2 by Valerie Ellery, Lori Oczkus, and Timothy V. Rasinski. © 2020 ASCD. Readers may duplicate this figure for noncommercial use within their school.

FIGURE 2.16
Oh, A-Hunting I Will Go for Nouns

Name: _____
Date: _____

Noun (practice word)	Context (text or page where the word was discovered)	Noun Type (person, animal, place, thing, or idea)	Singular Noun (word)	Plural Noun (word)	Plural Form (R = regular; I = irregular)
Example: frogs	"Jump or Jiggle" video	animal	frog	frogs	R: I just added -s.
1.					
2.					
3.					

Source: Literacy Strong All Year Long: Powerful Lessons for Grades K–2 by Valerie Ellery, Lori Oczkus, and Timothy V. Rasinski. © 2020 ASCD. Readers may duplicate this figure for noncommercial use within their school.

LESSON 10. MOTIVATION: MOTIVATING READERS

Title TAKE OFF AND PARTNER BOOK TALKS

Trailer "Tickets! Get your tickets!" Membership in the class book club includes a special ticket: one of the Take Off and Partner Talk bookmarks. Students gesture and share using prompts that motivate them to stay on topic as they discuss books and deepen their comprehension. Use these tools, one for fiction and one for nonfiction, to discuss books all year long!

Literacy Enhancer Motivation: Motivating Readers—Text Features: Book Talks, Predicting, and Summarizing

Key Academic Vocabulary Vocabulary from a previous lesson is marked with an asterisk (*).

Author*: The person who wrote the book

Predict*: To use information from a text to infer what the text will be about or what one might learn from it

Summarize*: To tell what has happened in the text by sharing important points and details

Title*: The name of the text or book; tells what it is about or gives clues to the content

Fiction*: The genre that includes stories that are make-believe; may also include poetry

Nonfiction*: The genre that includes factual or real information that is portrayed to answer, explain, or describe

Learning Objectives

- Discuss fiction and nonfiction with diverse partners using a variety of sentence stems before, during, and after reading that promote comprehension.
- Follow simple rules for discussion that include taking turns, making eye contact, active listening, and politely adding comments and questions.

Essential Questions

- What are the rules for discussing a book with a partner or in a group?
- What are some prompts to discuss a book before, during, and after reading with a partner or group?

STEP 1: PREPARATION

Organize Materials

- Fiction or informational books
- Leveled texts
- *Take Off and Partner Talk Bookmark: Fiction* reproducible (copies or enlarged for display)
- *Take Off and Partner Talk Bookmark: Nonfiction* reproducible (copies or enlarged for display)
- *Take Off and Partner Talk Guidelines* reproducible (copies or enlarged for display)
- Literacy notebooks

STEP 2: INITIATION

Club Member Chats!

Invite students to gather on the rug or floor. Explain to them that clubs often conduct meetings and have their own special codes to communicate. Ask students if they watch any shows or read books in which clubs use secret handshakes or talk in a secret language. Tell students they are going to learn how to turn and talk to partners about their reading using hand signals and conversational starters during class book club meetings.

STEP 3: DEMONSTRATION

Take Off and Partner Talk

For Fiction

1. Display a fiction book cover. Explain that when good readers talk about their reading, they get better at reading! Display the *Take Off and Partner Talk Bookmark: Fiction* reproducible (Figure 2.17) or provide a copy for each student.

2. Before reading, lead the class in a preview discussion by studying the text features (e.g., cover, title, a few pages of the text). Look for clues to predict what the text is about. Model for students the before-reading sentence stems. Say, "I think this is about _____ because _____." Use examples from the text to support your prediction. Invite students to turn to a partner and repeat the prompt. They may repeat your response.

3. During reading, pause to model each of the Take Off and Partner Talk during-reading sentence stems. For each one, pause on a page and model your thinking. Then, invite students to turn and share their thoughts with a partner and use gestures for each of the sentence stems as shown in the following chart.

During-Reading Sentence Stem	Gesture
• So far, _____ happened.	• Hold up your hands like you're taking a photograph to summarize what has happened in the text so far. • *Additional gesture:* Ask students to sketch in the air with their fingers what has happened in the text so far or show pages from the book if they're holding copies.
• Next, I think _____ will happen because _____.	• Sketch in the air what action you think will happen next. What do you predict?
• I want to know the word _____. • I think the author picked the word _____ because _____.	• Start with your index finger high in the air and land on the word that you want to know or to discuss why the author picked it.

4. After reading, pause to model each of the Take Off and Partner Talk after-reading sentence stems (see chart). Allow partners to repeat each of the sentence stems right after you model it and to use gestures for each one.

After-Reading Sentence Stem	Gesture
I liked the part where _____.	• Smile! Then, point to the part you liked in the text.
The character _____ felt _____ (happy, sad, angry, jealous) because _____.	• Point to your heart. Then, point to the character and tell the feeling.
I was surprised when _____.	• Make a surprised face. Hold both hands up to your cheeks. Open your mouth into an O position. Then, point to the page where you were surprised.

After-Reading Sentence Stem	Gesture
This book was about _____. At the beginning, _____. In the middle, _____. At the end, _____.	• Be a storyteller to summarize. Sketch each part of the story in the air with your fingers or show pages from the book.
This book reminds me of _____.	• Link your two index fingers together. The link stands for a text-to-self, text-to-text, or text-to-world connection.

For Nonfiction

1. Select a nonfiction book and display the book cover. Explain that good readers often talk to their friends as they read to help understand the reading better. Display the *Take Off and Partner Talk Bookmark: Nonfiction* reproducible (Figure 2.18) or provide a copy for each student.
2. Before reading, lead the class in a preview discussion of the text by studying the cover, title, and a few of the pages. Explain that you're looking for clues to predict what the text is about. Model for students the before-reading sentence stems. Say, "I think I will learn _____ because _____." Use examples from the text to support your prediction. Invite students to turn to a partner to repeat the prompt. They may repeat your response.
3. During reading, pause to model each of the Take Off and Partner Talk during-reading sentence stems using the text (see chart). For each one, pause on a page and model your thinking. Then, invite students to turn and share their thoughts with a partner. They may repeat your sentence stems and use gestures for each one.

During-Reading Sentence Stem	Gesture
So far, I have learned _____.	• Hold up your hands like you're taking a photograph to summarize what has happened in the text so far. • *Additional gesture:* Ask students to sketch in the air with their fingers what has happened in the text so far or show pages from the book if they're holding copies.

I want to know the word _____. I think the author picked the word _____ because _____.	Start with your index finger high in the air and land on the word that you want to know or to discuss why the author picked it.

4. After reading, pause to model each of the Take Off and Partner Talk after-reading sentence stems. Allow partners to repeat each of the sentence stems right after you model it and use gestures for each one.

After-Reading Sentence Stem	Gesture
I liked the part where _____.	Smile! Then, point to the part you liked in the text.
Something new I learned was _____.	Raise your eyebrows and draw an exclamation point in the air with your index finger.
I was surprised when _____.	Make a surprised face. Hold both hands up to your cheeks. Open your mouth into an O. Then, point to the page where you were surprised.
This book was about _____. At the beginning, I learned _____. In the middle, I learned _____. At the end, I learned _____.	Be a reporter. Sketch each part of the book in the air with your fingers or show pages from the book.
This book reminds me of _____.	Link your two index fingers together. The link stands for a text-to-self, text-to-text, or text-to-world connection.

STEP 4: COLLABORATION

Guidelines for the Club

Share with students some guidelines for partner talking. Show students the Take Off and Partner Talk bookmarks. Invite either one student to demonstrate with you or two students to role-play with a few talking points from one of the bookmarks. Conduct a quick demonstration of each of the guidelines in the *Take Off and Partner Talk Guidelines* reproducible (Figure 2.19).

STEP 5: APPLICATION

Partner Up and Conversational Coaching

Pass out books for partners to read and discuss. The books may be familiar or new to students. Encourage them to use the Take Off and Partner Talk bookmarks on their own with partners for conversational coaching.

Stroll Line

Line students up in two lines facing each other. Show the cover of a book and invite students to take turns discussing their predictions with the student across from them. Then, signal one of the lines to move one person to the right and the student at the end to move to the front of the line. Read further in the text and ask the new facing pairs to talk to each other about one of the during-reading sentence stems. Continue reading aloud and switching partners so students have the opportunity to discuss more of the reading sentence stems.

STEP 6: REFLECTION

Written Response

In their literacy notebooks, have students record their responses to the following sentence stems.

For Fiction

- This book reminds me of _____ because _____.
- I liked the part when _____ because _____.
- The character was _____ because _____.

For Nonfiction

- This book was about _____.
- Something new that I learned was _____.
- I liked the part about _____ because _____.
- The author used the word _____ because _____.

ADAPTATION/EXTENSION

- Give the Take Off and Partner Talk bookmarks to the big buddies or cross-age tutors as they read together. Teach the big buddies the gestures to engage little buddies during the reading session.
- Invite several students to join an informal lunch bunch and eat lunch in the classroom with you. Use the Take Off and Partner Talk bookmarks to discuss books they've read.

- *English Language Learner Suggestion:* Read aloud a text to a small group. Throughout the reading, pause every few pages and invite partners to use the gestures and sentence stems to discuss the story. Model and guide throughout using all the prompts or a select few.
- *Struggling Reader Suggestion:* During small-group instruction, guide students to respond to the texts they are reading using the appropriate Take Off and Partner Talk bookmark.

EVALUATION

"I Can . . ." Statements

- I can talk about a book with a partner and follow the Take Off and Partner Talk Guidelines.
- I can talk to my partner before and during reading to make predictions about a text.
- I can talk to my partner during reading to share my favorite part or a summary of a text, with the beginning, middle, and end.
- I can talk to my partner during reading and identify words I want to know.
- I can give reasons with evidence from a book for my comments.

BEHAVIOR INDICATORS

- Participates in discussion with a partner by making eye contact, actively listening, and adding related comments.
- Predicts what a book will be about before and during reading.
- Provides reasons for predictions.
- Summarizes what a book was about during and after reading by sharing a favorite part and a summary of the text, including the beginning, middle, and end.
- Provides text evidence for the summary.
- Identifies unknown words throughout the reading process.

FIGURE 2.17
Take Off and Partner Talk Bookmark: Fiction

Take Off and Partner Talk Bookmark: Fiction

Before reading:
- I think this is about ___ because ___.
- This reminds me of ___ because ___.

During reading:
- I want to know the word ___.
- So far, ___.
- Next, I think ___ will happen.
- I think the author picked the word ___ because ___.

After reading:
- In the beginning, ___.
- During the middle ___.
- At the end, ___.
- My favorite part was ___.
- I was surprised when ___.

Take Off and Partner Talk Bookmark: Fiction

Before reading:
- I think this is about ___ because ___.
- This reminds me of ___ because ___.

During reading:
- I want to know the word ___.
- So far, ___.
- Next, I think ___ will happen.
- I think the author picked the word ___ because ___.

After reading:
- In the beginning, ___.
- During the middle ___.
- At the end, ___.
- My favorite part was ___.
- I was surprised when ___.

Source: Adapted from *Best Ever Literacy Survival Tips: 72 Lessons You Can't Teach Without* (p. 26), by L.D. Oczkus. Copyright 2012 by International Reading Association, Newark, DE.

FIGURE 2.18
Take Off and Partner Talk Bookmark: Nonfiction

Take Off and Partner Talk Bookmark: Nonfiction

Before reading:
- I think I will learn ___ because ___.
- This reminds me of ___ because ___.

During reading:
- I want to know the word ___.
- So far, I have learned ___ from the text.
- Next, I think I will learn ___ because ___.
- I think the author picked the word ___ because ___.

After reading:
- The book was about ___.
- I liked the part where ___.
- Something new I learned was ___.
- I was surprised when ___.
- This book reminds me of ___.

Take Off and Partner Talk Bookmark: Nonfiction

Before reading:
- I think I will learn ___ because ___.
- This reminds me of ___ because ___.

During reading:
- I want to know the word ___.
- So far, I have learned ___ from the text.
- Next, I think I will learn ___ because ___.
- I think the author picked the word ___ because ___.

After reading:
- The book was about ___.
- I liked the part where ___.
- Something new I learned was ___.
- I was surprised when ___.
- This book reminds me of ___.

Source: Adapted from *Best Ever Literacy Survival Tips: 72 Lessons You Can't Teach Without* (p. 26), by L.D. Oczkus. Copyright 2012 by the International Reading Association, Newark, DE.

FIGURE 2.19
Take Off and Partner Talk Guidelines

LOOK at your partner.

LISTEN at your partner.

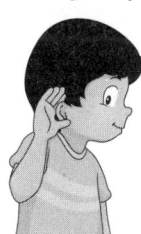

TAKE TURNS

ADD

- "I also think _____."
- "I agree _____."

QUESTIONS

- Ask *who, what, when, where,* and *why* questions.
- "I wonder _____."

LOOK at your partner.

LISTEN at your partner.

TAKE TURNS

ADD

- "I also think _____."
- "I agree _____."

QUESTIONS

- Ask *who, what, when, where,* and *why* questions.
- "I wonder _____."

Source: Literacy Strong All Year Long: Powerful Lessons for Grades K–2 by Valerie Ellery, Lori Oczkus, and Timothy V. Rasinski. © 2020 ASCD. Readers may duplicate this figure for noncommercial use within their school.

Ending the Year Literacy Strong

There is no real ending. It's just the place where you stop the story.
—Frank Herbert

A teacher affects eternity:
He can never tell where his influence stops.
—Henry Adams

It's been many months since the school year began. Motivation for learning and reading may be low as students begin to anticipate a break from school. You may even feel a bit tired after working so hard over the past school year. However, now is not the time to take it easy; it is the time to remain literacy strong! The final few weeks of the school year are a perfect time to continue the great progress that your students have made in their literacy development. It is also the time to set the stage for even more student reading. In this chapter are lessons that your students will find enjoyable and that you will find effective for maintaining and extending their literacy growth.

Let's look at a few classrooms that are ending the year literacy strong.

Literacy-Strong Classroom Scenarios

What do literacy-strong classrooms look like toward the end of the year? Terms that come to mind include *engaged, purposeful, creative,* and *fun-filled.* Here are some quick classroom stories for inspiration as you draw nearer to the end of the school year.

Fixated on Prefixes

Mrs. Fodorski's kindergarten students are doing amazing work. She has explained what a prefix is to them and asked them to untie their shoelaces. Once untied, she asks them to retie the laces. "What is the same in both of these words: *tie* and *untie*?" she asks. Lacy, in the back of the room, answers: "It's the word *tie*." "That's right," responds Mrs. Fodorski. "*Tie* is in both words." Next she asks what is different about the two words. This time Marcus answers: "The beginning of the words is what is different." "Perfect, you are right," replies Mrs. Fodorski. "They do not have the same beginning." She then provides students with a set of base words (*fold*, *lock*, *usable*, and *zip*) and asks them to add the prefixes *un-* and *re-* to the bases. As students write the combinations on their own sheets of paper, Mrs. Fodorski says each new word and asks students if it is a real word and what it means.

Tip for 1st and 2nd grades: This lesson can easily be expanded for 1st and 2nd grades by adding new prefixes to the lesson (e.g., *anti-*, *bi-*, *de-*, *dis-*, *sub-*, *tri-*, *uni-*). You can provide students with additional base words to combine and create.

Going on a Text Trip

Mr. Kennedy knows that his students need to have a good understanding of how texts are organized to bring meaning to the texts that they read. Because his 1st graders need more experience with informational texts, he has decided to take them on a text trip with a new informational book. The book he is sharing—*National Geographic Little Kids First Big Book of Space* by Catherine D. Hughes—is about space, so he holds a toy rocket ship in his hand and proceeds to move it across the pages of the book. The first stop on the trip will be the title page. He asks his students to identify what they think they'll find here. Kerry Ann says, "The title of the book and the author and illustrator." She has learned this from earlier trips in fiction books. Mr. Kennedy continues the class's journey through the book (and on subsequent days, other informational books), making stops at the table of contents, illustrations, photographs, headings, charts, graphs, index, and glossary. At each stop, he asks students to share what they know about the text feature and then provides his own elaboration on the feature. He then marks the features on the nonfiction text map displayed in the room. Over the course of several days, students' understanding of the critical and distinct features of informational texts crystalizes. With little assistance, students can determine the nature of a book by simply thumbing through the pages.

Tip for kindergarten and 2nd grade: Kindergartners will need more support in examining text structure. You may wish to limit your stops on your text trips to fewer items, such as the title, the author, chapters, and illustrations. As 2nd graders become more independent, you may wish to ask them to work in pairs or groups to complete their own text trips.

Word Association: Shade of Meaning

Second graders in Mrs. Wasabi's classroom think of themselves as word wizards. She has been exploring words and word meanings with students throughout the year. Because English is a rich language with multiple words that have the same or similar meanings, Mrs. Wasabi's students have recently been exploring shades of meaning. In today's lesson, she displays the following synonyms for *run* that she found by consulting her online thesaurus: *dash*, *jog*, *race*, *sprint*, and *trot*. She provides a brief explanation and an example sentence for each word and asks students to share their own understandings of the words. Then, she hands out a yellow paint chip and asks students to organize the words on the chip in terms of speed, from fast to fastest. Pairs of students have five minutes to discuss the words and their placement on the chip. When the time is up, Mrs. Wasabi asks individual pairs to explain their organization of the words. Did all pairs of students have the same organization? Is there only one way to organize the words? What patterns do students see in their organizations?

Tip for kindergarten and 1st grade: This lesson can easily be modified for younger students. Simply put fewer words in your word groups (e.g., kindergarten: *jog*, *run*, and *walk*; 1st grade: *race*, *stroll*, *trot*, and *walk*). You may also wish to make the shades of meaning more distinct for younger students. Instead of including words from fast to fastest, you might use slow to fast as the two endpoints on the shades-of-meaning continuum.

Addressing End-of-Year Challenges

As the end of the school year approaches, anticipation of the break from school begins to consume students' minds. The two major challenges for literacy-strong teachers are how to maintain and extend students' growth in reading and how to set the stage for continued reading during vacation. We present here some suggestions for making the most of these important challenges.

Questions Teachers Ask to Address End-of-Year Challenges

- How do I motivate students to continue to read when their minds are drifting off toward vacation?
- What valuable work can my community of literacy learners engage in collaboratively?

- What skills and strategies must I emphasize so my students finish the year as literacy-strong readers?
- How do I identify the literacy needs of my students so that when they return to school, their new teachers will be able to address their needs immediately?
- How do I continue to connect with parents and families?

Essential Strategies for Ending the Year Literacy Strong

1. Continue the Inspiration by Reading to Your Students

Even though the end of the school year is in sight, don't stop reading to your students. Research shows that children who are read to regularly have larger vocabularies, increased comprehension, and more motivation for reading (Rasinski, Padak, & Fawcett, 2009). Although many students look forward to the end of the school year, this can also be a time of anxiety as students anticipate end-of-year testing, leaving their friends, and moving on to the next grade level. Be sure to explain to your students that books can help them understand and deal with new and exciting, often worrisome, end-of-year changes.

2. Develop a Classroom Literacy Community Where Students Share Their Own Books

As anticipation grows, allow students to recommend some of their favorite books to their classmates. Provide a special time each day for one or two students to do a quick book talk about a favorite book from this school year. Be sure to remind each student presenter to bring in a copy of the book (so others can browse it), to give a brief summary of the book, and to share with classmates what they liked about the book. Make a list of the titles recommended and send it home with students the last week of school.

3. Harvest Words from Read-Alouds

Vocabulary growth is crucial to early reading success. What better place is there to find interesting words than in the books that you read to your students? As you read aloud each day, ask students to listen for any interesting words that the author may have used in the text. Then, at the end of the read-aloud, have students call out the words that they chose. Write the words on a chart and discuss their meanings. Read the words regularly and encourage students (including yourself) to use them in their oral and written language over the next several days. If you harvest five words per day over the last three months of the school year, you will have introduced your students to over 200 new and interesting words that are sure to add to their vocabularies.

4. Focus on Fluency

Fluency is a critical competency in the primary grades, and research indicates that many of our young readers struggle to achieve fluency in their reading. One way to focus students' attention on fluency is to develop a rubric that you display as a poster in your classroom (Rasinski, 2010). Your rubric should focus on these aspects of oral fluency:

- Word recognition accuracy
- Reading at an appropriate pace
- Reading with good phrasing
- Reading with good volume and confidence
- Reading with good expression

Each of these categories can be rated on a 1–4 scale, with 4 indicating strong performance and 1 indicating a need for improvement. Once the rubric is completed, your students can rate their own fluency while reading. They could even rate your reading when you read aloud to them. By rating and talking about fluency in your classroom, students will develop a deeper understanding of what is meant by *reading fluency* and how they might become more fluent readers.

5. Creative Response to Reading: Tableau

We often support students' reading comprehension by asking them to respond in some way to the reading. The response is often in the form of a discussion or writing assignment. A different way to respond to a reading is to ask students to form groups and create a tableau that represents a scene from the story. In a tableau, students use their bodies to portray the scene for their classmates. They must plan how to position themselves in relation to one another and what sort of hand, facial, or other gestures will accompany the tableau. When they are ready, have them form into their tableau, and then say, "Freeze!" At that point, the performing students must freeze in their tableau. Other members of the class are then challenged to determine the scene from the book that the tableau represents. The student discussion that precedes and comes after the tableau truly leads students to deep analysis and understanding of the text.

6. Singing Is Reading, Too!

Sometimes we forget that singing songs and reciting poetry are forms of reading —reading that is enjoyable and relatively short and, with practice, can be mastered by most students. Find songs about the season of the year, put the lyrics on display, demonstrate the melody, and have students sing a new song multiple times over the course of several days or a week.

7. Create Lifelong Readers

Our ultimate goal in literacy-strong instruction is to develop our students into lifelong readers—readers who will find value in literacy throughout the rest of their lives. For this reason, it is a good idea for students to hear the stories of others who have lived literacy-strong lives. Invite fellow teachers and school staff members, parents and other older family members, and members of the community to come into your classroom to share with students their own literacy lives and how reading and writing have enriched their lives. You might give your visitors an outline of some suggested topics that they could touch on in a 10-minute presentation, such as these:

- What was/is your favorite book as a child or adult?
- Did you find reading difficult as a child? How did you improve your reading?
- Describe a situation in which reading played an important role.
- Describe your personal preferences for reading.
- Describe your own personal reading habits: when and where you read.

By hearing the stories, students are more likely to view reading as an important part of their own reading lives and perhaps will make an even greater effort to read over the school break.

8. Anticipate Out-of-School Reading

As the school year winds down, it is a good idea to get students thinking about their out-of-school reading plans. Invite the librarian from your local public library to come to your classroom to speak to students about what the library has to offer them. These offerings can range from reading programs to special events held at the library. The librarian should also be asked to bring registration forms so students who do not have a library card can apply for one.

9. Continue the Parent Connection

Clearly, the need to connect with parents is as important now as it was during the earlier part of the school year. Create a reading recommendations flyer with ideas of what parents can do to help their children maintain and expand on their growth in reading. The flyer can discuss the following:

- Working on recognizing high-frequency words
- Parent read-alouds
- Parents listening to their child's read-alouds
- Playing word games
- Taking time for library and bookstore visits
- Intervention programs for struggling readers

10. Quick Assessment

The end of the year is a good time to check students' progress in reading. Here's a simple and quick way to assess their reading growth. Work individually with your students. Provide each student with a grade-level passage. Ask the student to read the passage aloud to you in his or her best (not fastest) reading voice. Mark any uncorrected word errors that the student makes and the point of progress after one minute. Toward the end of the school year, students should be reading at or above the following levels:

- *Kindergarten:* Five words read correctly in one minute
- *First grade:* Fifty words read correctly in one minute
- *Second grade:* Eighty words read correctly in one minute

This assessment provides a good measure of students' growth in their foundational reading competencies. Students whose scores are significantly below the levels indicated may be good candidates for additional instruction or reading assistance.

Although we are essentially measuring reading speed in this assessment, we should never focus students' attention on attempting to read quickly. Speed in reading is acquired simply through plenty of authentic and engaging reading experiences.

11. Try These Suggested Read-Alouds

- *The Berenstain Bears' Graduation Day* by Mike Berenstain
- *Last Day Blues* by Julie Danneberg
- *The Big Test* by Julie Danneberg
- *Field-Trip Fiasco* by Julie Danneberg
- *Testing Miss Malarkey* by Judy Finchler
- *Mrs. Spitzer's Garden* by Edith Pattou
- *Miss Bindergarten Celebrates the Last Day of Kindergarten* by Joseph Slate

12. End-of-School-Year Word Ladder

Start with a word that means "to conclude."

Finish	Take away two letters to make an animal that lives in the water.
Fish	Change one letter to make another word for a dinner plate.
Dish	Change the vowel to make a short running race.
Dash	Change the first letter to make a long cut on the skin.
Gash	Take away one letter to make a fuel most cars need.
Gas	Rearrange the letters to make a word that means to droop or hang down.
Sag	Add one letter to make the past participle of *sing*.
Sang	Change one letter to make a composition of words that are sung.
Song	Add two letters to make the opposite of *weak*.
Strong	Now, fill in the blanks below with appropriate words from the word ladder:

Now that we are close to the end of the school year, we need to keep our literacy tank filled with _____ so we can _____ the year literacy _____!

Overview of Chapter 3 Lessons

Lesson 1. Phonological Awareness and Phonics: Isolating and Identifying Sounds—Digraph Hero Teams

Lesson 2. Phonological Awareness and Phonics: Blending and Segmenting—The Blend Factor

Lesson 3. Phonics: Decoding—Fixated on Prefixes: Divide and Conquer

Lesson 4. Fluency: Phrasing—Text Road Signs: Marking Phrase Boundaries

Lesson 5. Comprehension: Craft and Structure Previewing—We're Going on a Text Trip

Lesson 6. Comprehension: Key Ideas and Details—Determining Importance and Summarizing—Finding the Topic: It's a Snap!

Lesson 7. Comprehension: Key Ideas and Details—Questioning for Close Reading—Question the Character

Lesson 8. Vocabulary: Associating Words—Shades of Meaning

Lesson 9. Vocabulary: Analyzing Words—Hunting to Position Prepositions and Verify Verbs

Lesson 10. Motivation: Motivating Readers—Ready, Set, Read!

LESSON 1. PHONOLOGICAL AWARENESS AND PHONICS: ISOLATING AND IDENTIFYING SOUNDS

Title DIGRAPH HERO TEAMS

Trailer Unity is key to being on a winning team. Working together side by side is vital. In much the same way, letters and sounds can act as teams working toward a seamless flow of language. Students practice isolating and identifying two consecutive letters creating one distinct sound—a phoneme!

Literacy Enhancer Phonological Awareness and Phonics: Isolating and Identifying Sounds—Digraphs

Key Academic Vocabulary Vocabulary from a previous lesson is marked with an asterisk (*).

Alliteration*: A figure of speech in which a series of words repeat the same initial sound

Digraph: Two consecutive vowels or consonants that represent a single speech sound (phoneme)

Isolate*: To separate sounds from other sounds in a word

Long vowel*: A speech sound produced without obstructing the flow of air from the lungs; the letters *a, e, i, o, u,* and sometimes *y*; long vowels make the same sound as the letter name

Phoneme*: The smallest unit of sound

Short vowel*: A speech sound produced without obstructing the flow of air from the lungs; the letters *a, e, i, o, u,* and sometimes *y*; short vowels do not make the sound of the letter name

Learning Objectives

- Isolate and identify digraph sounds by positioning the mouth, lips, jaw, and tongue to correspond with the appropriate digraph in single-syllable words.
- Distinguish the common consonant digraphs.

Essential Questions

- How do you position your mouth for the /_/ digraph sound in the word _____?
- What digraph sound is in the word _____?
- What other words have the same digraph sound as the word _____?

STEP 1: PREPARATION

Organize Materials

- Handheld mirrors
- Multimodal text sets with samples of digraphs
- *Digraph Picture Cards* reproducible (one copy of each card for each team)
- *Digraph Team Captain Cards* reproducible (one copy of each card)
- Literature notebooks

STEP 2: INITIATION

Team Power

Ask students to name different types of sports (e.g., basketball, football, soccer) and create an alliteration of sports team names (e.g., Pacers, Packers, Patriots, Pirates; Rams, Ravens, Rays, Royals). Share other types of teams (e.g., organizational, school, political). Discuss the characteristics that make a good team. Highlight that a good team always works together as one unit and tell students that they are going to study letter–sound teams.

STEP 3: DEMONSTRATION

Introducing the Digraph Team Captains

1. Say three words with the same initial digraph sounds (e.g., *chick, chip, chocolate*). Remind students how these three words make up an alliteration because they all have the same initial sound.
2. Use a handheld mirror to isolate the *ch* digraph sound in each word and describe the position of your mouth for that particular digraph. Introduce the *ch* digraph "Chocolate Chip Charlie" team captain from the *Digraph Team Captain Cards* reproducible (Figure 3.1). You can also review short- and long-vowel sounds in words (e.g., short *i* in *chip* and *chick* vs. the mouth position in *check* [short *e*] and *cheese* [long *e*]).
3. Read aloud from a text that has multiple uses of a digraph sound you are highlighting. Isolate and identify the digraph sound in the word by demonstrating how to position your mouth for the digraph sound and how to make the specific digraph sound.
4. Create anchor charts for the digraphs you are studying. Make sure to note the position of the mouth for each digraph. Use the *Digraph Team Captain Cards* or objects that have the digraph sounds as anchor images for each digraph team. Demonstrate examples where the digraph is positioned at the beginning, middle, or end of words.

5. Introduce the other digraph team captains ("Photo Phillip," "Thunderbolt Thad," "Sharky Sheila," and "Wheelbarrow Whitney") and explain to students that they are going to work in teams to learn how letters work together as one sound (e.g., *ch, ck, gh, kn, ph, sh, th*).

STEP 4: COLLABORATION

Digraph Superheroes and Conversational Coaching

Distribute a *Digraph Team Captain Card* to each team. Have students in each team work together to draw images or list words that correspond to each team player. Have teams engage in conversational coaching:

- How do you position your mouth for the digraph?
- Do the other images or words have that same position for the digraph sound?
- Do you hear the digraph at the beginning, middle, or end of the word?
- Which two letters form your digraph team's name?

STEP 5: APPLICATION

Sorting Digraphs

At a center or literacy station for word work, have students sort items or the picture cards in Figure 3.2 to correspond with the digraph teams' names. Students can record their results in their literacy notebooks for review and as their personalized anchor chart. Remind them to use the class digraph anchor charts as they reflect on the characteristics of each consonant digraph and the positioning of their mouth for each digraph sound.

STEP 6: REFLECTION

Oral or Written Response

Have students independently demonstrate the sound that each digraph makes. Have them respond to the essential questions orally or by writing in their literacy notebooks:

- How do you position your mouth for the digraph in the word _____?
- What digraph sound is in the word _____?
- What other words have the same digraph sound as the word _____?

ADAPTATION/EXTENSION

- Have teams create a silly poem or story with their digraph team captain as the main character, using the highlighted digraph as many times as they can in the story or poem.

- Create a digraph collage from clip art or magazines and place it on a picture digraph word wall.
- Create a class digraph rap. Use a YouTube video to model (e.g., "Digraph Rap by Mr. Thompson": www.youtube.com/watch?v=eEXUzXZjno4).
- Form teams for other digraphs, such as *ck*, *ng*, *tch*, *wh*, and *wr*.
- *English Language Learner Suggestion:* Create a model of what each digraph mouth position looks and sounds like. Place this in a sample digraph folder on a computer. Have students watch each digraph demonstration and then use a webcam on a computer or tablet to record themselves making the various digraph sounds as an anchor chart for their digital portfolio.
- *Struggling Reader Suggestion:* Have students work in groups to sort beginning and ending digraphs from predetermined images. Take a digital picture of the mouth position of the digraphs being practiced. Place these sample digraph mouth cards for the students to practice checking their mouth as they look at each picture card. Have them sort the digraph images as they watch and listen for the position of their mouth and where they hear the digraph in the word. Here are some sample Digraph Sort Cards:

Beginning Digraphs		Ending Digraphs	
ch__	th__	__ch	__th
chick	thorn	branch	earth
cheese	thirteen	beach	tooth
chair	three	bench	bath

EVALUATION

"I Can . . ." Statements

- I can identify the consonant digraph sounds in words.
- I can produce the consonant digraph sounds in words.
- I can tell the difference between different digraph sounds in words.

BEHAVIOR INDICATORS

- Isolates and identifies selected digraphs by positioning the mouth, lips, jaw, and tongue to correspond with the appropriate digraph in single-syllable words.
- Distinguishes consonant digraphs in words when reading regularly spelled, one-syllable words.
- Generates words with similar digraphs.

FIGURE 3.1
Digraph Team Captain Cards

ch: Chocolate Chip Charlie

ph: Photo Phillip

th: Thunderbolt Thad

sh: Sharky Sheila

wh: Wheelbarrow Whitney

Source: Literacy Strong All Year Long: Powerful Lessons for Grades K–2 by Valerie Ellery, Lori Oczkus, and Timothy V. Rasinski. © 2020 ASCD. Readers may duplicate this figure for noncommercial use within their school.

FIGURE 3.2
Digraph Picture Cards

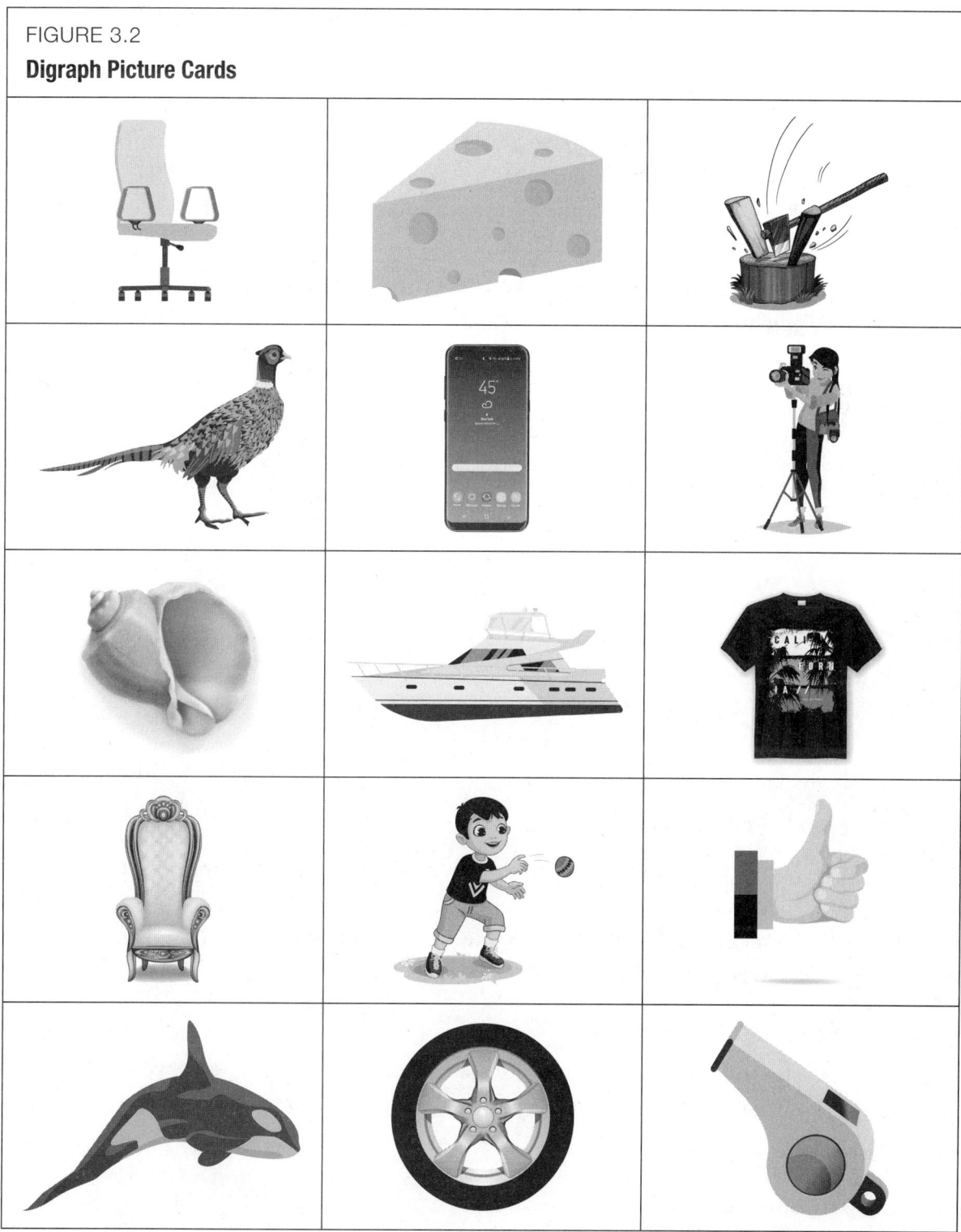

Note: These are the words by row: *chair, cheese, chop; pheasant, phone, photographer; shell, ship, shirt; throne, throw, thumb; whale, wheel, whistle.*

Source: Literacy Strong All Year Long: Powerful Lessons for Grades K–2 by Valerie Ellery, Lori Oczkus, and Timothy V. Rasinski. © 2020 ASCD. Readers may duplicate this figure for noncommercial use within their school.

LESSON 2. PHONOLOGICAL AWARENESS AND PHONICS: BLENDING AND SEGMENTING

Title THE BLEND FACTOR

Trailer Both colors and consonants can have the "it" factor! They can blend together well with their counterparts to create smoothness. Use the blend factor to combine consonant sounds and syllables on a perfect palette. Help readers create a complete masterpiece by blending and segmenting just the right mix of sounds and syllables for smooth reading.

Literacy Enhancer Phonological Awareness and Phonics: Blending and Segmenting—Consonant Blends and Multisyllabic Words

Key Academic Vocabulary Vocabulary from a previous lesson is marked with an asterisk (*).

Blending*: Combining a sequence of two or more sounds to form a word

Consonant blend: A voiced combination of a group of two or three consonants in a word

Multisyllabic word: A word that has more than one syllable

Onset*: The part of a syllable before the vowel; not all syllables have onsets

Rime*: The part of a syllable beginning with the sounded vowel and any consonants that follow

Segmenting*: Breaking a word by phonemes (sounds) and syllables

Syllable*: A part of a word that contains only one sounded vowel; words can be made up of one or more syllables

Learning Objectives

- Orally produce single-syllable words by segmenting and blending sounds (phonemes).
- Segment single-syllable words into their complete sequence of individual sounds (phonemes).

Essential Questions

- How do you orally produce consonant blends?
- How many syllables do you hear in the word _____?

STEP 1: PREPARATION

Organize Materials

- Glass bowl
- Water

- Food coloring
- Flashlight
- Handheld mirrors
- Multimodal text set for the topic of study
- *The Blend Factor* reproducible (copies or enlarged for display)
- Literacy notebooks

STEP 2: INITIATION

Blending Colors

Ask the students, "How do we make the color green?" Chart their responses, highlighting key terms (e.g., *combine, blend, put two colors together*). Squeeze a drop of yellow food coloring into a clear bowl of water. Ask, "What color is this? Are there any traces of blue in the bowl?" Share with students that there is only yellow in the bowl. Now, add a drop of blue to the yellow. Discuss how we are actually making a math sentence. By adding another color to the equation, we will have a new sum: a new color. We are color blending!

What do color blending and consonant blending have in common? Each color has a separate blend factor, and so does each sound. Blending colors means creating an area between two colors where they gradually mix, so you can get a gentle transition from one color to the other. Today we are going to focus on consonant clusters and how we can gradually mix two sounds together to get the blend factor.

STEP 3: DEMONSTRATION

The Blend Factor

1. For the read-aloud, select a text that focuses on consonant blends and multisyllabic words (e.g., *The Grouchy Ladybug* by Eric Carle, poems from *A Light in the Attic* by Shel Silverstein).
2. From the text, select several multisyllabic words that also have consonant blends.
3. Say a selected word aloud (e.g., *grouchy*). Isolate the /gr/ consonant blend sound. Share how this sound is part of the blend factor: "These two sounds (/g/ and /r/) mix together to make one smooth sound." Remind students how we made word smoothies (see Chapter 2) and how each sound could stand alone, but when blended together, we can get a smooth read.
4. Create a class chart for consonant blends (i.e., contains two or three consonant sounds that cluster together; each consonant sound is distinct in the blend and can be heard within the cluster; each consonant blend can be pronounced or

they can glide together with a smooth flow; they can be found at the beginning, middle, and end of a word).

5. Display the selected blended, multisyllabic word (*grouchy*). Highlight the *gr* consonant blend with a flashlight. Focus the light on the *g* and say its sound, /g/. Begin to create the math sentence by saying, "/g/ + __ = /gr/." Focus the light on the *r* and say its sound, /r/. Next, with a smooth glide of the flashlight, complete the equation by blending the two sounds together.

6. Pick up a mirror and say the complete multisyllabic word in the mirror (*grouchy*). Think aloud about what you noticed when you said the word (e.g., "My mouth formed the /g/ and /r/ sound together, my chin moved twice, and my chin dropped down").

7. Continue to practice other words from the text with student volunteers and compare what they notice with the class chart, adding any other observations to the chart for both consonant blends and multisyllabic words (e.g., "Each time my chin dropped, I noticed a vowel within that section of the word").

STEP 4: COLLABORATION

Conversational Coaching

Engage in conversational coaching by asking students to discuss the following questions with diverse partners:

- "How many syllables do you hear in the word _____?"
- "How do you know?"
- Ask them to describe the blend factor for both consonant clusters and multisyllabic words.

STEP 5: APPLICATION

Mirror, Mirror

Have students work in groups or individually to select multisyllabic words with consonant blends to segment and blend. Distribute small mirrors and have students look in the mirror and say the selected words. Have them notice the number of times their mouths open when saying each word. They can also place their hand under their chin and feel the number of times it drops when they say the word. Have them use *The Blend Factor* reproducible (Figure 3.3) to record their observations and identify which part of the word causes their jaw to drop. Remind them to use the class chart.

STEP 6: REFLECTION

Written or Oral Response

Have students review one of their independent writing pieces (e.g., interpretation/response to literature, argumentative or persuasive) in their literacy notebooks. Have students select three multisyllabic words with consonant blends from their writing piece to analyze and record as a "math sentence" in their notebook. Have them respond to the essential questions orally or in writing:

- How do you orally produce consonant blends?
- How many syllable parts do you hear in the word _____?

ADAPTATION/EXTENSION

- Include verbal and kinesthetic actions (e.g., jumping, clapping, tapping, or marching in place to the syllables).
- *English Language Learner Suggestion:* Use the online Syllable Dictionary at www.howmanysyllables.com as a reference for finding out how many syllables are in a word and how to pronounce a word. Have students sort the words by how many syllables are in each word. Then have them try to find the blend in the word and stretch the two sounds slowly to hear how they pronounce both consonant letters in the blend. Here are some sample blend words:

    One syllable
    - drum
    - crab
    - frog

    Two syllables
    - drag/on
    - cray/on
    - fro/zen

- *Struggling Reader Suggestion:* Create Bingo blend boards with picture cards or consonant blend letter cards. After each picture or word is called out, have the students use the word in a sentence, then isolate the consonant blend within the word. Create cards online for free using a website like www.print-bingo.com. When students mark a consonant blend for a Bingo, they have to generate another word that has the same consonant blend.

EVALUATION

"I Can . . ." Statements

- I can identify and produce consonant blends.
- I can identify how many syllables are in a word.
- I can examine a syllable and determine the vowel in each syllable.

BEHAVIOR INDICATORS

- Produces a word by blending sounds, including consonant blends.
- Identifies the number of syllables in a word.
- Determines the vowel in each syllable.

FIGURE 3.3
The Blend Factor

Name: _____

Date: _____

Directions: In your reading materials, search for at least two words with consonant blends that have more than one syllable. Draw a paint swatch on the palette to represent each syllable.

Write the letter or letters in each syllable segment swatch. Then, create a paint swatch palette to highlight just the blend in the selected word. Blend the sounds and syllables back together and read the word in context or share the word in a sentence.

Example:
Word: *grouchy*
Number of syllables: 2

grouchy (word)

g, r, grou, chy

Word: _____
Number of syllables: _____

_____ (word)

Word: _____
Number of syllables: _____

_____ (word)

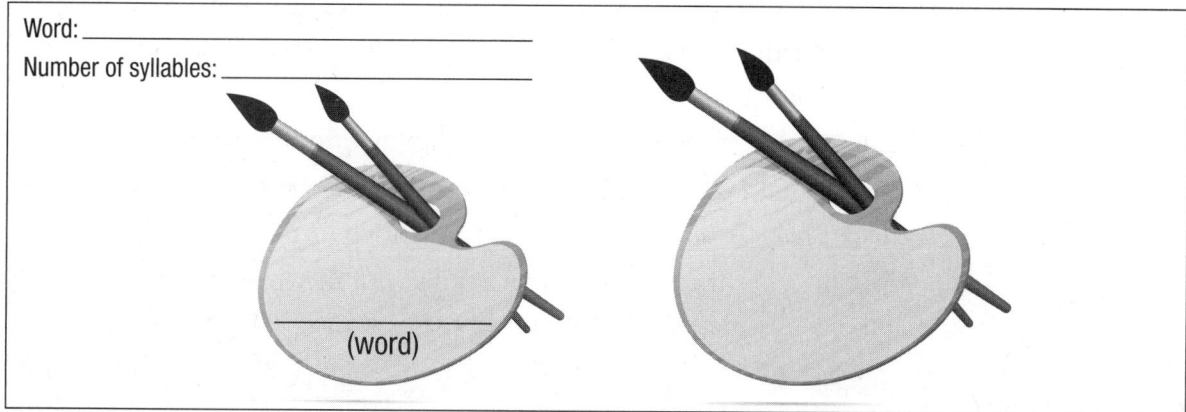

Source: Literacy Strong All Year Long: Powerful Lessons for Grades K–2 by Valerie Ellery, Lori Oczkus, and Timothy V. Rasinski. © 2020 ASCD. Readers may duplicate this figure for noncommercial use within their school.

LESSON 3. PHONICS: DECODING

Title FIXATED ON PREFIXES: DIVIDE AND CONQUER

Trailer Focus fast! It is important in the primary grades to fixate on words and word parts to decode for meaning. To understand words, readers divide them into parts and conquer their pronunciation and meaning. Readers are like knights in armor riding through text, armed with strategies as their swords. Students practice decoding words by dividing them into syllables, analyzing letter–sound connections with a focus on vowels, and determining prefixes among root words to bring meaning to what is read.

Literacy Enhancer Phonics: Decoding—Multisyllabic Words: Prefixes

Key Academic Vocabulary Vocabulary from a previous lesson is marked with an asterisk (*)

Closed syllable: A syllable that ends in a vowel sound

Decode*: The ability to apply letter-sound relationships to read and pronounce a written word

Grapheme*: The written symbol (letters) used to represent a phoneme (sounds)

Long vowels*: The letters *a, e, i, o, u,* and sometimes *y*; long vowels make a speech sound produced without obstructing the flow of air from the lungs; make the same sound as the letter name

Multisyllable word*: A word made up of more than one syllable

Open syllable: A syllable that ends in a consonant sound

Prefix: A meaningful group of letters added to the beginning of a root or base word to modify its meaning

Root (base) word: The primary part of a word that does not require a prefix or suffix

Short vowels*: The letters *a, e, i, o, u,* and sometimes *y*; short vowels make a speech sound produced without obstructing the flow of air from the lungs; do not make the sound of the letter name

Syllable*: A basic unit of spoken language containing a vowel sound

Vowel: A speech sound produced without obstructing the flow of air from the lungs; the letters *a, e, i, o, u,* and sometimes *y* in written form

Word family: The portion of a syllable that begins with the vowel and vowel sound and contains any other letters after the vowel (e.g., *-at, -ate, -it, -ight*); also known as phonograms or rimes

Learning Objectives

- Decode regularly spelled two-syllable words.
- Decode and generate words with common prefixes.
- Demonstrate how prefixes affect words and their meanings.

Essential Questions

- How do you decode the meaning of a new word with the prefix?
- How do the vowels help you determine the number of syllables in a word?
- How does knowledge of prefixes impact your ability to read?

STEP 1: PREPARATION

Organize Materials

- Shoes that tie
- Chart paper or interactive whiteboard
- Paper
- Multimodal text sets with multisyllabic words with prefixes
- *Divide and Conquer Prefix Venn Diagram* reproducible (copies or enlarged for display)
- *Syllable Structure and Vowel Jingles* reproducible (copies or enlarged for display)
- *Instructions for Prefix Flap Book* reproducible (copies or enlarged for display)
- *Commonly Used Prefixes* reproducible (copies or enlarged for display)
- Literacy notebooks

STEP 2: INITIATION

Do and Undo

Look at students with a big smile on your face to demonstrate the word *happy*. Twirl around and change the look on your face to now be unhappy. Ask students to describe what emotions you shared by your facial expressions. If they describe sad as one of your emotions, elicit other words for *sad* until the word *unhappy* is given. Discuss how *sad* can also mean unhappy.

Next, look down at your shoes and say, "I am *unhappy* because my shoes are hurting my feet. I *tied* my shoelaces a little too tight." Place an emphasis on the word *tied* with your voice to encourage students to fixate on that word. Stop and bend down as you say, "I am going to need to *untie* my shoelaces." Again, emphasize with your voice the word *untie*, with extra stress on the prefix *un-*. (*Note:* You will need to wear shoes that can tie or use a student volunteer who has shoes with shoelaces to demonstrate.)

Create a T-chart on chart paper or the interactive whiteboard and write the word *happy* on one side and *unhappy* on the other side. Ask partners to share what makes these two words similar and how they are different. Encourage partners to think about the vowels in the words, what they mean, and how they sound. Have partners share their responses with the group. Explain that students are going to continue to practice decoding words that have prefixes—groups of letters in front of a root word that have their own meaning, cannot form a word by themselves, and change the meaning of the root word.

STEP 3: DEMONSTRATION

Divide and Conquer Prefixes

1. Revisit the prefix T-chart and highlight the prefix in the word *unhappy*.
2. Draw a Venn diagram or use the *Divide and Conquer Prefix Venn Diagram* reproducible (Figure 3.4) to model how to decode the word *unhappy* by breaking it up using syllable patterns (e.g., CVC, CVVC, CVCe) and the word's definition to read and bring meaning to words. To determine the structure of the syllable (e.g., closed or open), use the *Syllable Structure and Vowel Jingles* reproducible (Figure 3.5) as a guide. Think aloud to model the process. For example, "When I hear two vowel sounds in the word *happy*, that means there are two syllables in the word. The first syllable, *hap-*, is a closed syllable because it ends in a consonant and the vowel has a short-*a* sound. The second syllable, *-py*, is an open syllable because it ends in the *y* acting as a long-*e* vowel sound. I would make the syllable break between the two *p* consonants."

Here's a sample Venn diagram for *happy* and *unhappy*:

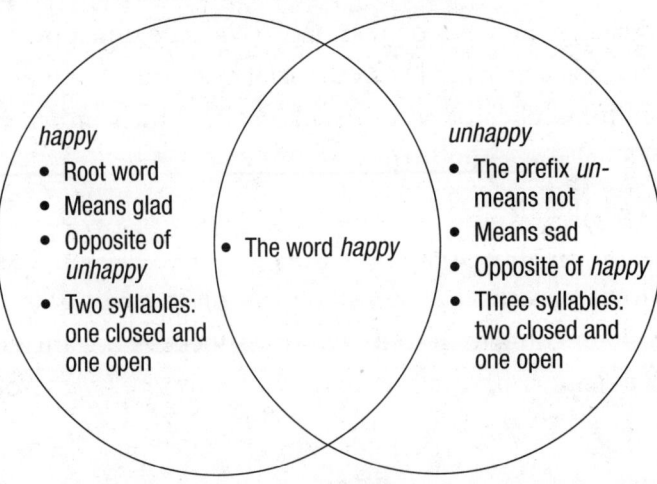

- Short-vowel sound
- The letter *y* as the long *-e* vowel sound
- Double consonant

3. Add *tie* and *untie* to the prefix T-chart. You can create a Venn diagram about these two words or begin to compare *unhappy* and *untie*. For example, "As I look at these two words, I notice that they both added *un-* to the root word, which changed the meaning to form an opposite."

4. Add the *re-* prefix by saying, "I need to *retie* my shoes again." Have students pretend to tie and untie by acting out the motions and clapping out the words by syllables (i.e., one clap for *tie*, two claps for *retie*). Explain how adding the prefix to the word changed it to two syllables. Ask, "What is the prefix in the word *retie*? Based on the way the word *retie* was used in the sentence, what do you think the prefix *re-* means when added to root words?"

5. Read aloud a section from a selected text and think aloud as you model decoding words with common prefixes. Create an anchor chart for each prefix studied.

STEP 4: COLLABORATION

Divide and Conquer Venn Diagrams and Conversational Coaching

Divide students into teams and assign each team a prefix or have them search from text to locate a word that aligns with the prefix that you are studying. Invite the teams to complete their own *Divide and Conquer Prefix Venn Diagram* (see reproducible) as they engage in conversational coaching about these questions:

- What does the prefix mean?
- What is the root word?
- How many syllables are in the word? How do you know?
- What parts do the two words have in common?
- What parts do the two words not have in common?
- What does the prefix _____ do when added to the start of the word _____?

STEP 5: APPLICATION

Flap Book

Assign students a prefix and a root word. Using the *Instructions for Prefix Flap Book* reproducible (Figure 3.6), assist students in making a flap book for their assigned prefix and root word. Remind them to use the class anchor chart about prefixes. Display all the completed trifold prefix flap books to create a prefix word wall. Display or distribute the *Commonly Used Prefixes Chart* reproducible (Figure 3.7) to be used as a resource for reading and writing prefixes.

STEP 6: REFLECTION

Oral or Written Response

In their literacy notebooks, have students create sentences using words that have prefixes. Have students respond to these essential questions orally or in writing:

- How does knowledge of prefixes affect your ability to understand words and read?
- How do the vowels help you determine the number of syllables in a word?

ADAPTATION/EXTENSION

- Write a story using as many of the studied prefixes and the words that contain them.
- Create a prefix word sort center for students to practice identifying the prefix in a word.
- Have students keep a log in their literacy notebooks to record the number of times they use one of the studied prefixes in either their personal oral conversations or their writing. Students can also record each time they read one of the studied prefixes in a text.
- Create a prefix/root word matching game with index cards or puzzle pieces.
- *English Language Learner Suggestion:* Play online animated prefix clips for the students to see and hear prefix words in context. (Sample animated clip: "The Un People," produced by the PBS Kids series *Between the Lions*, about the prefixes *un-* and *re-*: www.youtube.com/watch?v=B-hwHUDbakw.) After watching a clip, have a search-and-find time where the students can look through books for the prefix words being highlighted and create a list.
- *Struggling Reader Suggestion:* Have the students use a mirror to watch how many times their chin drops when they pronounce a word. Remind them that for every syllable their chin will drop. They can use online tools such as the examples below to check and compare the definition and syllable count in words to how many times their chin drops in the mirror:
    - Syllable Counter (syllablecounter.net)
    - Syllable Counter & Word Count (www.wordcalc.com)
    - Dictionary.com (dictionary.reference.com)
    - OneLook (www.onelook.com)

EVALUATION

"I Can . . ." Statements

- I can decode two-syllable words following basic patterns by breaking the words into syllables and using the vowels to help identify the number of syllables in a word.
- I can identify common prefixes in words.
- I can use the prefix to determine the new meaning of a root word.

BEHAVIOR INDICATORS

- Decodes two-syllable words following basic patterns by breaking the words into syllables.
- Identifies the prefix and the root word.
- Determines the meaning of a newly formed word when a common prefix is added to a root word.

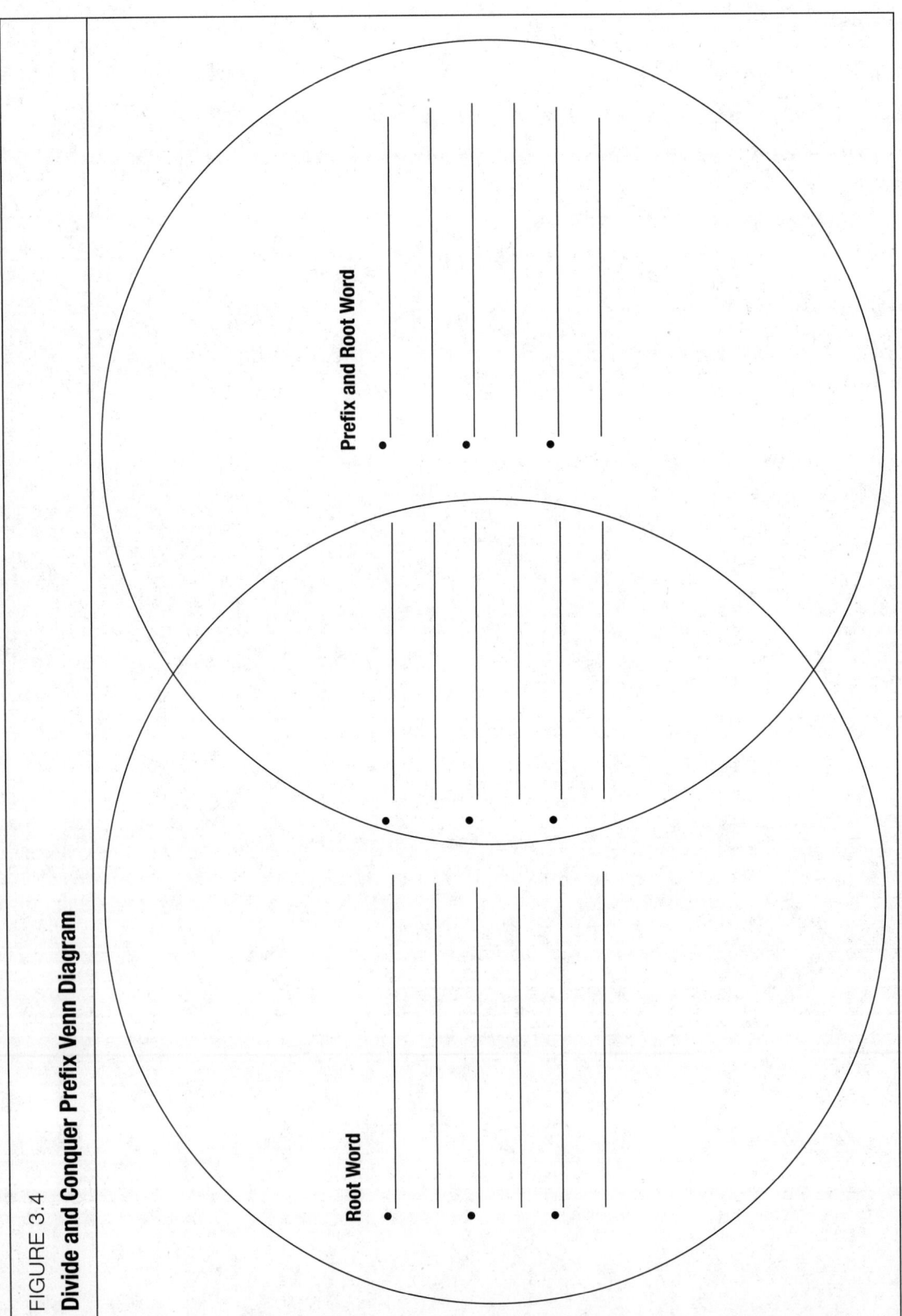

FIGURE 3.4
Divide and Conquer Prefix Venn Diagram

Source: Literacy Strong All Year Long: Powerful Lessons for Grades K–2 by Valerie Ellery, Lori Oczkus, and Timothy V. Rasinski. © 2020 ASCD. Readers may duplicate this figure for noncommercial use within their school.

FIGURE 3.5
Syllable Structure and Vowel Jingles

Steps to Syllable Structure Segmenting
Step 1. Determine how many vowels are in the word. Syllables are formed by vowel sounds.
Step 2. Subtract any silent vowels, silent e, or vowel teams (i.e., -ou, -ea, -ie, -oa)
Step 3. Determine the number of vowel sounds left. This is the number of syllables in the word.
Step 4. Analyze the structure of the word by asking questions, and divide the word accordingly.

Types	Does it have...	Divide	Examples	Exception if...
Suffix	a suffix	**before** a suffix from root word	price/less sharp/en	
Consonant + -le	-le at the end of the word	**before** consonant -le	a/ble pur/ple	the letter before the -le is a vowel (i.e., sale, file, ale)
Vowel with -l	-al, el, il at the end of word	-al, -el, -il	me/dal **ho/tel**	-ckle at the end of word (i.e., ta/ckle)
r-controlled	The letter r followed by a vowel (ar, er, ir, or, ur) neither long or short	**before** consonant when next to r-controlled vowel	doc/tor har/bor	-r controlled vowel comes after a root word (singer, jumper) If only one vowel, then it has only one syllable (i.e., star).
Compound Words	two words making a compound word	**between** the two word within the compound word	rain/bow, foot/ball	
Closed Syllable	two middle consonants, usually short-vowel sound	**between** two middle consonants next to each other with a vowel on each side vc/cv pattern	ob/ject	two consonants make one sound—digraphs (i.e., ch, th, sh, wh)
	double consonants	**between** double consonants	hap/pen din/ner	two consonants that make one sound (i.e., ff)
	a single-letter vowel followed by consonant— usually short	**after** the consonant when the nearby vowel is short cvc pattern	plan/et nap/kin cat duck	
Open Syllable	a single-letter vowel at the end of the syllable, not closed in by a consonant	**after** an open syllable with a long-vowel sound v/cv pattern	me cry pro/tect	words that make the long-vowel sound with one vowel (i.e., co/met) vc/v pattern
Prefix	a prefix	**after** a prefix	re/wind pre/view	
Silent -e	an -e at the end of the word is silent and makes the next vowel before it a long-vowel sound	vce pattern	ride mis/take	

Source: Literacy Strong All Year Long: Powerful Lessons for Grades K–2 by Valerie Ellery, Lori Oczkus, and Timothy V. Rasinski. © 2020 ASCD. Readers may duplicate this figure for noncommercial use within their school

FIGURE 3.6
Instructions for Prefix Flap Book

Directions:

1. Fold a sheet of paper lengthwise and cut it on the fold.

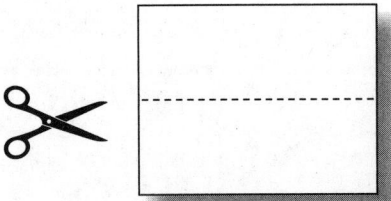

2. Take one piece and pull the two short ends to meet in the center. Crease the paper.

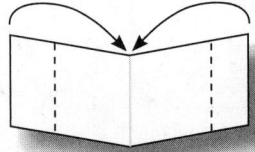

3. On the front left panel, write the prefix. On the front right panel, write the root word.

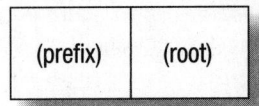

- On the inside center panel, write the combined prefix and root word and the new word's meaning.
- On the inside left panel, write the features of the prefix.
- On the inside right panel, write the features of the root word.

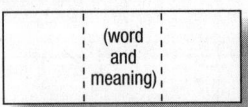 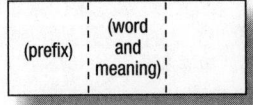 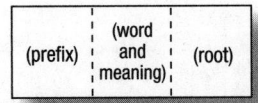

5. On the back of the flap book, write a sentence using the prefix word in context.

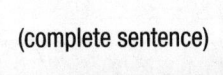

6. Repeat with the other piece of paper using a new prefix and sentence.

Source: Literacy Strong All Year Long: Powerful Lessons for Grades K–2 by Valerie Ellery, Lori Oczkus, and Timothy V. Rasinski. © 2020 ASCD. Readers may duplicate this figure for noncommercial use within their school.

FIGURE 3.7

Commonly Used Prefixes

Prefix	Meaning	Examples
auto-	self	autopilot, autograph, automobile
bi-	two	bicentennial, bicycle, bilingual
de-	reverse action, remove, away	decrease, detach, deflect
dis-	apart, negative, away	disinterest, disagree, disappoint
in-	not, free from, out	informal, invisible, incorrect
mis-	wrong	mislead, misplace, misbehave
pre-	before	preview, premade, prepare
re-	back, again	redo, recount, reapply
tri-	three	triangle, tricycle, tripod
un-	not	uncover, unhealthy, unhappy

Source: Literacy Strong All Year Long: Powerful Lessons for Grades K–2 by Valerie Ellery, Lori Oczkus, and Timothy V. Rasinski. © 2020 ASCD. Readers may duplicate this figure for noncommercial use within their school

LESSON 4. FLUENCY: PHRASING

Title TEXT ROAD SIGNS: MARKING PHRASE BOUNDARIES

Trailer Punctuation in text is a bit like road signs when driving. It informs readers about the type of sentence they are reading and the appropriate places for chunking a text into meaningful units. However, phrase boundaries are not always marked by commas or other punctuation. Students learn to infer and mark phrase boundaries in texts and then read those texts with appropriate fluency and phrasing.

Literacy Enhancer Fluency: Phrasing—Chunking Texts into Meaningful Units and Phrase Boundaries

Key Academic Vocabulary Vocabulary from a previous lesson is marked with an asterisk (*).

Comma*: A punctuation mark used within a sentence to set off meaningful phrases or other meaningful chunks of text

Narrative text: A text that tells a story

Period*: A punctuation mark used at the end of a sentence that is a statement

Phrase*: A sequence of two or more words that form a meaningful unit, often preceded and followed by a brief pause when read orally

Poem*: A text in verse form that is often characterized by alliteration, assonance, rhyme, or rhythm to express meaning

Punctuation*: Marks in writing or printing that are used to separate meaningful elements and make the meaning of the text clear

Sentence*: A unit of one or more words that expresses an independent statement, question, request, command, or exclamation

Learning Objectives

- Identify and mark phrase and sentence boundaries in grade-appropriate texts.
- Rehearse and perform the marked texts with fluency that reflects the meaning of the texts.

Essential Questions

- What is a phrase?
- What is a sentence?
- Why is reading text in appropriate chunks important for comprehension?

STEP 1: PREPARATION

Organize Materials

- Collections of poetry for primary-grade students
- Grade-appropriate narrative passages (100–200 words) with all punctuation removed
- Chart paper or a device for displaying texts
- *Text Road Signs: Phrase Boundaries* reproducible (copies or enlarged for display)
- Literacy notebooks

STEP 2: INITIATION

Perform a Poem

Use the poem below or find a poem that is familiar to most of your students. Display the poem on chart paper or on a whiteboard in your classroom. Read the poem aloud to your students multiple times, changing your phrasing of the text in each reading. Discuss with students which phrasing scheme was best for reflecting the meaning of the passage. Share how the punctuation is like a road sign on the journey of reading and how these text signs provide a natural phrase boundary for reading fluently.

Spring into Spring

Spring oh spring what a glorious thing

Spring oh spring oh spring,

Oh spring you make the birdies sing

And the bees start to sting,

Spring oh spring dear spring.

Spring into Spring (with phrase boundaries)

Spring / oh spring / what a glorious thing //

Spring / oh spring / oh spring //

Oh spring / you make / the birdies sing //

And the bees / start to sting //

Spring / oh spring / dear spring. //

Spring into Spring (with fewer phrase boundaries)

Spring oh spring / what a glorious thing //

Spring oh spring oh spring //

Oh spring / you make the birdies sing //

And the bees start to sting //

Spring oh spring / dear spring. //

STEP 3: DEMONSTRATION

Mark and Read

1. Use a marker to draw slash marks in the poem to demonstrate the phrase boundaries that reflect the best phrasing scheme.
2. As a class, chorally read the poem several times, emphasizing the marked phrase boundaries. After reading the poem several times with different phrasings to discover which set of phrases best reflected the meaning of the poem, discuss with students how the phrase boundaries were determined.
3. Display a second poem and use the same process as above to mark the appropriate phrase boundaries in the text.
4. Discuss with students the importance of phrase boundaries in other texts, including narrative and informational texts. Use the *Text Road Signs: Phrase Boundaries* reproducible (Figure 3.8) as a visual guide to emphasize punctuation and how each punctuation mark has a different function for proper flow of reading. Note that punctuation is often used to mark phrase and sentence boundaries. However, in many texts, not all phrase boundaries are marked by punctuation. Indicate to students that when the phrase boundaries are not marked, it is up to the reader to determine the phrase boundaries. This is often done through multiple readings of the passage.

STEP 4: COLLABORATION

Partners Phrase and Perform and Conversational Coaching

Distribute a copy of the narrative text that does not have punctuation to each student. Have students work in pairs or groups of three. Ask students to read the narrative text several times and determine the appropriate sentence and phrase boundaries. Students should mark the sentence and phrase boundaries with slash marks.

Once their text is marked, allow students several minutes to rehearse it. Then, have each pair or group perform their text for another pair or group. Emphasis should be placed on reading the text with good fluency and phrasing. Have listening students provide conversational coaching to the pair or group reading the passage aloud.

STEP 5: APPLICATION

More Phrasing on Their Own

Over the next several days, assign a new grade-appropriate narrative passage with punctuation removed. Allow students to repeat step 4 with each new text. Emphasize to students that their job is to find the most appropriate phrase boundaries that best reflect a fluent and meaningful reading of the text.

STEP 6: REFLECTION

Oral Response

After students perform their marked narrative texts, invite classmates in the audience to make specific, positive comments about the performances. Be sure to emphasize the importance of expressive phrasing that reflects the intended meaning of the passage.

Written Response

After they've had several opportunities to mark phrase boundaries in narrative texts, ask students to write personal responses in their literacy notebooks about the experience. Have students comment on what they had to focus on to identify and mark phrase boundaries that best reflected the meaning of the text. You may also ask students to complete the following sentence stems in their literacy notebooks:

- Phrase boundaries in texts are important because _____.
- Besides looking for punctuation, a good way to determine phrase boundaries in a text is to _____.

ADAPTATION/EXTENSION

- Have students go through the process of marking phrase boundaries in informational texts. Discuss with students how phrase boundaries in these texts are alike and different from phrase boundaries in narrative texts and poetry.
- Invite students to create their own poetry by taking words and phrases from a text and arranging them into a poem. Remind students to focus on the phrase boundaries for a smooth read.
- *English Language Learner Suggestion:* Record yourself reading additional narrative texts; provide oral emphasis on the phrase and sentence boundaries as you read. Provide students with written copies of the text. During center time, have students mark phrase boundaries on the text as they listen to your recorded reading of it.

- *Struggling Reader Suggestion:* Have students take home texts that they have marked appropriately (see steps 4 and 5) and read their texts to their parents and other family members a minimum of five times. Ask family members to sign the text and comment positively on the student's reading. This repeated reading at home will improve students' sight vocabulary and overall reading fluency.

EVALUATION

"I Can . . ." Statements

- I can read any grade-appropriate text with good expression and phrasing.
- I can determine phrase boundaries in texts that are not marked by punctuation.
- I can experiment with different phrasing schemes by rehearsing a passage orally.
- I can use my listening skills and be a good audience member to someone reading orally.
- I can be expressive when reading a narrative text aloud.

BEHAVIOR INDICATORS

- Independently engages in rehearsal of a narrative text.
- Performs a narrative text with good fluency and phrasing.
- Identifies phrase boundaries in narrative texts that are not marked by punctuation.
- Listens attentively as an audience member while another person reads orally.
- Provides positive and constructive feedback when listening to a classmate read a narrative passage.

FIGURE 3.8
Text Road Signs: Phrase Boundaries

Punctuation: Comma

Purpose: To slow down and pause for a moment to separate a thought in a sentence

Punctuation: Period

Purpose: To come to a complete stop at the end of a sentence

Punctuation: Exclamation Point

Purpose: To demonstrate strong feelings, often with high volume, at the end of a sentence

Punctuation: Question Mark

Purpose: To demonstrate a question being asked (who, what, when, where, why) at the end of a sentence

Source: Literacy Strong All Year Long: Powerful Lessons for Grades K–2 by Valerie Ellery, Lori Oczkus, and Timothy V. Rasinski. © 2020 ASCD. Readers may duplicate this figure for noncommercial use within their school.

LESSON 5. COMPREHENSION: CRAFT AND STRUCTURE—PREVIEWING

Title WE'RE GOING ON A TEXT TRIP

Trailer Maps help travelers find their way. Like maps, the structures and features of fiction and nonfiction texts assist readers as they move through a text. With fiction, readers rely on the route of beginning, middle, and end. Informational text includes road signs such as headings, bold words, and charts. Knowing which map you need makes all the difference for the reading journey!

Literacy Enhancer Comprehension: Craft and Structure—Previewing

Key Academic Vocabulary Vocabulary from a previous lesson is marked with an asterisk (*).

Author*: The person who wrote the book

Back cover*: The back side of a book that often contains information about the book and its author and illustrator

Book cover*: The front of a book that contains the title, author, and illustrator

Character: The who in the story; often a person or animal in the text

Fiction*: The genre that includes stories that are make-believe; may also include poetry

Illustrator*: The person who drew the pictures or illustrations that go with the book's content

Informational text*: A type of nonfiction text

Nonfiction*: The genre that includes factual/real information that is portrayed to answer, explain, or describe

Photographer*: The person who took the photos that go with the book's content

Predict*: To use information from a text to infer what the text will be about or what a reader might learn from it

Problem: The challenge that the character(s) face and need to overcome

Setting: Where the story takes place

Story sequence mapping: Fiction stories are usually organized around what happens at the beginning of the story, in the middle, and at the end.

Text features*: Parts of the text that support the reader in navigating through key characteristics of a text for locating and accessing meaning from the text (e.g., title, headings, photographs, bold words, maps)

Text walk: A preview of a fiction or nonfiction text to see what it is about and gather clues to determine what text features the author has included

Title*: The name of the book, which usually tells what it is about or gives clues to the content

Learning Objectives

- Recognize that fiction texts have a beginning, middle, and end.
- Recognize that fiction texts have characters, a setting, a problem/solution, and main events.
- Recognize that nonfiction texts have special, distinguishing text features, including headings, photographs, diagrams, maps, graphs, and sometimes an index and glossary.
- Choose a fiction or nonfiction map and use it to preview a text and throughout the reading process.

Essential Questions

- How are fiction texts organized?
- How can the fiction text map of beginning, middle, and end guide our reading?
- How can the characters, setting, problem/solution, and main events help us preview a text and keep track of our comprehension of it?
- What do nonfiction text features look like? How are they like the "road signs" of nonfiction text? How can nonfiction text features help us preview a text?

STEP 1: PREPARATION

Organize Materials

- Two maps of different places (e.g., state, local) or in different styles (e.g., topographical, weather)
- Toy car
- *Fiction Map* reproducible (copies or enlarged for display)
- *Nonfiction Map* reproducible (copies or enlarged for display)
- *We're Going on a Text Trip* reproducible (copies or enlarged for display)
- *Nonfiction Road Signs* reproducible (copies or enlarged for display)
- Multimodal text set for the topic of study
- Literacy notebooks

STEP 2: INITIATION

Map Metaphor

Show students a map. Invite them to share what they know about maps and how people use them. Mention that you may need a different map for each place you travel to. Show maps of two different locations (e.g., state, local) or two different kinds of maps (e.g., topographical, weather). Tell students that today they will learn how good readers can use a map to help them read as they go through a text.

STEP 3: DEMONSTRATION

Going on a Text Trip

Hold up a small toy car. Tell students that you are going to take a trip through a book, so you need to see which map you will need. Demonstrate taking a fiction and nonfiction journey through books.

For Fiction

1. Hold up the fiction text and drive the toy car across the cover. Tell students that as you plan for your trip into this book, you will use the *Fiction Map* reproducible (Figure 3.9). Show the Fiction Map and tell students that this map goes with fiction, or make-believe, stories. Explain the elements of the map: beginning, middle, and end. Drive the car across the title, cover art, and first few pages. Ask students to turn and talk to discuss what they think the story will be about. Tell students that the story will have a beginning, middle, and end. Show the beginning, middle, and end on the map and ask students to repeat the three terms aloud.

2. Return to the text and read a few pages as you drive the car across the pages. Explain that the characters are the people or animals in the story and that the setting is where it takes place. Have students help you figure out the setting and characters to put on the Fiction Map. Read enough of the story aloud with students to identify the story's problem and record it on the map. Ask students to turn and talk to repeat the characters, setting, and problem.

3. Continue to use the Fiction Map throughout the reading to record events. Emphasize the beginning, middle, and end. When you are finished reading the story and recording on the map, use it as a guide for retelling. Model using the following language:
    - The characters are _____.
    - In the beginning the story, takes place at _____.
    - The problem is _____.

- In the middle, _____ (describe the events).
- At the end, _____ (if the story has a problem, share the solution).
- The theme or lesson of the story is _____.

4. To reinforce the concepts, sing or chant "Going on a Story Hunt" from the *We're Going on a Text Trip* reproducible (Figure 3.10). As you sing each verse, return to the text and ask students to look for the various elements of fiction (characters, setting, problem, beginning, middle, and end).

For Nonfiction

1. Hold up a nonfiction book. Ask students to tell you what type of book it is and how they know. Explain that this kind of book requires some unique road signs. Drive the toy car across the title, cover art, and first few pages as you show how to use text features to preview the text.
2. As you drive through the text, pause and discuss text features, such as the table of contents, headings, bold words, photographs, illustrations, captions, maps, graphs, and charts. On the *Nonfiction Map* reproducible (Figure 3.11), record information from the text features as you read parts of the text aloud.
3. Demonstrate how to find information in the text using the text features. Ask students, "What if I wanted to know about _____? Which text features might help me find that information?" Show students how to find information in a text by using the following text features: the table of contents, headings, photographs, maps, glossary, and index.
4. As you discuss each text feature, ask students, "Why do you think the author included this text feature?"
5. To reinforce text features, sing or chant "Going on a Text Feature Hunt" (from the *We're Going on a Text Trip* reproducible). As you sing each verse, return to the text and ask students to look for the various elements of nonfiction text features (e.g., headings, visuals, glossary, index).

STEP 4: COLLABORATION

Continue the Journey and Conversational Coaching

Have students each draw a paper car and use it and either a fiction or nonfiction text to drive to the various parts of the text as they demonstrate using text features. Encourage students to engage in conversational coaching by asking partners to discuss the following questions:

- What text features did you notice on your journey through the text?
- How did a particular text feature help you navigate your way?

Have students explain how they use text features to gain an awareness of a text and go deeper in their journey for meaning.

STEP 5: APPLICATION

Drive It!

Ask pairs of students to reread a familiar text and identify either the elements of fiction or the text features of nonfiction as they drive their paper cars through the text.

Draw It!

Have students fold a paper into thirds. Have them write "Beginning" at the top of the first column, "Middle" at the top of the second column, and "End" at the top of the third column. Ask students to sketch the beginning, middle, and end parts of the book. Share with partners.

STEP 6: REFLECTION

Written Response

Students choose one fiction book and one nonfiction book to write about in their literacy notebooks. Ask them to use the following sentence stem for each: "I like the book _____ because _____."

Invite students to share with the whole group their favorite titles and their literacy notebook entry.

ADAPTATION/EXTENSION

- Either sketch or enlarge giant versions of the *Fiction Map* and *Nonfiction Map* reproducibles. Using books that the class has read, fill in the maps together to post in the hallway, library, or classroom.
- Provide a pile of cutouts of the *Nonfiction Road Signs* reproducible (Figure 3.12) for students to use in pairs. Have them take turns selecting a road sign from the pile and finding that text feature in a text.
- *English Language Learner Suggestion:* Work with students in a small group using one of the text maps and the song that goes with it. Read aloud from a fiction or nonfiction text and fill in the text map together. Provide small toy cars to "run" across the texts!
- *Struggling Reader Suggestion:* Work with students in a small group. Provide a pile of cutouts of the *Nonfiction Road Signs* reproducible for students to use in pairs. Guide students as they take turns selecting a road sign from the pile and finding that text feature in a text.

EVALUATION

"I Can . . ." Statements

- I can tell which map I need, fiction or nonfiction, by previewing the text.
- I can use the front cover and a text walk of a fiction book to preview and predict the beginning, middle, and end.
- I can use the text features, such as headings and photographs, to help me preview and predict what a nonfiction text will be about.
- I can identify at least three of the following nonfiction text features: table of contents, heading, photograph, map, bold words, glossary, and index.
- I can use text features to help me find information in a nonfiction text.

BEHAVIOR INDICATORS

- Identifies a fiction book by looking at the cover and taking a text walk.
- Identifies fiction elements in a fiction book (i.e., characters, setting, problem, main events).
- Identifies the story sequence in a fiction book (i.e., beginning, middle, end).
- Identifies a nonfiction book by previewing the cover and taking a text walk.
- Distinguishes at least three text features in a nonfiction book (e.g., table of contents, headings, photographs, maps, bold words, glossary, index).
- Applies nonfiction text features to locate information in a nonfiction book.

FIGURE 3.9
Fiction Map

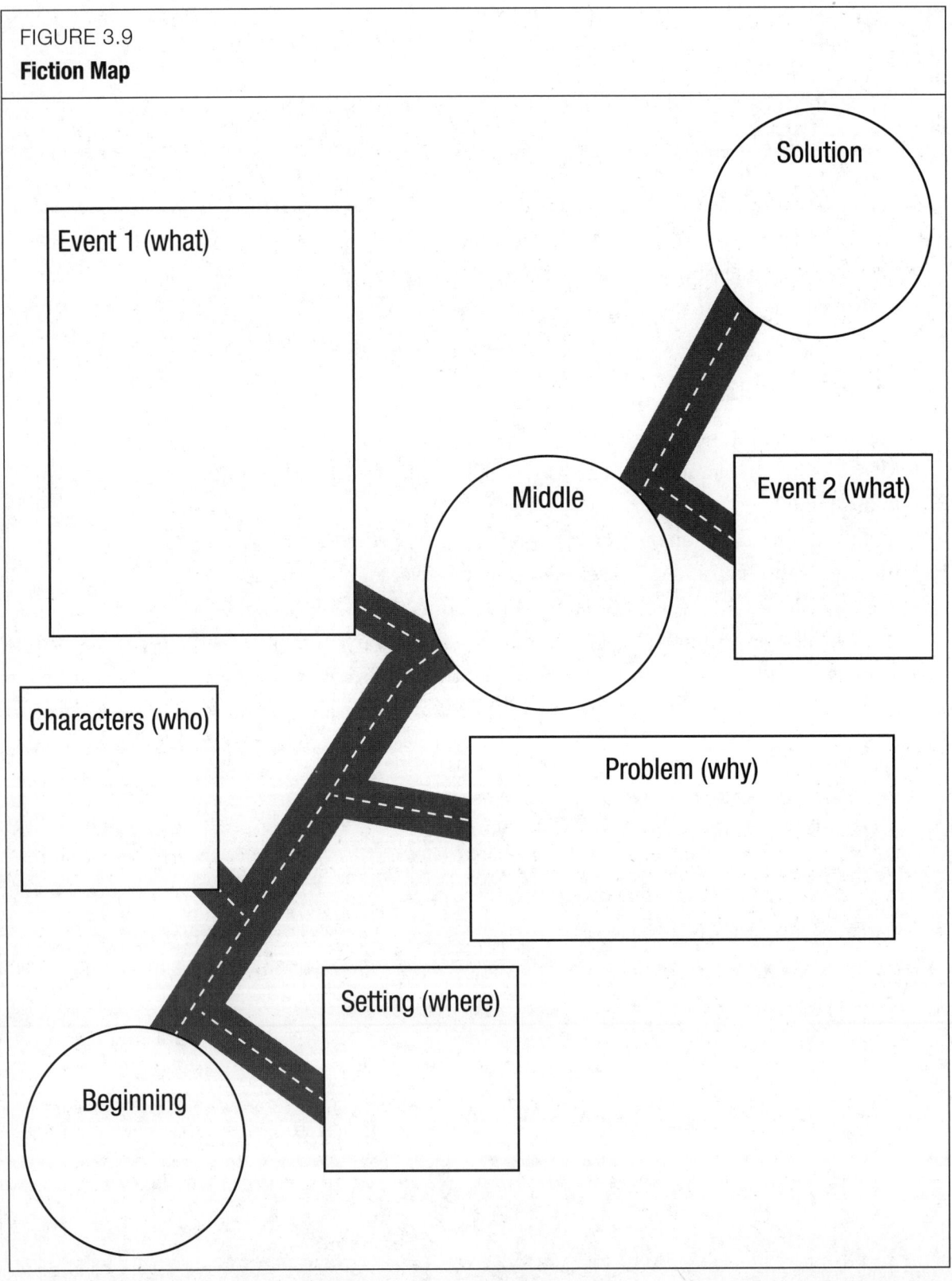

Source: Literacy Strong All Year Long: Powerful Lessons for Grades K–2 by Valerie Ellery, Lori Oczkus, and Timothy V. Rasinski. © 2020 ASCD. Readers may duplicate this figure for noncommercial use within their school.

FIGURE 3.10
We're Going on a Text Trip

Going on a Story Hunt (Fiction)
We're going on a story hunt. We're going on a story hunt.
Can't go over it. Can't go under it.
Gotta read through it!

I see the characters. I see the characters.
Who is in the story? Who is in the story?
Can't go under them. Can't go over them.
Gotta go meet them!

I see the setting. I see the setting.
Where does the story take place? Where does the story take place?
Can't go under it. Can't go over it.
Gotta read through it!

I see the story problem. I see the story problem.
What's the problem? What's the problem?
Can't go under it. Can't go over it.
Gotta read to solve it!

I see the beginning. I see the beginning.
Then comes the middle and the end.
Gotta read it all!

Going on a Text Feature Hunt (Nonfiction)
We're going on a text feature hunt. We're going on a text feature hunt.
Can't go under them. Can't go over them.
Gotta read and study them!

I see the table of contents. I see the table of contents.
Can't go under it. Can't go over it.
Gotta read and study it!

I see a heading. I see a heading.
Can't go under it. Can't go over it.
Gotta read though it!

I see a photo. I see a photo.
Can't go under it. Can't go over it.
Gotta look and study it!

I see a map. I see a map.
Can't go under it. Can't go over it.
Gotta read and study it!

I see the glossary. I see the glossary.
Can't go under it. Can't go over it.
Gotta find the words!

I see the index. I see the index.
Can't go under it. Can't go over it.
Gotta find the page numbers!

Source: Literacy Strong All Year Long: Powerful Lessons for Grades K–2 by Valerie Ellery, Lori Oczkus, and Timothy V. Rasinski. © 2020 ASCD. Readers may duplicate this figure for noncommercial use within their school.

FIGURE 3.11
Nonfiction Map

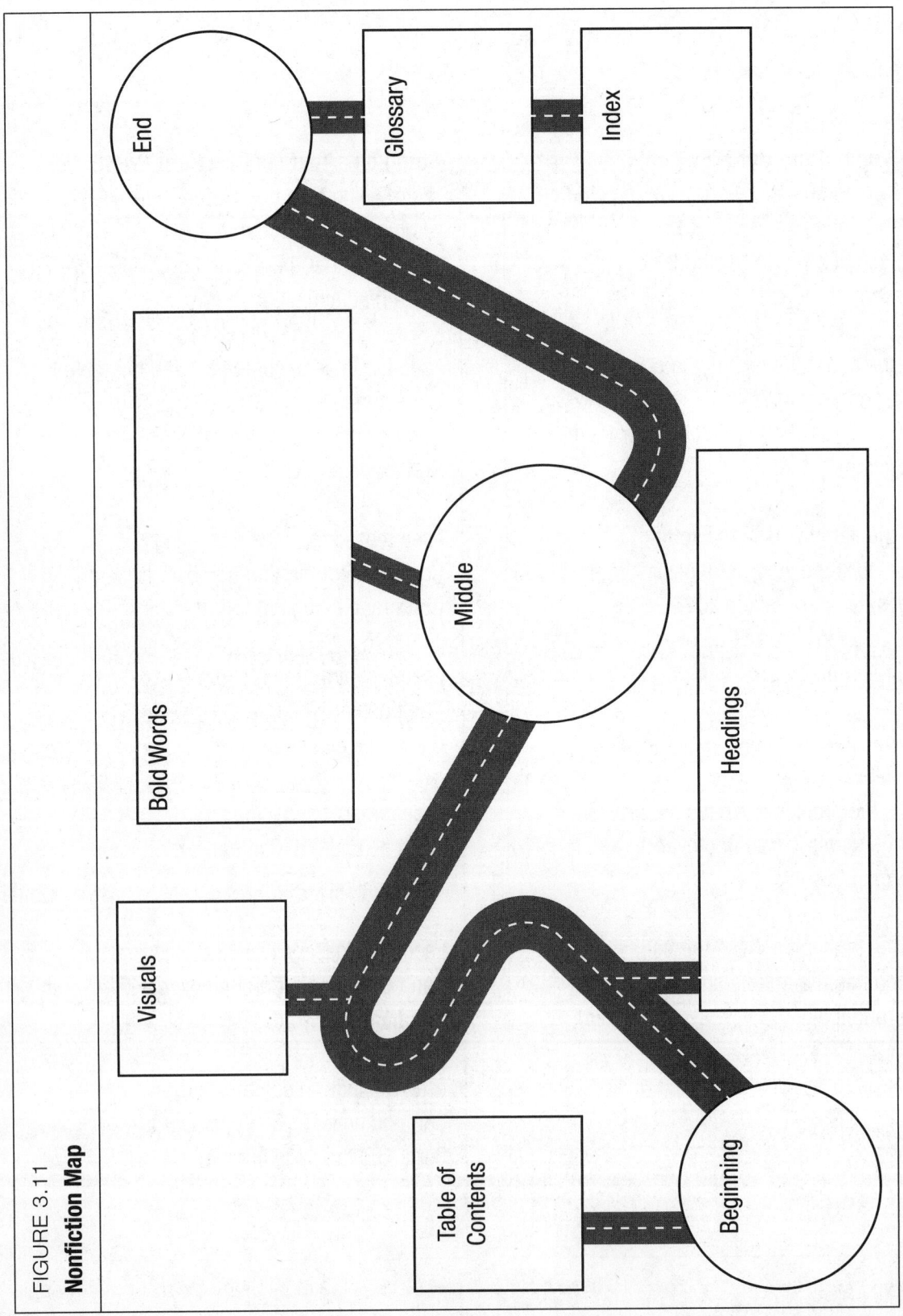

Source: *Literacy Strong All Year Long: Powerful Lessons for Grades K–2* by Valerie Ellery, Lori Oczkus, and Timothy V. Rasinski. © 2020 ASCD. Readers may duplicate this figure for noncommercial use within their school.

FIGURE 3.12
Nonfiction Road Signs

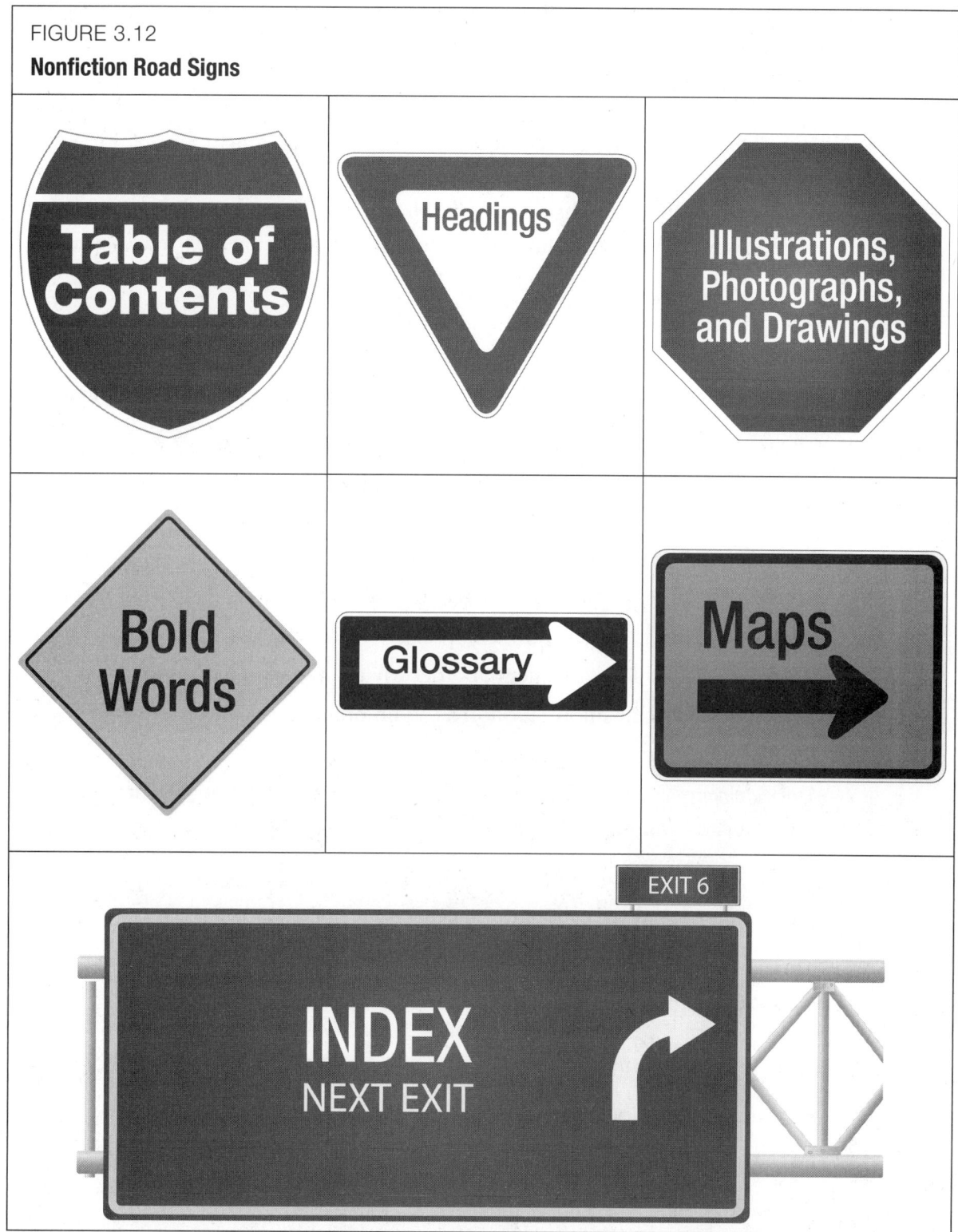

Source: Literacy Strong All Year Long: Powerful Lessons for Grades K–2 by Valerie Ellery, Lori Oczkus, and Timothy V. Rasinski. © 2020 ASCD. Readers may duplicate this figure for noncommercial use within their school.

LESSON 6. COMPREHENSION: KEY IDEAS AND DETAILS—DETERMINING IMPORTANCE AND SUMMARIZING

Title FINDING THE TOPIC: IT'S A SNAP!

Trailer Information, information, information! There's so much information in a text that it can be overwhelming at times for readers. How can they identify key details within the text to begin grasping the main reason for it? The answer is only a snap away! Readers learn how to get the gist of identifying details to discover the main topic.

Literacy Enhancer Comprehension: Key Ideas and Details—Determining Importance and Summarizing and Key Details and Main Topic

Key Academic Vocabulary Vocabulary from a previous lesson is marked with an asterisk (*).

Essential*: Necessary for the meaning and purpose

Gist*: The main point or overall part of a text

Information*: Gathered knowledge; facts or ideas

Key detail*: An important feature, fact, or item that supports the overall meaning

Main topic: The gist or general thought of the whole concept

Retelling*: Recalling in a sequential order what is happening in a text

Sequencing*: Placing information in a certain order

Sift*: To filter and examine what is most important

Story elements*: Parts (ingredients) of a story: characters, setting, events, plot, problem, and solution

Learning Objectives

- Determine key details about the specific topic being studied.
- Identify the main topic of the content being studied.

Essential Questions

- What is a key detail?
- How do you determine the main topic?
- What is the relationship between key details and the main topic?

STEP 1: PREPARATION

Organize Materials

- Index cards for words or pictures from the unit of study

- Multimodal text set for the topic of study
- *Finding the Topic: It's a Snap!* reproducible (copies or enlarged for display)
- Literacy notebooks

STEP 2: INITIATION

It's a Snap!

Ask students to snap their fingers and think about how many fingers are active when they are snapping. Have them hold open their hands and then try to snap their thumb and index finger without moving any other fingers. Have students share with a partner what they noticed. Continue having them practice snapping with the other fingers, noting how all the fingers play some part in creating a strong snap. Tell the students, "In today's lesson, we are going to use our fingers to point out and collect information from the text. We will then bring all the information together by snapping when we think we have the gist of how all the important facts on our fingers go together." Remind students that the information we are collecting on our fingers are the story elements, as in our Retell Recipe (see Chapter 1) or the important information that would have been on the stones in our Sifting Details lesson (see Chapter 2).

STEP 3: DEMONSTRATION

Getting the Gist

1. Gather several photos for the topic of study (e.g., community workers, weather) to display or select several illustrations from a text. While thinking aloud, examine one photo at a time, describing certain details that you notice in the illustration. For example, "I see a white jacket, medicine, and a stethoscope. Those details help me determine that this picture is mainly about a doctor or nurse."
2. Hold up your hand and count aloud and with your fingers as you say each detail from the images again. Explain how the details represent key facts and are represented on each finger as you count them out.
3. Next, snap your fingers together and say, "I've got the gist of all of these details!" Say the main topic of all the details as you snap your fingers again (e.g., doctors as community helpers).
4. Based on the unit of study, select a text and read aloud, noting along the way the key details (e.g., characters, setting) that support the topic. Count on your fingers as you say aloud a detail, and then snap when you connect all the details to the main topic within the text. It is important to explain why you chose a certain detail to point out on your finger and possibly how you sifted the detail as either information that was just interesting or information that is

important. Inquire aloud, "What made that piece of information so important?" (e.g., "The keywords gave the important details to help visualize where the story is taking place.")

STEP 4: COLLABORATION

Conversational Coaching

Engage in conversational coaching by asking students to discuss the following questions with diverse partners:

- What information is represented on the fingers?
- What is happening with that information when you snap your fingers?
- What is the relationship between the details (i.e., what's on the fingers) and the main topic (i.e., the snap)?
- What topic keeps occurring in the text?

STEP 5: APPLICATION

Helping Hand

Using the *Finding the Topic: It's a Snap!* reproducible (Figure 3.13), have students work in groups to determine details (e.g., narrative text: characters, setting, events; informational text: concept, ideas) about a main topic that you assign them to investigate from a text or topic that you are studying. Post these hands and give the display a title that represents the main topic.

STEP 6: REFLECTION

Written Response

Have students independently select a hand from the display and write or draw in their literacy notebooks about the main topic written in the palm of the hand. Remind them to use the details on the fingers to support the main topic.

ADAPTATION/EXTENSION

- Collect the completed *Finding the Topic: It's a Snap!* reproducibles and place them in a class book. Students can practice orally retelling the text, using each page as a springboard for discussion.
- Students can write from the perspective of a character to describe in detail what the character does in the story.
- Create an ad or commercial about the topic of study. Have students design an avatar (talking character) on the Voki website (www.voki.com) to say details about the main topic.

- Using the iMovie app on an iPad (www.apple.com/ios/imovie/?cid=wwa-us-kwg-ipad-com), create a text trailer with the topic and five essential details from the *Finding the Topic: It's a Snap!* reproducible.
- *English Language Learner Suggestion:* Select four to five items that are related and place them in a bag (e.g., swim goggles, inflatable beach ball, plastic shovel, bag of sand). Pull out one item at a time and have the students describe what it is and when, where, how, and why you would you use it. Continue until all the items in the bag have been displayed and discussed. Ask, "How are all of these items connected?" Explain to students that their answers help describe the topic of the items in the bag. Name the items as you count them on your fingers and then snap your fingers and name the topic (e.g., beach).
- *Struggling Reader Suggestion:* Give students a magnifying glass and tell them "We are going on a search for details that will help us determine the main topic." Walk them through a text on their reading level. Begin with the cover. Have them locate with their magnifying glass images on the cover that are clues to what the text will be about. List their findings on a chart. Read the title and determine how the images support the text and can help determine the topic of the text they will read. Create several detail statements from the text. Read each one to the students and have them search in the text for text features that support the statements. Then ask, "How are these details related?" Capture students' thoughts as you scaffold a main idea statement together based on their conversations on the connections of the details. Compare their findings with the cover examination and review how the details support the main idea and also help categorize them into creating a topic.

EVALUATION

"I Can . . ." Statements

- I can determine three key details about a specific topic.
- I can identify the main topic based on specific details.
- I can answer questions using specific details from the text.

BEHAVIOR INDICATORS

- Uses supporting details from a text to clearly explain the main topic.
- Asks and answers questions about key details in a text: who, what, when, where, why, and how.
- Uses the illustrations and details in a text to describe its key ideas.

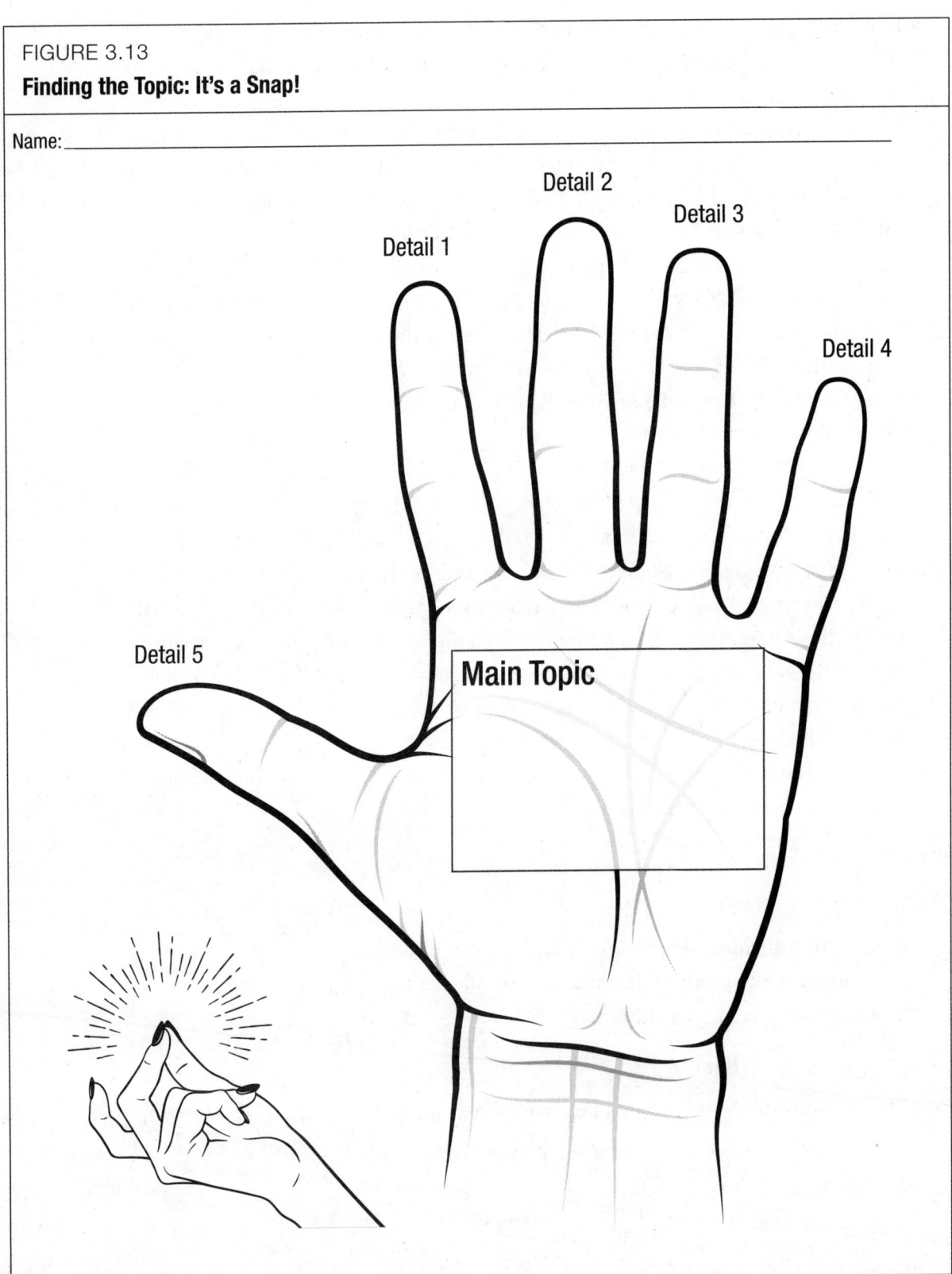

FIGURE 3.13
Finding the Topic: It's a Snap!

Name: _____

Source: *Literacy Strong All Year Long: Powerful Lessons for Grades K–2* by Valerie Ellery, Lori Oczkus, and Timothy V. Rasinski. © 2020 ASCD. Readers may duplicate this figure for noncommercial use within their school.

LESSON 7. COMPREHENSION: KEY IDEAS AND DETAILS—QUESTIONING FOR CLOSE READING

Title QUESTION THE CHARACTER

Trailer What a character! Teaching young children to interview characters during reading deepens their comprehension and ramps up their critical thinking. By imagining a conversation with the characters from a text, students use text clues to learn to infer. This lesson provides many creative opportunities for thinking to grow, whether students are reading fiction to question motives, feelings, and actions or nonfiction to inquire about a creature or object.

Literacy Enhancer Comprehension: Key Ideas and Details—Questioning for Close Reading and Character's Point of View

Key Academic Vocabulary Vocabulary from a previous lesson is marked with an asterisk (*).

Answer clues*: General knowledge information from a text that aligns with *who, what, when, where,* or *why* questions

Character*: A person or animal in a text

How: A question word that asks for the means, procedure, or quality of something

What*: A question word that asks about the events or things that happened

When*: A question word that asks the time of day or year

Where*: A question word that asks about the place

Who*: A question word that asks about the people or animals in the text

Why: A question word that asks for a reason

Learning Objectives

- Create questions about key ideas and details in the text with the question words *who, what, when, where, why,* and *how*.
- Answer questions about key ideas and details in the text using the question words *who, what, when, where, why,* and *how*.
- Pretend to pose questions to the characters in a text to show understanding of the key ideas and details in the text.
- Pretend to pose questions to the characters in a text to infer understandings about key ideas and details in the text, using text evidence as clues.

Essential Questions

- What questions can I ask and answer that start with *who, what, when, where, why,* and *how*?
- How do I ask and answer questions using text evidence?

STEP 1: PREPARATION

Organize Materials

- Plastic microphone (optional)
- Multimodal text set for the topic of study (fiction and nonfiction texts)
- *Question the Character* reproducible (copies or enlarged for display)
- Literacy notebooks

STEP 2: INITIATION

Role-Play Warm-Up

- Ask students to name some famous people they would like to meet, or suggest a few well-known celebrities, athletes, musicians, or cartoon characters your students might know. Ask them what they would like to ask the character or person if they could meet him or her in real life. Record the questions on the board. Tell students that they are about to learn a fun way to think about the characters they meet in books. Students will have the opportunity to conduct pretend interviews as they talk to the characters from fiction and nonfiction texts. *Optional:* Bring in a stuffed animal of a character featured in familiar books, such as Clifford or Curious George. Brainstorm questions to ask the character and invite a volunteer to be the voice of the animal (or do it yourself). As you record each question, write the character's name first. For example, "George, why do you like to be so mischievous?" Encourage students to use text evidence and examples from the text as they answer questions.

STEP 3: DEMONSTRATION

Read Aloud to Question

1. Read aloud from a fiction picture book that features either animal or human characters. Display the *Question the Character* reproducible (Figure 3.14). Begin reading from the text and pause after a few pages to invite students to act out the story.
2. Model how to ask questions about another's actions, wishes, feelings, or dialogue. Use a plastic microphone as you interview. Record the questions you ask

on the *Question the Character* reproducible. After modeling questions, invite students to turn to partners to repeat your questions and answers. Read more pages from the book and invite a different set of students to act out the reading and to interview with you in front of the class.

3. Explain to students that asking characters questions helps you better understand what you are reading and gives you the character's point of view. *Optional:* Conduct the same lesson with informational text. If the text doesn't feature characters or people, personify objects, creatures, or things. For example, interview the planets in the solar system, a seed as it grows into a plant, or a bird digging for worms.

STEP 4: COLLABORATION

Conversational Coaching

Read aloud from a text. Pause frequently throughout to question the characters. Invite volunteers to act out scenes from the text in front of the class. Assign each table (or pairs) in the class one question stem, such as "Why did you _____?" Invite teams to engage in conversational coaching by verbally creating questions and posing them to the actors. Students record their questions on the *Question the Character* reproducible or a strip of paper. Show students how to use text evidence when role playing to answer questions about feelings, motives, and actions. Provide question stems as necessary. Here are some examples:

- What did you want _____?
- Why did you _____?
- How did you _____?
- How did you feel when _____?

STEP 5: APPLICATION

The Character and the Interviewer

Pair up students. Ask them to read together and pause throughout the text to pose questions to the characters. Pairs should take turns reading and role playing as the character and the interviewer. Students record one question for each character on the *Question the Character* reproducible. *Optional:* Read the text multiple times, focusing on one character at a time and creating questions for just that character. Reread and pose questions to a different character.

Question the Character Show

Students work independently to sketch characters from the text and write questions to ask them on the Question the Character reproducible. Next, students pose their questions to classmates while acting as characters on a pretend Question the Character Show.

STEP 6: REFLECTION

Oral or Written Response

Encourage students to write questions in their literacy notebooks for characters, using *who, what, when, where, why,* and *how*. Have them put a star next to their best question and pose it to a partner, who role-plays that character. Also, students may respond to these essential questions in their literacy notebooks:

- What questions can I ask and answer that start with *who, what, when, where, why,* and *how*?
- How do I ask and answer questions using text evidence?

ADAPTATION/EXTENSION

- Read aloud biographies and invite your students to ask questions of famous people throughout the reading. Take turns role-playing the interviewer and the famous person.
- Read David A. Adler's Picture Book Biography series. It comprises 23 titles, including *A Picture Book of Helen Keller, A Picture Book of Jackie Robinson,* and *A Picture Book of Sitting Bull.*
- Try Brad Meltzer's delightful picture book series Ordinary People Change the World, which is especially geared at motivating emerging readers. The series includes childhood stories that happened to the well-known individuals highlighted. The growing series includes such titles as *I Am Amelia Earhart, I Am Abraham Lincoln, I Am Rosa Parks,* and *I Am Albert Einstein.*
- *English Language Learner Suggestion:* Select a fiction text with characters. Read the text multiple times, focusing on one character at a time and creating questions for just that character. Reread and pose questions to a different character. Use a toy microphone.
- *Struggling Reader Suggestion*: Students decorate paper-bag puppets of the characters in a story. Students role play in pairs or teams, asking and answering questions using pages from the text to find answers and evidence. Students record questions for characters on the *Question the Character* reproducible.

EVALUATION

"I Can . . ." Statements

- I can create questions for the characters in a text and focus on asking about key ideas and details by using the question words *who*, *what*, *when*, *where*, *why*, and *how*.
- I can role play a character from a text and answer questions by using key ideas, details, and evidence in the text.
- I can infer a character's feelings, motives, thoughts, and actions by using text evidence and connections to my life, other books, and the world around me.

BEHAVIOR INDICATORS

- Poses questions to characters in a text, focusing on key ideas and details and using the question words *who*, *what*, *when*, *where*, *why*, and *how*.
- Answers questions in complete sentences to clarify comprehension.
- Answers questions while role-playing a character in a text and uses evidence from the text to answer questions that begin with *who*, *what*, *when*, *where*, *why*, and *how*.
- Infers what a character thinks, feels, and does by using text evidence and connections to his or her own life, other books, and the world.

FIGURE 3.14
Question the Character

Directions: Write the name and draw a picture of a character from your text. Then, write a question to ask the character.

Question words: Who   What   When   Where
                     Why   How

Draw the Character	Question the Character
	Example: Mr. Lion, (name of character), why do you roar so loudly? _____(name of character), _____ _____?
	_____(name of character), _____ _____?
	_____(name of character), _____ _____?
	_____(name of character), _____ _____?

Source: Literacy Strong All Year Long: Powerful Lessons for Grades K–2 by Valerie Ellery, Lori Oczkus, and Timothy V. Rasinski. © 2020 ASCD. Readers may duplicate this figure for noncommercial use within their school.

LESSON 8. VOCABULARY: ASSOCIATING WORDS

Title SHADES OF MEANING

Trailer Carefully choosing just the right word at the right time makes a powerful impact in every aspect of life. Shades of meaning matter in life and in literacy. Understanding synonyms and their levels of meaning helps students expand their vocabulary, strengthen their comprehension, and dramatically improve their writing. Teach students to abandon old, tired words such as *walk, said,* and *mad* by inviting them to joyfully saunter, stroll, scurry, and race to grasp wonderful words for every occasion!

Literary Enhancer Vocabulary: Associating Words—Synonyms, Adjectives, and Verbs

Key Academic Vocabulary Vocabulary from a previous lesson is marked with an asterisk (*).

Adjective*: A word that describes a noun (a person, place, or thing)

Antonym*: A word that has an opposite meaning of another word

Homograph*: A word that has more than one meaning

Homonym*: Another name for a homograph

Noun*: A person, place, or thing

Opposite*: Two words or concepts that are in some way related but distinctly different in meaning from each other

Shades of meaning*: Words that are synonyms with varying degrees of different meanings

Synonym*: A word that has a similar meaning to another word

Verb*: An action word

Learning Objectives

- Identify and demonstrate the varying shades of meaning among commonly used verbs.
- Identify and demonstrate the varying shades of meaning among commonly used adjectives for emotions.

Essential Questions

- How do varying shades of meaning of common verbs relate to one another?
- How do varying shades of meaning of common adjectives for emotions relate to one another?

STEP 1: PREPARATION

Organize Materials

- Index cards or sticky notes
- Several different paint swatches with various shades of a color on one strip from a paint store
- Multimodal text set for the topic of study
- *Shades of Meaning Word Cards for Emotions* reproducible (copies or enlarged for display)
- *Shades of Meaning Word Cards for Verbs* reproducible (copies or enlarged for display)
- Literacy notebooks

STEP 2: INITIATION

Happy Song

- Write the word *happy* on a large sticky note or an index card with tape and post it on the board or a chart. Ask students to define the word. Discuss what makes them happy.
- Sing the song "If You're Happy and You Know It." Tell students that today they will explore many other words that mean the same thing as *happy* and that they will learn how using different words for the same concept will help their reading and writing.

STEP 3: DEMONSTRATION

Happy Song and Human Word Web

1. Tell students that the word *happy* is an adjective, or a describing word, for a feeling or emotion. Ask students to turn to a partner and name at least two other words that also mean happy. Record some of their responses. Introduce other words for *happy* and list them on the board on sticky notes or index cards with tape. As students share words, ask the class to make faces to demonstrate the intensity of each word. For example, "How happy is *overjoyed*? Show me with your face!" Use sentences with your students' names to show the difference in intensity of emotion for each word. Here are some examples:
    - "Juan was excited that his dog finally rolled over on command."
    - "Anna felt joyful that her grandmother was coming over for a visit."
    - "Derek was overjoyed that his birthday party would be at the pool."

2. Create a human word web (Roth, 2012). Write synonyms for *happy* (e.g., *excited, joyful, cheerful, overjoyed, ecstatic*) in large letters on 8.5-by-11-inch sheets of paper, one word per sheet. Invite one student to stand in front of the classroom and hold up the word *happy*. Invite five more volunteers to hold the other words. Position the five students in a circle around the student holding the word *happy*. Have the five students in the circle stretch out their right arms and point to the student in the middle, who is holding the word *happy*. Invite each of the five students in the circle to hold up a word card and substitute the synonym for *happy* as you sing "If You're Happy and You Know It."
3. Sing the song "If You're Happy and You Know It" and replace the word *happy* with other synonyms. Explain to students that they are going to explore lots of interesting and wonderful words. Using different words that mean the same thing but are slightly different makes reading and writing more interesting and fun!
4. Begin to build a word wall or chart by using several different paint swatches in various shades of one color on one strip to show shades of meaning for emotion words. Using a strip of happy colors, write the synonyms for *happy* in order of emotional intensity on the strip, like this:

| *happy* |
| *glad* |
| *cheerful* |
| *joyful* |
| *excited* |
| *ecstatic* |

Repeat this lesson to demonstrate other emotion words and synonyms. Sing the song "If You're Happy and You Know It," substituting *sad*, *angry*, and other examples of emotion words. Repeat the word web and paint swatch activities with these new words, too. Use the *Shades of Meaning Word Cards for Emotions* reproducible (Figure 3.15). Here are some examples of common emotion adjectives and their synonyms for the swatches:

Common Adjective for an Emotion	Synonyms in Order of Intensity	Suggested Base Color for Paint Swatches
mad	*angry* *furious* *enraged*	*red*
sad	*disappointed* *upset* *depressed*	*blue*
scared	*afraid* *frightened* *petrified*	*purple*

STEP 4: COLLABORATION

Line Up the Words and Conversational Coaching

Cut apart the word cards from the *Shades of Meaning Word Cards for Emotions* reproducible or the *Shades of Meaning Word Cards for Verbs* reproducible (Figure 3.16). Call up volunteers to help you sort the words by level of intensity of meaning. Order the words in a row either vertically (like the paint swatches) or horizontally. Invite partners to engage in conversational coaching by acting out the words and then sharing which words they think will be next in order, explaining their rationale for the order. *Optional:* Give each table one word. Invite the groups to act out their word, share its meaning using a strip of happy colors (e.g., a paint swatch of yellows), and stand in order from left to right to indicate intensity of meaning, from least to most.

STEP 5: APPLICATION

Word Sorts and Games

Students work independently or in pairs to sort words from the Shades of Meaning Word Cards for either emotions or verbs. Select any of the following ways for students to respond:

- Place the words in horizontal order and glue them on a paper strip or use index cards or sticky notes for repeated use. Place the words in order of intensity from left to right, for least to most intensity.
- Glue the words on a vertical strip (or paint swatches with multiple colors on one strip) or use index cards or sticky notes for repeated use.
- Use the cards for classic games:

- *Charades:* A student selects a card and acts it out. The partner guesses the word.
- *Race the Clock:* Students take turns in pairs or work as a team to dump the cards, mix them up, and order the synonyms. Students work on beating their own time, not their partner's or teammate's time.

STEP 6: REFLECTION

Written Response

In their literacy notebooks, have students write and illustrate their favorite synonyms. Ask students to make a journal entry in which they describe their day, using as many different words as they can think of.

ADAPTATION/EXTENSION

- Repeat the lesson to demonstrate other common verbs and synonyms using a human word web or word chant. Use the Shades of Meaning Word Cards for Verbs. Invite students to act out the words and form a human word web. *Optional:* Sit in a circle and guide students to clap the pattern; clap hands first and then thighs as the class chants together the following verse. Going around the circle, students take turns and substitute words. Encourage students to use the words you've displayed on the chart or word wall. Invite a volunteer to act out each new word in the center of the circle. Try snapping fingers, stomping feet, or tiptoeing during the chant.

    I know another word for *said, said.*
    I know another word for *said, said:*
    Whispered, whispered, whispered.

    I know another word for _____, _____.
    I know another word for _____, _____.
    _____, _____, _____.

- Have students use ReadWriteThink.org's interactive theme poems (www.readwritethink.org/classroom-resources/student-interactives/theme-poems-30044.html) to create their own poems with shades of meaning.
- *English Language Learner Suggestion:* Use the Shades of Meaning Word Cards for Verbs to act out the various verbs with the group. Select related words such as *eat, nibble, gobble,* and *chomp* that each student acts out for others to guess.

- *Struggling Reader Suggestion*: Try using the semantic gradients lesson and video on the Reading Rockets website (www.readingrockets.org/strategies/semantic_gradients). Follow the steps to introduce your students to word gradients.

EVALUATION

"I Can . . ." Statements

- I can identify and demonstrate the meanings of words that are synonyms for emotion words.
- I can identify and demonstrate the meanings of verb synonyms.
- I can order a series of synonyms for emotions in order of intensity.
- I can categorize a series of synonyms for verbs.

BEHAVIOR INDICATORS

- Identifies, names, and categorizes synonyms for emotions.
- Orders emotion words according to level of intensity.
- Identifies, names, and categorizes synonyms for common verbs.
- Groups common verbs according to meaning.

FIGURE 3.15
Shades of Meaning Word Cards for Emotions

Directions: Cut the cards apart, mix them up, sort them into emotion categories, and then put them in order by intensity.

happy	sad	mad	scared
joyful	disappointed	angry	afraid
excited	upset	furious	frightened
ecstatic	depressed	enraged	terrified

Source: Literacy Strong All Year Long: Powerful Lessons for Grades K–2 by Valerie Ellery, Lori Oczkus, and Timothy V. Rasinski. © 2020 ASCD. Readers may duplicate this figure for noncommercial use within their school.

FIGURE 3.16
Shades of Meaning Word Cards for Verbs

Directions: Cut the cards apart, mix them up, sort them into categories by meaning, and then put them in order by intensity.

say	walk	eat	see
whisper	stroll	nibble	peek
exclaim	march	gobble	look
shout	strut	chomp	stare
throw	jog	clean	cry
toss	skip	rinse	whimper
pitch	run	wash	sob
hurl	gallop	scrub	bawl

Source: Literacy Strong All Year Long: Powerful Lessons for Grades K–2 by Valerie Ellery, Lori Oczkus, and Timothy V. Rasinski. © 2020 ASCD. Readers may duplicate this figure for noncommercial use within their school.

LESSON 9. VOCABULARY: ANALYZING WORDS

Title HUNTING TO POSITION PREPOSITIONS AND VERIFY VERBS

Trailer Hunters love the thrill of a pursuit and the search for a rare find! Proficient readers also love the pursuit of finding meaning from text and reading phrases smoothly. Readers, like hunters, need to be prepared to analyze a situation to capture a prize. Students will hunt for ways to capture the meaning of prepositions and analyze regular and irregular verbs.

Literacy Enhancer Vocabulary: Analyzing Words—Parts of Speech: Regular and Irregular Verbs, Prepositions

Key Academic Vocabulary Vocabulary from a previous lesson is marked with an asterisk (*).

Common noun*: A nonspecific type of noun that names any regular, ordinary person, animal, place, thing, or idea

Irregular plural noun*: A type of noun that changes its spelling in the plural form in ways other than what is normal by adding -s or -es to the end of the noun; can end in a variety of ways, with no consistent pattern (e.g., foot→feet, man→men, mouse→mice, person→people)

Irregular verb: A type of verb that changes its form for the past tense and can also completely change for the past participle, rather than just adding a letter or letters, such as -ed or -d; can end in a variety of ways, with no consistent pattern (e.g., sing→sang, go→went)

Noun*: A part of speech that is a type of naming word that represents a person, animal, place, thing, idea, or concept; there are more nouns in the English language than any other words; usually followed by a verb

Parts of speech*: Categories of words used in English grammar (e.g., nouns, verbs, adverbs, adjectives, prepositions)

Plural*: A form of a word that conveys quantity (more than one)

Preposition: A part of speech that shows the logical relationship of a noun to the rest of the sentence through words that specify where (spatial), when (temporal), and why (logical) something is taking place (e.g., *at, before, beside, by, to, with*); always followed by a noun or pronoun in a phrase; never followed by a verb, and a verb is never a part of a prepositional phrase

Proper noun*: A specific type of noun that names a particular person, animal, place, thing, or idea and begins with a capital letter

Regular verb: A type of verb whose past tense and past participle forms end by adding a *-d* or *-ed* (e.g., *dance → danced, roll → rolled*)

Verb*: A part of speech that is a type of word that demonstrates an action (physical or mental); tells what the subject (noun) of a simple sentence is doing; without a verb, a sentence would not exist

Learning Objectives

- Identify and use the most frequently occurring prepositions (e.g., *beyond, by, during, for, from, in, of, off, on, out, to, toward, with*).
- Identify and use the past tense of frequently occurring regular verbs (e.g., *smile → smiled*) and irregular verbs (e.g., *sit → sat, tell → told*).

Essential Questions

- What is the difference between regular and irregular verbs?
- How can you identify and correctly place prepositional phrases in sentences?
- Why is it important to have command of parts of speech?

STEP 1: PREPARATION

Organize Materials

- Stuffed animal, preferably a bear
- Medium-sized empty box
- Items or pictures for a treasure hunt
- Multimodal text set for the topic of study with a focus on regular and irregular verbs or prepositions
- *Verb Verifier* reproducible (copies or enlarged for display)
- *Positioning Prepositions Cards* reproducible (copies or enlarged for display)
- Literacy notebooks

STEP 2: INITIATION

Going on a Bear Hunt and Pantomiming Prepositions

Prior to the lesson, hide a stuffed animal inside a medium-sized box. Tell students, "We're going on a bear hunt today!" Have students march in place and repeat each line of the "Preposition Hunt Chant" after you while making the pretend motions for each sentence until you get to the one about the box. Pull the bear out of the box when the students say, "He's here!" at the end.

Preposition Hunt Chant

We're going on a bear hunt! Let's climb up the hill.

He's not here!

Let's go around this log. He's not here!

Let's look inside this box. He's here!

Next, share that the bear is going to pantomime (act out) different situations. Invite students to look for his action clues and follow him like they would if they were hunting him. Begin to pantomime the bear going into the box. Ask students to share with a partner what the bear is doing. Continue to use the box and pantomime with the bear pretending to do a variety of different things. For each pantomime, have students describe the situation (i.e., what the bear is doing and where he is doing the action in relation to the box). Record their responses. Here are some suggested ideas for the various pantomime situations:

Action/Verb	Prepositions
lying	*beside, under*
dancing	*beside, on*
hopping	*around, over*

Highlight all the preposition words that students shared throughout the chant, and pantomime and tell them that they are going to use these words on a treasure hunt.

STEP 3: DEMONSTRATION

Defining and Pantomiming Prepositions

1. Revisit the recorded prepositions. Ask students, "How are all of these words alike?" Explain that these words are all called prepositions. Write the word *preposition* on the board and circle the root word *position*. Have students think again about the words from the bear hunt (e.g., *around, beside, on, under*), and discuss how they are about positions or locations, as in the circled word on the board. Continue to share how prepositions are a group of words that represent the part of speech that helps readers and writers figure out the relationship of the noun to the rest of the sentence. Explain that prepositions can also help readers understand temporal (e.g., *after, before*) relationships of words.
2. Highlight the verbs that you used with the class during the bear hunt and when pantomiming prepositions. Use the *Verb Verifier* reproducible (Figure 3.17) as a guide to analyze each action word. Share how it is in a reader's best interest to

examine a few of these frequently occurring irregular verbs and learn to understand them in the world of words.

Present Tense (doing)	Past Tense (did)
climb, climbing	*climbed*
dance, dancing	*danced*
go, going	*went*
hop, hopping	*hopped*
lie, lying	*laid*
look, looking	*looked*

3. Read aloud from picture books about verbs and prepositions. You can also use wordless picture books and have students orally use prepositions and verbs to create a storyline based on the illustrations. On the board or a chart, create a list of verbs collected from the reading. Explain how learning about parts of speech, such as verbs, helps to structure our sentences and expand our vocabulary. Here are some suggested verbs and preposition mentor books:
    - *If You Were a Verb* by Michael Dahl
    - *Nouns and Verbs Have a Field Day* by Robin Pulver
    - *Under, Over, by the Clover: What Is a Preposition?* by Brian P. Cleary
    - *Hunters of the Great Forest* by Dennis Nolan (wordless picture book)

STEP 4: COLLABORATION

Treasure Hunt and Conversational Coaching

Prior to class, hide a few objects or pictures in a certain area of the room. These items can correlate with a topic you are studying to continue to build vocabulary and integrate content. Invite a student volunteer to go on a treasure hunt for one of these items by asking yes/no questions (e.g., Is it beside the desk? Is it under the table? Is in on the chair?). Once the student locates the item or picture card, have students engage in conversational coaching by asking one another these questions:

- *For nouns:* What is it? Who is it? What type of noun is it?
- *For verbs:* What does it do? What can it do? What do you do with it? What action can take place with it?
- *For prepositions:* When? Which one? Where? Which direction or position?

STEP 5: APPLICATION

Positioning Prepositions

Distribute copies of the *Positioning Prepositions Cards* reproducible (Figure 3.18) and ask students to sort the cards. Have students position prepositions under their appropriate heading and give an example of each one's use in a complete sentence. *Optional:* Create a basket of texts and have students go on a hunt for these prepositions in use.

Verifying Verbs

Have students practice transforming verbs from present to past tense and record the results on the Verb Verifier. *Optional:* Create a basket of texts and have students go on a hunt for regular and irregular verbs in use.

STEP 6: REFLECTION

Written Response

In their literacy notebooks, have students record verbs and prepositions that they encounter while reading. Have students respond to these essential questions:

- What is the difference between regular and irregular verbs?
- How can you identify and correctly place prepositional phrases in sentences?
- Why is it important to have command of parts of speech?

ADAPTATION/EXTENSION

- Display a list of some prepositions in alphabetical order. Have students select a preposition and think of a noun and a verb that also begin with the same letter as the preposition. For example, if the preposition is *at*, a noun could be *apples* and the verb *ate*. Next, have students try to create sentences using all three words to create an alliteration (e.g., "Ally ate apples at home").
- *English Language Learner Suggestion:* Set up an Animation Station with building blocks, toy people, cards, animals, and other small items. Ask students to build a town and then, using the *Positioning Prepositions Cards* reproducible, animate the prepositions in action as they manipulate the toys in the town. Invite students to write complete sentences to increase their language development by practicing using prepositions, or have students record sentences on index cards.
- *Struggling Reader Suggestion:* Play online preposition games for students to practice building their vocabulary and strengthening their grammar development. Here are some suggested games:

- "Prepositions" by SpellingCity.com: https://www.spellingcity.com/prepositions.html
- "Prepositions" by Turtlediary.com: www.turtlediary.com/grade-1-games/ela-games/prepositions.html
- "Preposition Song Introducing Prepositions to Young Students" by BusyBeavers.com: www.watchknowlearn.org/Video.aspx?VideoID=26871&CategoryID=8771

EVALUATION

"I Can . . ." Statements

- I can identify frequently occurring preposition words in a sentence.
- I can use frequently occurring prepositions in my writing.
- I can identify frequently occurring irregular verbs.

BEHAVIOR INDICATORS

- Demonstrates the ability to identify prepositions in sentences.
- Demonstrates the ability to identify irregular verbs in sentences.
- Correctly forms and uses the past tense of irregular verbs while speaking and writing.

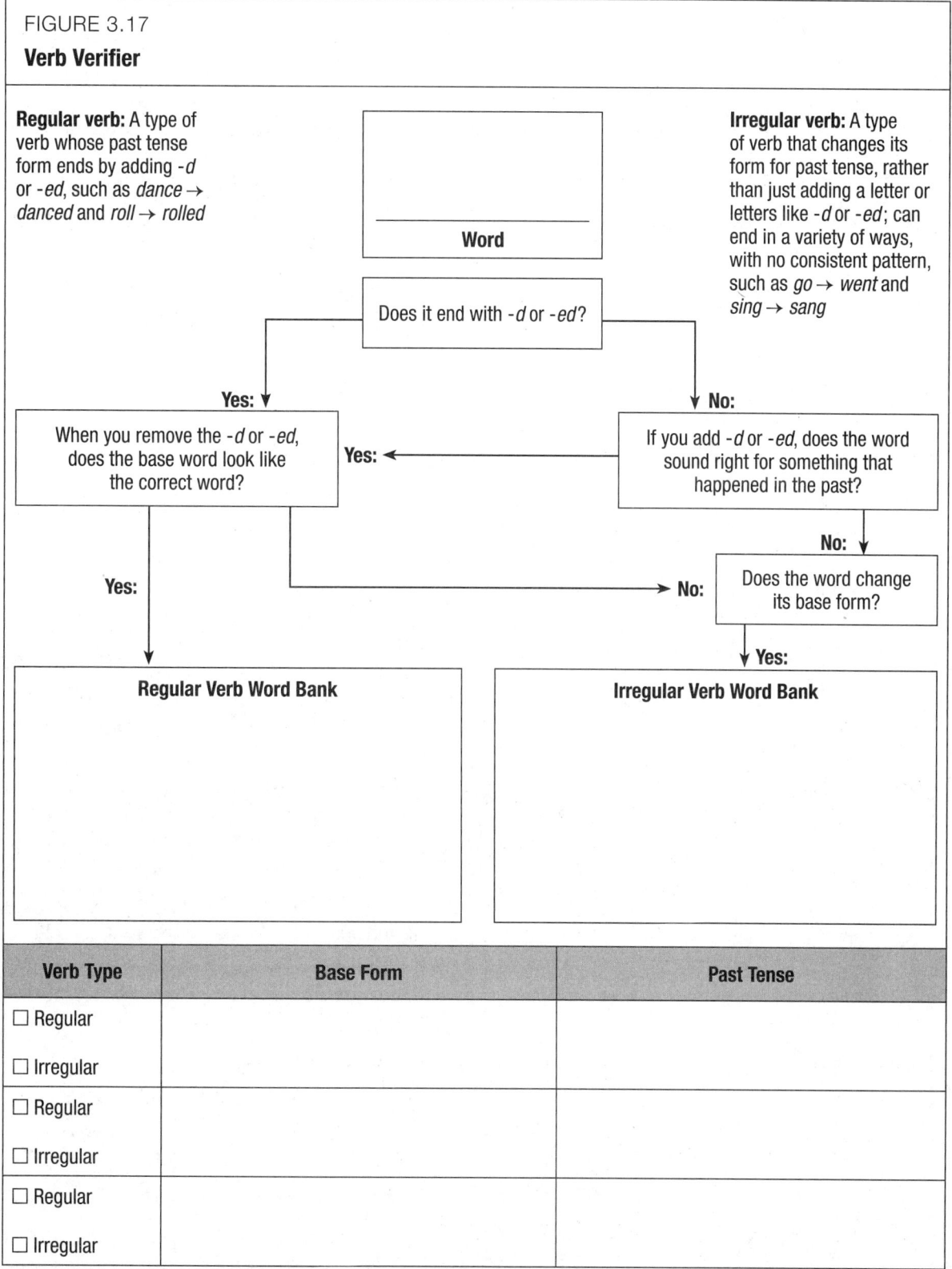

FIGURE 3.17
Verb Verifier

Source: Literacy Strong All Year Long: Powerful Lessons for Grades K–2 by Valerie Ellery, Lori Oczkus, and Timothy V. Rasinski. © 2020 ASCD. Readers may duplicate this figure for noncommercial use within their school.

FIGURE 3.18
Positioning Prepositions Cards

Directions: Cut the cards apart. Have students sort the cards and position the prepositions under the appropriate heading (When? Where? Which one?). Ask students to write a complete sentence using each preposition (an example of how the preposition may be used is provided below each word).

When? (Time)	Where? (Direction/Position)	Where? (Location/Place)	Which one? (Description)
after after school	**in** in the room	**across** across the street	**about** about him
at at recess	**near** near the tree	**from** from the store	**by** by the author
before before lunch	**on** on the table	**into** into the car	**except** except my brother
during during class	**toward** toward her	**through** through the city	**with** with the boys
until until tomorrow	**under** under the bed	**to** to school	**without** without her

Source: Literacy Strong All Year Long: Powerful Lessons for Grades K–2 by Valerie Ellery, Lori Oczkus, and Timothy V. Rasinski. © 2020 ASCD. Readers may duplicate this figure for noncommercial use within their school.

LESSON 10. MOTIVATION: MOTIVATING READERS

Title READY, SET, READ!

Trailer No matter your goal, planning small, realistic action steps makes reaching it a reality. The same holds true for students' reading goals. Broad goals such as "I want to be a better reader" or "I will read more books" tend to be too vague and not motivating for students. However, by breaking the goals into smaller steps that are measurable and attainable, students will recognize and experience success along the way. Harness the power of goal setting!

Literacy Enhancer Motivation: Motivating Readers—Reading Goals: Goal Setting, Text Features, Book Talks, Predicting, and Summarizing

Key Academic Vocabulary Vocabulary from a previous lesson is marked with an asterisk (*).

Author*: The person who wrote the book

Fiction*: The genre that includes stories that are make-believe; may also include poetry

Goal: An ideal or objective to achieve

Nonfiction*: The genre that includes factual or real information that is portrayed to answer, explain, or describe

Plan: A specific action that is measurable for working toward a goal

Predict*: To use information from a text to infer what the text will be about or what one might learn from it

Stamina: The ability to focus on reading for set amounts of time

Summarize*: To tell what has happened in the text by sharing important points and details

Title*: The name of the text; tells what it is about or gives clues to the content

Learning Objectives

- Identify and establish personal, measurable reading goals that center around reading more books and a variety of book genres.
- Identify and establish personal, measurable reading goals that center around reading stamina (i.e., number of minutes of uninterrupted reading).
- Identify and establish personal, measurable reading goals that center around increasing the volume of reading (e.g., books, pages) and the rigor of the material.

- Identify and establish personal, measurable reading strategy goals that center around comprehension, fluency, and decoding words.

Essential Questions

- What are some ways that you can improve your reading by setting goals?
- What goals can you set for reading a variety of genres, improving stamina, increasing the amount of reading you do, and increasing the difficulty of the reading materials?

STEP 1: PREPARATION

Organize Materials

- Ruler
- Fiction or informational books
- Leveled texts
- *Ready, Set, Read! Class Book Club Goals* reproducible (copies or enlarged for display)
- *Ready, Set, Read! My Reading Goals* reproducible (copies or enlarged for display)
- *My Reading Goals and Plans* reproducible (copies or enlarged for display)
- Literacy notebooks

STEP 2: INITIATION

Setting Goals

Explain to students that athletes often set goals and practice to improve their performance in their sport. Invite a student volunteer to demonstrate for the class how to do a long jump. Mark a spot on the floor and have the student jump just a little way across the floor and mark the landing spot. Measure the distance and ask the student if she would like to set a goal to jump farther. Write on the board, "I want to jump ____ inches farther." Show the student the ruler and have her fill in the blank with the extra number of inches as a goal. Applaud the student's progress and explain to the class that when setting a goal, it is helpful to come up with a plan and provide a specific, doable number of steps to achieve that goal.

STEP 3: DEMONSTRATION

How to Set Reading Goals

1. Display the *Ready, Set, Read! Class Book Club Goals* reproducible (Figure 3.19). Explain that you are going to model how to set goals for the class book club. Ask students to be on the lookout for numbers as the class sets its goals.

Explain that good readers often set goals and use numbers to improve their reading. Share an example from your own reading to show how to set a goal. You might say, "I read lots of mysteries because they're my favorite kinds of books. This year my goal is to read more nonfiction books so I can learn more about lots of things, like dogs and places to go on vacation." Write on the board, "I want to read more nonfiction books."

2. Point out that in order to reach your goal of reading more nonfiction, you need a plan. Invite the class to chant the question "How many nonfiction books will you read?" Next, write your specific goal on the board: "I will read _____ (number) nonfiction books _____ (a certain number of times or by a certain deadline)." Also, share the topics that you are interested in learning about.

STEP 4: COLLABORATION

Walk to the Goal

1. Display at least four different book types in different spots around the room. Give a brief book talk about each title. Invite several students to take turns walking over to the book they would like the class to read or for you to read aloud, and share why. Encourage students to say, "We will read _____ (title), and it is a _____ (genre) book."

2. Ask students to help you make a list of books you've read aloud or together as a class (see the *Class Book Club Reading Log* reproducible from the "Take Off with Reading! Class Book Club" lesson in Chapter 1; Figure 1.17). Share the goal "We want to read more books." Discuss the number of books that students would like to read together as a class and within what time frame. Invite them to chant the refrain "How many books will we read?" Discuss and select a doable plan that includes the number of books and a time frame. On the board, write, "We will read _____ (number) books _____ (a certain number of times or by a certain deadline)."

3. Share with students the class goal "We want to read different kinds of books." Ask students to repeat the chant "How many books will we read?" Explain to students that the goal of reading different kinds of books is a great one, but it helps to set a goal to read one type of book and a target number.

4. Study a list of books with the students and come up with a genre that they need to read for their goal. Select a number and a time to fill in the frame "We will read _____ (one kind of book) _____ (a certain number of times or by a certain deadline)."

5. Discuss the goal "We want to read longer." Ask students to think of questions they could ask about this goal. Invite the class to chant "How long should we read?" Come up with appropriate minutes for school and home. Tell students that as they become stronger readers, the class can increase the reading time in five-minute increments.
6. Discuss the goal of reading more challenging or harder books. Ask students to share what makes a book hard or easy. Share with them the points listed on the *Ready, Set, Read! Class Book Club Goals* reproducible. Hold up books and ask students what is hard about them (i.e., more words on the pages, more pages, fewer illustrations, and chapters). Discuss the goal of reading more challenging books and encourage students to work with you to set some goals.

Class Book Club Chant

Display the *Ready, Set, Read! Class Book Club Goals* reproducible and fill it out as a class. Practice chorally reading each of the goals together. Then, as a class, chant after each goal, "How many books do we want to read?"

Individual Goals

- Cut the *Ready, Set, Read! My Reading Goals* reproducible (Figure 3.20) into the four parts. Select just one part to focus on and pass it out to all students. Call up several students to tell what their goal is and their plan to reach that goal. Invite the class to turn to partners and share their goals.
- Display the reproducible. Invite one student to be interviewed by you about his or her goal. Use that student's goal to model how to fill in the reproducible. Encourage students to talk to partners about their own plans for their goals and then fill in the reproducible.
- On subsequent days, repeat the process of talking, modeling with a student, and filling in each of the other three parts of the *Ready, Set, Read! My Reading Goals* reproducible.

STEP 5: APPLICATION

Individual Conferences and Big Buddies

Meet with each student to discuss each *Ready, Set, Read! My Reading Goals* reproducible. Prompt students to come up with a plan for each goal that outlines specific timelines and book titles. Make sure students can verbalize their goals and plans. Have students complete their *Ready, Set, Read! My Reading Goals* reproducible independently or in small groups that you call up to a table. The cross-age big buddy tutors may also help the younger students fill out their forms. Make sure the older buddies are first trained in how to prompt younger students and how to model if necessary.

STEP 6: REFLECTION

Written Response

Have students complete the *My Reading Goals and Plans* reproducible (Figure 3.21). Students may also want to keep a running list of book titles that they are currently reading or interested in reading in their literacy notebooks using these sentence stems:

- I want to read _____ because _____.
- I am reading _____ because _____.

ADAPTATION/EXTENSION

- Invite students who have similar goals to eat lunch with you to discuss their books. For example, students who wish to read more fairy tales or books by a particular author may meet to discuss books over their lunch.
- A shelfie is a photograph taken of the reader and a chosen book or books (Miller, 2009). A shelfie may also be a photograph of the book or books and the student's name if you don't want to post student faces. Take photographs of your students with their favorite books or books they want to read. Post the photographs in the room or on the class or school website, with permission from their parents.
- Steven L. Layne shares the following idea in *Best Ever Literacy Survival Tips: 72 Lessons You Can't Teach Without* (Oczkus, 2012):

  > My elementary and middle school classes loved poetry breaks, when I would cease instruction in a manner that appeared completely impromptu and wildly yell something like "POETRY BREAK!" They were trained to know that this meant everyone was to grab any poetry book from my large collection, find a comfy spot, and read some poems—or grab a partner and read them aloud together. (p. 6)

  Keep poetry in students' reading bins or on their desks so they will be ready when you choose a random time to signal for a poetry break!
- *Nonfiction break:* This idea is a spin-off of the poetry break. Simply alert your students that it is time to drop everything and read a nonfiction book. Keep the books in table bins or students' bags so they can access them quickly. Make the nonfiction and poetry breaks complete surprises—and add a healthy snack for fun.

- *English Language Learner Suggestion:* Discuss one reading goal at a time using realia: number of books (bring a stack of books), kinds of books (bring variety), time spent reading (bring a clock), and challenge level (show a variety of reading levels). Assist students as they fill out *Ready, Set, Read! My Goals* reproducible.
- *Struggling Reader Suggestion:* Bring specific titles for students to peruse and model goal setting using the language provided on the reproducible. Encourage students to share their goals with a partner and guide the discussions.

EVALUATION

"I Can . . ." Statements

- I can set a goal for reading and make a plan to reach it.
- I can set goals and specific plans for reading more books.
- I can set goals and specific plans for reading for more minutes.
- I can set goals and specific plans for reading different types of books.
- I can set goals for reading more challenging books.

BEHAVIOR INDICATORS

- Identifies a goal for reading more books by setting a goal with a number of books and a timeline for reading them.
- Identifies a goal for reading different kinds of books.
- Names genres or types of books to read in a given time frame.
- Identifies a goal for spending more time reading by setting minute goals for home and school.
- Identifies a goal for reading more challenging books by identifying what makes them challenging: more words on the pages, more pages, or chapters.
- Sets a goal to read more challenging books in a given time frame.

FIGURE 3.19
Ready, Set, Read! Class Book Club Goals

Week: _____ Month: _____

Number of Books

Our Goal
We want to read more books.

Our Plan
We will read ____ (number) books _____ (by when) or every _____ (week/month).

Our Drawing

Title(s):_____
_____

Time for Reading

Our Goal
We want to spend more time reading.

Our Plan
We will read for ____ minutes at school every day.
We will read for ____ minutes at home every day.

Our Drawing

Title(s):_____
_____

Kinds of Books

Our Goal
We want to read different kinds of books.

Our Plan
We will read ____ (number) books (by when) _____ or every (week/month).
Kinds of books: adventure, autobiography, biography, fables, fairy tales, mysteries, nonfiction, poetry, realistic fiction, science fiction

Our Drawing

Title(s):_____
_____

Challenge of Books

Our Goal
We want to read harder books.

Our Plan
We will read ____ (number) books that have
- more words on the page
- more pages
- more chapters

Our Drawing

Title(s):_____
_____

Source: Literacy Strong All Year Long: Powerful Lessons for Grades K–2 by Valerie Ellery, Lori Oczkus, and Timothy V. Rasinski. © 2020 ASCD. Readers may duplicate this figure for noncommercial use within their school.

FIGURE 3.20
Ready, Set, Read! My Reading Goals

Name: _____ Week: _____ Month _____

Number of Books

My Goal
I want to read more books.

My Plan
I will read ____ (number) books _____ (by when) or every _____ (week/month).

My Drawing

Title(s): _____
_____

Time for Reading

My Goal
I want to spend more time reading.

My Plan
I will read for ____ minutes at school every day.
I will read for ____ minutes at home every day.

My Drawing

Title(s): _____
_____

Kinds of Books

My Goal
I want to read different kinds of books.

My Plan
I will read ____ (number) books (by when) _____ or every (week/month).
Kinds of books: adventure, autobiography, biography, fables, fairy tales, mysteries, nonfiction, poetry, realistic fiction, science fiction

My Drawing

Title(s): _____
_____

Challenge of Books

My Goal
I want to read harder books.

My Plan
I will read ____ (number) books that have
- more words on the page
- more pages
- more chapters

My Drawing

Title(s): _____
_____

Source: Literacy Strong All Year Long: Powerful Lessons for Grades K–2 by Valerie Ellery, Lori Oczkus, and Timothy V. Rasinski. © 2020 ASCD. Readers may duplicate this figure for noncommercial use within their school.

FIGURE 3.21
My Reading Goals and Plans

My Goal

I want to_____.

My Plan

- I will_____.
- I will_____.

My Drawing

My Goal

I want to_____.

My Plan

- I will_____.
- I will_____.

My Drawing

My Goal

I want to_____.

My Plan

- I will_____.
- I will_____.

My Drawing

My Goal

I want to_____.

My Plan

- I will_____.
- I will_____.

My Drawing

Source: Literacy Strong All Year Long: Powerful Lessons for Grades K–2 by Valerie Ellery, Lori Oczkus, and Timothy V. Rasinski. © 2020 ASCD. Readers may duplicate this figure for noncommercial use within their school.

~4

Stopping the Summer Slide

Summer afternoon—summer afternoon; to me those have always been the two most beautiful words in the English language.
—Henry James

Success is not final, failure is not fatal: it is the courage to continue that counts.
—Winston Churchill

Summer is a wonderful time for playing, swimming, riding bikes, picnicking, and much more. However, for many students, summer is not a time for reading. This is unfortunate, as research has shown that if children do not continue reading during the summer months, they are likely to regress in their reading—reading at a lower level of proficiency at the end of the summer than at the beginning (Allington & McGill-Franzen, 2013; Kim & White, 2011). According to some studies, students can lose up to three months of reading achievement over the summer break by not engaging in reading. Between grades 1 and 6, the cumulative regression in reading achievement can be 1.5 years (Mraz & Rasinski, 2007). Of course, there is a flip side to summer reading: Those students who engage in reading and reading-related activities can increase their reading achievement over the summer.

Summer is a time for fun, but it is also a critical time for continuing students' reading success that began during the school year. Through the previous chapters, we provided you with lessons on various key competencies for reading success. These lessons spiraled through the school year, so the individual competencies were given continued and increasingly complex focus throughout the year. In this chapter, you will find that we have continued our focus on the same essential reading competencies but with an emphasis on how parents, caregivers, out-of-school providers, and teachers can continue students' reading development through the summer. Here you will find instructional tools and approaches that you can share to make reading fun and educational and to keep students literacy strong!

Literacy-Strong Summer Scenarios

Summer is a great time for students to grow by reading more at home. At the end of the school year, share with parents ways they can help their children read. Also, be sure to discuss and share specifics on summer reading, including where, what, and when to read. Here are some classroom stories for promoting summer reading.

Describe It in Five!

Mr. and Mrs. Kistler learned about the Describe It in Five! strategy at the end-of-year parent meeting that Ms. Granger, their son's kindergarten teacher, hosted during the last week of school. They have been doing the activity at least twice a week during the summer months. Every evening, one parent reads to Michael. At the end of the read-aloud, the parent and Michael discuss the story and pick out a couple of interesting words that can be described using the five categories that Ms. Granger shared with them: size, color, shape, touch, and weight. After writing the words on a sheet of paper, the parent and child try to come up with other words that describe the chosen words. Both parents report that the discussion that comes from this activity is rich. They have noticed that Michael has been using both the words and the descriptors in his own oral language.

Tips for grades 1 and 2: The beauty of Describe It in Five! is that it can be used at any grade level. For older students, the more sophisticated books that they are exposed to will reveal more sophisticated words to be described in five.

Splash into Reading

Mr. Evans, a 1st grade teacher, is delighted with the progress that his students have made during the year. However, he knows that much of that progress is at risk if students don't continue to read over the long break. He spent time over the last week of school splashing into reading with his students. For the last 15 minutes of each day, he spent time talking with students about summer activities, including reading. He taught his students the "Splash into Summer Reading Song," singing it himself at first and then, as the days passed, getting individual students to respond to the song's questions: "What are you reading, where do you read, when do you read, and who do you read with?" By the end of the week, all students had sung with Mr. Evans and completed the Summer Reading Club form. Mr. Evans's students have set plans for their summer reading.

Tips for kindergarten and grade 2: The last few days of school are always a good time to talk about summer activities. Certainly, we should be talking about traditional activities, such as swimming and playing ball, but it is equally important for teachers to chat with students about summer reading as well. Regardless of whether you use a song or a poem as a starter, spend time talking about your own summer reading plans and encourage students to make their own as well. Invite students to take photographs of themselves reading, and when school is back in session, ask them to bring in their photos for the first bulletin-board display of the year.

Summer Poetry Reading

"What fun!" are the first two words that Hallie Brady said when asked about Summer Poetry Reading. Mrs. Brady heard about the activity from a video posting on her daughter Simone's classroom website, where Simone's 2nd grade teacher, Ms. Jan, has regularly posted information and ideas on reading for parents. During the last month of school, she posted three ideas on continuing the development of students' reading during the summer months, and Summer Poetry Reading caught Mrs. Brady's attention. Each week, she and Simone went online and found four poems that they thought were interesting and touched on a different summer theme (e.g., swimming, baseball, picnics). They printed out the poems together and assigned one to every member of the family (Mom, Dad, Simone, and older brother Jonathan). During the week, each family member was expected to spend five minutes per day rehearsing a poem. Then, on Friday evenings, they would have a family poetry slam. Each member performed the poem and was greeted with applause and clicking fingers. The positive feedback that Simone received from these weekly slams kept her motivated to read poetry and books throughout the summer.

Tips for kindergarten and grade 1: Summer Poetry Reading is an activity suitable for any grade or age level. The critical feature is the difficulty of the poems chosen to be read. For kindergartners, nursery rhymes are excellent choices, as they help develop students' phonemic awareness. Assign poems to pairs to support younger readers and to help model good expression and phrasing.

Addressing Summer Challenges

Summer is near, and Mrs. Jacoby is worried. Her 2nd grade son, Thomas, has struggled in reading since the start of 1st grade. Although he was initially excited about learning to read, his lack of progress has caused him to be discouraged and lose interest. The only reading activity that he seems to enjoy is when his parents read to him. Mrs. Jacoby wonders what she and her husband can do to help Thomas improve his independent reading.

Mrs. Jacoby knows that if she can get her son involved in reading and reading-related activities for as little as 20–30 minutes per day, it is likely that he may not only retain but also increase his reading achievement. Teachers can do much to support parents like Mrs. Jacoby who want to keep their children growing literacy strong.

Questions Teachers Ask to Address Summer Reading Challenges

- How can I, as the teacher, communicate with and influence reading at home during the summer months?
- How can families find time for reading and reading-related activities?
- In what ways can families integrate literacy into typical summer activities?
- What resources are available in my community to promote literacy during the summer months?
- How can I track students' reading over the summer?

Essentials for Stopping the Summer Slide

1. **You've Got Mail!**

    Children love receiving mail—snail mail or e-mail messages. Before the end of the school year, collect students' or families' e-mail addresses or have parents write their child's name and mailing address on two or three postcards. Then, over the course of the summer, drop notes to your students reminding them to read and perhaps even suggesting a couple titles for each student (make sure the title is available in the community library).

2. **Family Read-Alouds**

    The power of reading to children cannot be overstated. Children love to be read to. Children who are read to have larger vocabularies and better comprehension and are more enthusiastic about reading. Encourage parents to read to their children nightly. Not only are the children strengthening their literacy, but parents are also creating wonderful memories that will last a lifetime!

3. **Family Reads: Make It Interactive**

    Some books are meant to be read by more than one reader, such as these:
    - *Tell Me a Story, Mama* by Angela Johnson
    - *Joyful Noise* by Paul Fleischman
    - *I Am Phoenix* by Paul Fleischman
    - *I Am the Dog, I Am the Cat* by Donald Hall
    - *You Read to Me, I'll Read to You* by Mary Ann Hoberman
    - *Once Upon a Cool Motorcycle Dude* by Kevin O'Malley

Provide parents and caregivers with a list of such books and encourage them to divide up the reading parts and read with the children. Having read a book or poem once, family members can switch parts and read it again.

4. **Family Reads: Parents as Listeners**

    Research has shown that children can improve their reading by reading to their parents (Rasinski, Padak, & Fawcett, 2009). Parents who are positive and supportive as they listen to their children read allow the children to demonstrate their growing competence in reading. Encourage parents to take a few minutes to listen to their children read and to follow the reading with positive, enthusiastic, and encouraging comments. When children feel safe and successful in their reading, they are likely to read more. Brainstorm with parents or caregivers a list of comments that they could make in response to the children's reading (e.g., "I love how you read that story with expression!" "Wow, you impressed me with your word decoding! There were some difficult words in that passage" "It's so fun listening to you read! I hope we can do this every evening").

5. **Summer Songs and Rhythmical Words**

    Just as the summer air is filled with the rhythmical sounds of birds, crickets, and other creatures, summer can also be filled with the sounds of song and poetry. There are many poems available for children and families to read, rehearse, recite, and celebrate. Search online for "summer songs for children," "patriotic songs," and "summer poetry for children," and you will find more than enough rhythmical words to challenge even the most enthusiastic crickets!

6. **Fast Start for Reading**

    Fast Start is an early reading instructional routine designed for parents to get their children off to a good start in their reading (Padak & Rasinski, 2005, 2008). The challenge of Fast Start is for children to learn to read a poem or short text every single day. The daily routine looks like this:
    - Make a copy of a new poem or short text every day for your child to read.

- Read the poem or text to your child two or three times while she follows along silently.
- Talk about the content of the reading.
- Read the poem or text with your child two or three times. Make sure that you're reading in unison, at a pace that is not too fast for your child.
- Have your child read the poem or text aloud two or three times. Assist as necessary.
- Praise your child for efforts and improvements.
- Choose two to four words from the poem or text and write them on a sheet of paper. Analyze them together and have your child practice reading them alone.

Although the instructional lesson is short and sweet (10–15 minutes per day), research has demonstrated Fast Start's effectiveness in helping even less able readers become literacy strong (Rasinski & Stevenson, 2005).

7. **Summer Is the Right Time for Writing**

Think of all the things that children can write over the summer months with their parents and other family members. Consider this list:
- Keep a daily journal over the summer.
- Describe a summer trip through journal entries.
- Keep a dialogue journal, with the parent and child alternating days on which they make their entries.
- Write letters (snail mail or e-mail) to family members far away. (Of course, children may receive replies from their family members as well—what a treat!)
- Write and perform poetry. Learn how to write parodies of popular poems on the Giggle Poetry website (www.gigglepoetry.com).
- Author their own version of patterned books. Here are a few of our favorites:
    - *The Important Book* by Margaret Wise Brown
    - *Brown Bear, Brown Bear, What Do You See?* by Bill Martin, Jr.
    - *Fortunately* by Remy Charlip
    - *If You Give a Mouse a Cookie* by Laura Joffe Numeroff

8. **It May Be Television, but It's Still Reading**

What happens when you turn on the captioning feature on your home television? You instantly have the opportunity to read in a supported manner. When watching captioned television, children will hear the words being uttered by the speaker and see the very same words appear on the television screen. Moreover, we know that the eyes seem to be drawn to the words on the screen; we can't help ourselves from looking at the words. Although it may not be the best medium for children's reading, it is still reading.

9. Check Out Your Community

Families need to know that there may be many community resources that they can turn to in helping children remain literacy strong. Certainly, the community library offers a wide range of engaging programs to keep children reading over the summer months, but there also may be other organizations and programs that support summer literacy. Check out the local bookstores, the local newspaper, city government programs, the parks and recreation department, churches and other places of worship, the local university. Public libraries have apps for downloadable books, so parents and caregivers don't have to drive to the library. They can download books, perhaps on a family tablet or digital device, for their child.

Teachers and principals may wish to contact some local organizations in advance to ask if they would be willing to support literacy learning in some way. In many instances, these organizations only need to be asked.

10. Monitor Summer Reading

We're not talking about testing here. It is a good idea to try tracking the reading that students do over the summer. Perhaps give families a monthly calendar to put on their refrigerator. The calendar can be filled with literacy ideas for the summer. You can also ask caregivers to simply estimate and report the number of minutes their children read each day over the summer. The calendar can act as a reminder for parents to keep literacy on the front burner during the summer. It can also be used by teachers at the end of the summer to determine just how successful they were at encouraging children and families to engage in summer reading and writing.

11. Books for Summer Reading

Here is a list of books that anyone can use for reading aloud during the summer break:

- *And Then Comes Summer* by Tom Brenner
- *Time of Wonder* by Robert McCloskey
- *Blueberries for Sal* by Robert McCloskey
- *The Relatives Came* by Cynthia Rylant
- *The Night Before Summer Vacation* by Natasha Wing
- *Summer Days and Nights* by Wong Herbert Yee

12. Summer Word Ladder

On a blank sheet of paper, number the rows from 1 to 10. Write the word *summer* next to number 1. Then make 9 more words by adding, subtracting, and changing letters from the previous word. Listen closely to the clues. Then sort the words you made into those words that you think may have something to do with summer and those that don't. Be prepared to explain your choices.

1. Summer — Take away three letters to make the answer to an addition problem.
2. Sum — Change one letter to make the object that warms the earth.
3. Sun — Change one letter to fill in the blank: "Playing with my friends is ____."
4. Fun — Change one letter to make a machine that blows air to cool a room.
5. Fan — Change one letter to fill in the blank: "All my friends love Silly Bandz. They are the new ____."
6. Fad — Change one letter to make the opposite of *good*.
7. Bad — Change one letter to make a place to sleep.
8. Bed — Change one letter to make a color.
9. Red — Add one letter to make a fun activity to do in the summer.
10. Read

Overview of Chapter 4 Lessons

Lesson 1. Phonological Awareness and Phonics: Isolating and Identifying Sounds—I Spy! Capturing Sounds

Lesson 2. Phonological Awareness and Phonics: Blending and Segmenting Sounds—The Sweet Blend of Sounds

Lesson 3. Phonics: Decoding—Working Words Weekly Summer Plan

Lesson 4. Fluency: Phrasing—Weekly Summer Poetry Reading

Lesson 5. Comprehension: Craft and Structure—Previewing—Text Trip Travels

Lesson 6. Comprehension: Key Ideas and Details—Determining Importance and Summarizing—Home Run with Details

Lesson 7. Comprehension: Key Ideas and Details—Questioning for Close Reading—My Question, Your Question!

Lesson 8. Vocabulary: Associating Words—Describe It in Five!

Lesson 9. Vocabulary: Analyzing Words—Literary Scrapbooks: From Parts of Speech to a Whole Picture of a Text

Lesson 10. Motivation: Motivating Readers—Splash into Summer Reading!

LESSON 1. PHONOLOGICAL AWARENESS AND PHONICS: ISOLATING AND IDENTIFYING SOUNDS

Title I Spy! Capturing Sounds

Trailer I spy, with my little eye, sounds! Go on a hunt to capture sounds! Students will have a blast reviewing long and short vowels and digraphs and even creating alliterations using a variety of common objects in an I Spy guessing game. Students practice isolating and identifying specific sounds they find in this adventurous, rhythmic lesson.

Literacy Enhancer Phonological Awareness and Phonics: Isolating and Identifying Sounds—Initial, Medial, and Beginning Sounds; Vowels; and Digraphs

Key Academic Vocabulary Vocabulary from a previous lesson is marked with an asterisk (*).

Alliteration*: A figure of speech in which a series of words repeat the same initial sound

Digraph*: Two consecutive vowels or consonants that represent a single speech sound (phoneme)

Isolate*: To separate sounds from other sounds in a word

Long vowel*: A speech sound produced without obstructing the flow of air from the lungs; the letters *a, e, i, o, u,* and sometimes *y*; long vowels make the same sound as the letter name

Phoneme*: The smallest unit of sound

Short vowel*: A speech sound produced without obstructing the flow of air from the lungs; the letters *a, e, i, o, u,* and sometimes *y*; short vowels do not make the sound of the letter name

Learning Objectives

- Isolate and identify sounds by positioning the mouth, lips, jaw, and tongue to correspond with appropriate sounds in words.
- Capture and categorize images and create a digital sound picture book.

Essential Questions

- How do you position your mouth for the / / sound in the word? (fill in the identified sound)
- What sound is in the word?
- What sounds do all these images have in common?

STEP 1: PREPARATION

Organize Materials

- Handheld mirrors
- I Spy book series by Jean Marzollo
- Digital camera, smartphone, tablet, or any other device for taking pictures
- Objects aligned with the selected sound
- White poster board or chart paper
- Computer

Here are some options for organizing and differentiating the instructional setting:

- **Small-Group Instruction**
    - I Spy inspections and games
    - The I Spy sounds book
- **Families or Tutors**
    - I Spy inspections and games
    - Conversational coaching
- **Independent Work**
    - Application of an I Spy page from the I Spy sounds book
    - Reflection

STEP 2: INITIATION

I Spy with My Eye

Visit a local library and check out various I Spy books. Inspect the features of these books (e.g., photos, collage layouts, riddles). Think about how each page focuses on a specific topic and how all the photos are related to answering the riddles. Discuss the themes of the I Spy books and how objects are hidden or camouflaged and require a detail-catching eye to be able to spy the highlighted object. Highlight the rhythm of the text and how it resembles the folk song "Sweet Betsy from Pike." *Optional:* Download the folk song and listen to the tune: www.balladofamerica.com/music/indexes/songs/sweetbetsyfrompike/index.htm

STEP 3: DEMONSTRATION

Capturing Sounds for an I Spy Riddle

1. Say, "I am thinking of a specific sound. As I look around, I spy the sound in certain objects." Walk up to each object and pretend to take a photograph of it by using a hand gesture and a clicking noise as if you just took a picture—or use a digital camera or tablet and actually take the picture.

2. Share the pictures or say the objects' names aloud. Ask students, "What do these images all have in common?" If it is the beginning sound, remind students that these objects can form an alliteration. After the images have been identified, discuss how they all have the same sounds (e.g., short or long vowel, digraph, beginning or ending sound) in the words.
3. After the highlighted sound has been identified, use a handheld mirror to isolate the sound in each word and describe the position of your mouth for it. Use the tune from "Sweet Betsy from Pike" to create a riddle to align with your chosen sound items. Create an anchor chart for what is necessary to create the poetry format of the I Spy riddle. Here's a list of items you could use a sample anchor chart for I Spy poetry:
   - Each line begins with a capital letter.
   - There are four beats per line.
   - Lines 1 and 3 end with a comma.
   - A semicolon is at the end of line 2.
   - There is a period at the end of line 4.
   - The last words in lines 1 and 2 and lines 3 and 4 rhyme.

STEP 4: COLLABORATION

Conversational Coaching

Explore and play I Spy games (online games can be found at www.scholastic.com/ispy/games/index.htm). Assign partners or groups a particular sound to create a page for an I Spy sounds book. Engage in conversational coaching by asking students to discuss the following questions with diverse partners:

- What sounds do all these images have in common?
- How do you position your mouth for the common sound found in the images?

STEP 5: APPLICATION

Creating a Sound Collage

Have students collect at least two objects that correlate with a particular sound. Remind them that their objects need to rhyme so they can complete the riddle for their page. After collecting the items, have students arrange them on a white poster board or chart paper and take a bird's-eye overview picture with a digital camera, smartphone, or tablet. Visit Jean Marzollo's website (www.jeanmarzollo.com) and submit the student-created I Spy sounds book to her website for sharing.

STEP 6: REFLECTION

Oral or Written Response

Have students independently create a riddle for their I Spy poem page. Remind them to include four beats to a line, with every two lines rhyming. Have students respond to the essential questions through written response (or orally):

- What sounds connect all these images?
- How do you position your mouth for the sound in the word _____?

ADAPTATION/EXTENSION

- Revisit this section in the following lessons for a variety of examples for isolating and identifying sounds:
    - "Need to Know Names" in Chapter 1
    - "Mingle and Jingle with Vowels" in Chapter 2
    - "Digraph Hero Teams" in Chapter 3

- *English Language Learner Suggestion:* Give students a basket of objects or picture cards and have them select an item; say its name; pronounce its initial, medial, or final sound; and then sort the objects or cards to create categories for the chosen practice sounds.
- *Struggling Reader Suggestion:* Reinforce the position of students' mouths for selected sounds and check their mouth position using a handheld mirror. Have them describe the position of their mouth for each of the sounds to a partner. Revisit a leveled text to search and find other words that match the practiced sounds.

EVALUATION

"I Can . . ." Statements

- I can identify common sounds in words.
- I can categorize words by specific sounds in them.
- I can identify the rhythm and form of the I Spy poem.

BEHAVIOR INDICATORS

- Isolates and identifies selected sounds by positioning the mouth, lips, jaw, and tongue to correspond with a chosen word for the sound.
- Distinguishes specific sounds in words.
- Categorizes objects by a specific sound and justifies why they are together.

LESSON 2. PHONOLOGICAL AWARENESS AND PHONICS: BLENDING AND SEGMENTING

Title THE SWEET BLEND OF SOUNDS

Trailer Ice cream and summer are the perfect pair! The cool sensation and smoothness of ice cream are a sweet tooth's dream on a hot summer day. Help students find that same smoothness by whipping together individual sounds, like the ingredients in ice cream, to form delicious words. This lesson will help satisfy the summer desire for ice cream, while blending and segmenting just the right mix of sounds and syllables for a smooth taste of sweet sounds of blends to form words.

Literacy Enhancer Phonological Awareness and Phonics: Blending and Segmenting—Consonant Blends, Digraphs, and Single-Syllable and Multisyllabic Words

Key Academic Vocabulary Vocabulary from a previous lesson is marked with an asterisk (*).

Blending*: Combining a sequence of two or more sounds to form a word

Consonant blend*: A voiced combination of a group of two or three consonants in a word

Consonant digraph: A combination of two adjacent consonants in a syllable that represent only one sound

Multisyllabic word*: A word that has more than one syllable

Onset*: The part of a syllable before the vowel; not all syllables have onsets

Rime*: The part of a syllable beginning with the sounded vowel and any consonants that follow

Segmenting*: Breaking a word by phonemes (sounds) and syllables

Syllable*: A part of a word that contains only one sounded vowel; words can be made up of one or more syllables

Learning Objectives

- Orally produce single-syllable words by blending and segmenting sounds (phonemes).
- Blend and segment words into a complete sequence of individual sounds (phonemes) to form a word.

Essential Questions

- How many sounds or syllables do you hear in the word _____?
- What sounds did you combine to form the word _____?

STEP 1: PREPARATION

Organize Materials

- Ingredients for homemade ice cream (sugar, milk, cream, vanilla extract, rock salt, ice)
- Bowl
- Stirring and measuring spoons
- Dish towel
- One pint-sized and one gallon-sized resealable storage bag
- Assorted colors of modeling clay
- Plastic or paper ice-cream cone
- Multimodal text set for the topic of study
- Optional: *Sweet Tooth's Instant Ice Cream Recipe* reproducible (copies or enlarged for display)

Here are some options for organizing and differentiating the instructional setting:

- **Small-Group Instruction**
    - *Sweet Tooth's Instant Ice Cream Recipe* reproducible
    - Ice cream word list
    - Read-aloud
    - Word scoops

- **Parents or Tutors**
    - Modeling clay (to tangibly demonstrate segmenting and blending sounds)
    - Conversational coaching

- **Independent Work**
    - Word scoops
    - Reflection

STEP 2: INITIATION

The Perfect Blend for Ice Cream

Brainstorm a list of words associated with ice cream. Ask, "What are some ingredients that we might find in homemade ice cream?" Share *Sweet Tooth's Instant Ice Cream Recipe* (Figure 4.1) for making simple ice cream, highlighting individual ingredients (segmented parts) that can be blended together to make a refreshing sweet snack in five minutes. Make the homemade ice cream. As you are eating the ice cream, share how you are going to use modeling clay to represent ice-cream scoops of sounds.

STEP 3: DEMONSTRATION

Scoop It Up

- For the read-aloud, select a text that focuses on ice cream, consonant blends, or digraphs (e.g., *Curious George Goes to an Ice Cream Shop* edited by Margret and H. A. Rey, *Wemberly's Ice-Cream Star* by Kevin Henkes, *Should I Share My Ice Cream?* by Mo Willems, *The Ice Cream King* by Steve Metzger).
- From the text or the ice-cream word list, select several words that have consonant blends (e.g., *cream, strawberry, stir, star*) or digraphs (e.g., *chocolate chip, whip, shop, share*).
- Say a selected word aloud (e.g., *shop*). Roll a piece of modeling clay into a ball and share how it looks like a scoop of ice cream and will represent a "word scoop." Holding up the ball of clay, repeat the selected word and explain that the ball will now represent the word *shop*. Isolate the sounds in the word *shop* as you say it slowly: /sh/ /o/ /p/. Share how the word has three sounds. Remind students that the *sh* makes the /sh/ digraph sound because you only hear one sound for the two letters.
- Repeat the sounds in the selected word (*shop*) and divide the scoop of ice cream (clay ball) into the number of sounds heard in the word.
- Hold up each piece of the ball as you say each individual sound aloud. Begin to connect each sound by blending the sounds together as you pinch the clay pieces back into a whole ball to form the complete word.
- Review an anchor chart for consonant blends (i.e., containing two or three consonant sounds that cluster together, with each consonant sound distinct in the blend and heard within the cluster; can be found at the beginning, middle, and end of a word).
- Continue to practice with other words from the read-aloud. Pick up a mirror and say the complete word in the mirror. Think aloud about what you noticed as you said the word (e.g., "When my mouth formed the /sh/ sound, I noticed my lips come together toward the middle, making my lips pucker like a kiss, and the middle of my tongue go up slightly").

Have students compare what they notice about their mouth position and the number of phonemes each word produces.

STEP 4: COLLABORATION

Conversational Coaching

Engage in conversational coaching by asking the following questions:

- How many sounds or syllables do you hear in the word _____?
- How did you figure out how many sounds you hear in the word _____?
- Which sounds do you hear in the word _____?
- How do you position your mouth for the / / sound? (say specific isolated sound with the sound bracket)

STEP 5: APPLICATION

Word Scoops

Have students practice forming word scoops of ice cream with modeling clay to blend and segment sounds and syllables. They can use a plastic ice-cream cone to stack their word scoops. Distribute small mirrors and have students look in the mirror and say the selected words. To determine syllables, have students place their hand under their chin and feel the number of times their jaw drops when they say each word.

STEP 6: REFLECTION

Oral Response

Have students reflect on the specific sounds or syllables in selected words as they segment the words using modeling clay. As they blend sounds or syllables to form each whole word, have students use the newly formed word scoop in a sentence to bring application and meaning to the selected word. They can also take several word scoops (e.g., *creamy*, *snack*, *stir*, *strawberry*, *sweet*) and connect them into a delicious sentence (e.g., "I will make a sweet snack and stir in a strawberry to make it creamy"). Have students reflect on their word choices by answering the following questions:

- Which words have blends?
- Did you create an alliteration with your words?
- Are there any words that have a digraph in them?

ADAPTATION/EXTENSION

- Revisit this section in the following lessons for a variety of examples for blending and segmenting:
    - "The Blending Dance" in Chapter 1
    - "Making Word Smoothies" in Chapter 2
    - "The Blend Factor" in Chapter 3

- *English Language Learner Suggestion:* Partner students with a model English student to review a list of selected words with blends to match the ELL students' level. Have them practice segmenting how many sounds they hear in each word and then using the word in a sentence. Remind them that with a blend, you can hear both sounds.
- *Struggling Reader Suggestion:* Have students practice consonant blends online at Vocabulary Spelling City: www.spellingcity.com/consonant-blends.html

EVALUATION

"I Can . . ." Statements

- I can identify and produce consonant blends.
- I can identify and produce digraphs.
- I can identify how many syllables are in a word.

BEHAVIOR INDICATORS

- Determines the number of sounds in a word by segmenting the word.
- Identifies the digraph(s) in a word.
- Produces a word by blending sounds, including consonant blends.

FIGURE 4.1
Sweet Tooth's Instant Ice Cream Recipe

Makes two or three small servings

Ingredients

6 tbsp. sea salt

ice (enough to fill half of a one-gallon ziplock plastic bag)

1 tbsp. sugar

½ cup milk, sweetened condensed milk, cream, or half-and-half (*Note:* Cream will provide the highest calorie count.)

¼ tsp. vanilla extract (*Note:* May substitute other flavorings or chocolate chips.)

1 pint-size ziplock plastic bag

1 gallon-size ziplock plastic bag

1 small hand towel

Directions

1. Fill the large bag halfway with ice and add sea salt.
2. In a bowl, mix the other three ingredients.
3. Pour the mixture into the small bag and seal tightly.
4. Place the small bag into the larger one, making sure the small bag is immersed in the ice.
5. Place a towel around the outside of the bags.
6. Shake for 5 minutes.
7. Spoon the contents from the bag and enjoy!

> **Slime**
> If a sweet food treat isn't the best option, consider play materials such as homemade Slime.
>
> **Ingredients:**
> white school glue
> water
> liquid laundry detergent
> optional—food coloring and glitter
>
> **Directions:** Mix equal parts of glue and water in a bowl. Add ¼ cup (60 milliliters) of laundry detergent, using a fork to fold it in—and any optional ingredients. Knead for 1 or 2 minutes. Play! Then store in an airtight container.

Source: Literacy Strong All Year Long: Powerful Lessons for Grades K–2 by Valerie Ellery, Lori Oczkus, and Timothy V. Rasinski. © 2020 ASCD. Readers may duplicate this figure for noncommercial use within their school.

LESSON 3. PHONICS: DECODING

Title WORKING WORDS WEEKLY SUMMER PLAN

Trailer Life seems to go so much better with a plan! Winning teams have a plan and learn to execute it for success. Readers can have a plan, too! Students learn how to design and execute a routine to decode words as they make and break words, distinguish vowel sounds, and identify prefixes within root words. Get on the winning team for reading!

Literacy Enhancer Phonics: Decoding—Following a Plan to Practice Decoding Vowels and Prefixes

Key Academic Vocabulary Vocabulary from a previous lesson is marked with an asterisk (*).

*Decode**:* The ability to apply letter-sound relationships to read and pronounce a written word

*Grapheme**:* The written symbol (letters) used to represent a phoneme (sounds)

*Long vowel**:* The letters *a, e, i, o, u,* and sometimes *y;* long vowels make a speech sound produced without obstructing the flow of air from the lungs; make the same sound as the letter name

*Multisyllable word**:* A word made up of more than one syllable

*Prefix**:* A meaningful group of letters added to the beginning of a root or base word to modify its meaning

*Root (base) word**:* The primary part of a word that does not require a prefix or suffix

*Short vowel**:* The letters *a, e, i, o, u,* and sometimes *y;* short vowels make a speech sound produced without obstructing the flow of air from the lungs; do not make the sound of the letter name

*Syllable**:* A basic unit of spoken language containing a vowel sound

*Vowel**:* A speech sound produced without obstructing the flow of air from the lungs; the letters *a, e, i, o, u,* and sometimes *y* in written form

*Word family**:* The portion of a syllable that begins with the vowel and vowel sound and contains any other letters after the vowel (e.g., *-at, -ate, -it, -ight*); also known as phonograms or rimes

Learning Objectives

- Create a weekly word work plan to support decoding words and bringing meaning to the text.
- Decode and analyze word parts (the five major vowels and common prefixes).

Essential Questions

- How will having a weekly word work plan help you?
- How will recognizing the difference between short and long vowels help you read and write words?
- What is decoding, and what does it allow you to do?
- How do prefixes affect the meanings of root words?

STEP 1: PREPARATION

Organize Materials

- Multimodal text sets about setting goals and making a plan
- *Working with Words Weekly Plan* reproducible (copies or enlarged for display)
- Parent Letter for Working with Words Weekly Plan (copies)
- Literacy notebooks

Here are some options for organizing and differentiating the instructional setting:

- **Small-Group Instruction**
    - Team Wins Chart
    - Read-aloud about topic goals and creating a plan
    - *Working with Words Weekly Plan* reproducible
- **Parents or Tutors**
    - Parent Letter for Working with Words Weekly Plan
- **Independent Work**
    - *Working with Words Weekly Plan* reproducible
    - Books for independent reading
    - Literacy notebook

STEP 2: INITIATION

Team Wins Chart

Ask students to think about how teams (e.g., games, music, academics) win at what they do and what makes them great. Create a Team Wins Chart and list and discuss students' responses. Sample responses might include the following:

- Collaboration and communication (work together)
- Practice (hard work)
- Leadership (a good coach with team members listening to the coach)
- Commitment (sticking to it)
- Desire (to reach full potential)
- Goals (setting clear goals and monitoring progress)
- Focus (creating a plan)

Share how you are going to come together as a team to help continue working on becoming literacy strong.

STEP 3: DEMONSTRATION

Big Plans: Goal Setting

1. Read aloud from a text that inspires students to set goals, make a plan, and stick to it for success. Here are some suggested read-aloud texts:
   - *Big Plans* by Bob Shea. Have students repeat this line from *Big Plans*: "I GOT BIG PLANS! BIG PLANS, I SAY!" Ask the question from the book, "WHAT KIND OF PLANS?" (n.p.).
   - *Annie's Plan: Taking Charge of Schoolwork and Homework* by Jeanne Kraus
   - *Dream Big Little Pig!* by Kristi Yamaguchi
   - *Shh! We Have a Plan* by Chris Haughton

2. Discuss the theme of the book and relate it to making a plan of working on ways to strengthen reading and writing to include decoding word parts. Share how the easier it is for students to decode words, the smoother their reading will be, which will increase their fluency and ultimately bring deeper meaning to what is being read.

3. Brainstorm a list of reading and writing goals that students hope to accomplish over the summer. List strategies and techniques supporting those goals that could be included in a summer weekly plan.

4. Complete the *Working with Words Weekly Plan* reproducible (Figure 4.2) to design a structure of techniques that students can follow each day. This plan allows students to practice reading and writing words from text or an assigned word list to strengthen their decoding skills and improve their confidence as readers.

STEP 4: COLLABORATION

Conversational Coaching

Engage in conversational coaching by asking students to discuss the following question with diverse partners:

- How will having a weekly word work plan help you?
- What is decoding, and what does it allow you to do?

STEP 5: APPLICATION

Word Work Goals

1. Have each student complete the daily technique from the *Working with Words Weekly Plan* reproducible each day. Have students think about how the specific technique is helping them accomplish their word work goals.
2. Make copies of the *Parent Letter for Working with Words Weekly Plan* reproducible (Figure 4.3) and send one home with each student as an at-home application activity for continued practice, along with a list of appropriate words for the student to practice decoding and a suggested summer reading list of books. Also, include one copy of each of these reproducibles, which are discussed in the parent letter:
   - Where Is Short Vowel? from the "Vowel Changers" lesson in Chapter 1
   - If/Then Word Family Chart from the "Vowel Changers" lesson in Chapter 1
   - Vowel Transformers T-Chart from the "Vowel Transformers" lesson in Chapter 2
   - Divide and Conquer Prefix Venn Diagram from the "Fixated on Prefixes: Divide and Conquer" lesson in Chapter 3

STEP 6: REFLECTION

Written Response

In their literacy notebooks, have students write their summer goals for becoming stronger readers and writers. Have them record on their weekly word work plans what they did today to work toward meeting their goals and how it supported and strengthened their reading and writing.

ADAPTATION/EXTENSION

- Revisit this section in the following lessons for a variety of examples for decoding:
  - "Vowel Changers" in Chapter 1
  - "Vowel Transformers" in Chapter 2

- "Fixated on Prefixes: Divide and Conquer" in Chapter 3
- *English Language Learner Suggestion:* Revisit the Trifold Flap Prefix Book from Chapter 3. Have students work with a model English student to review common prefix words and their meanings. Remind them to explain the definition of each preview.
- *Struggling Reader Suggestion:* Create a Working with Words practice bin. Include a small mirror for isolating sounds, modeling clay for blending and segmenting sounds, word cards for reading and writing words, and a task chart for keeping track of the Working with Words Weekly Plan. Conference with students at the beginning of the week to determine tasks and goals for each day of the week. Have students work with a partner who is not struggling with the given tasks to check for understanding throughout the week. Revisit goal tasks at the end of week to modify for the following week's plan.

EVALUATION

"I Can . . ." Statements

- I can follow a weekly word work plan to practice decoding words.
- I can decode words following basic patterns by breaking the words into syllables and using the vowels to help identify the number of syllables in a word.
- I can identify root words and common prefixes in words.
- I can give a definition of a word based on analyzing the prefix for meaning.

BEHAVIOR INDICATORS

- Follows a weekly plan to practice decoding words.
- Decodes words following basic patterns by breaking the words into syllables.
- Decodes regularly spelled words with short and long vowels.
- Determines the meaning of a newly formed word when a common prefix is added to a root word.

FIGURE 4.2
Working with Words Weekly Plan

Monday	**Sing the "Where Is Short Vowel?" song** (page 25): Focus on a different short or long vowel, create the new words that would align with the chosen vowel, and complete the verse. Record in a notebook or on a chart and keep adding to it each week for review and for a completed vowel song book at the end of summer.
Tuesday	**Whip words and create the If/Then Word Family Chart** (page 26): Capture a few word family words and use shaving cream, whipped cream, or sand to make and break words in the chosen word family. Complete the If/Then Word Family Chart by using this week's selected words. Add to the chart each week with new "if/then" words.
Wednesday	**Transform and sort words by using the Vowel Transformers T-Chart** (page 102): Search through reading materials to find words that can transform from the consonant-vowel-consonant pattern to the pattern of consonant-vowel-consonant + silent *e*. Complete the chart and keep adding to it each week.
Thursday	**Divide and Conquer Prefix Venn Diagram** (page 180): Use the Venn diagram to analyze words for their parts, such as prefixes and root words: • What is the prefix, and what does it mean? • What is the root word? • How many syllables are in the word? How do you know? • What parts do the two words have in common? • What parts do the two words not have in common? • What does the prefix _____ do when added to the start of the word?
Friday	**Play online word games:** Use a different online resource to practice decoding words, focusing on vowels and prefixes. Here are some free online resources: • Diane Werner's "Short Vowel Sounds" (www.youtube.com/ watch?t=19&v=-8s1y3IFVO4) • Learning Games for Kids (www.learninggamesforkids.com) • ReadWriteThink.org's "Word Family Sort" (www.readwritethink.org/classroom-resources/student-interactives/word-family-sort-30052.html)

Source: Literacy Strong All Year Long: Powerful Lessons for Grades K–2 by Valerie Ellery, Lori Oczkus, and Timothy V. Rasinski. © 2020 ASCD. Readers may duplicate this figure for noncommercial use within their school.

FIGURE 4.3
Parent Letter for Working with Words Weekly Plan

Dear Parents and Caregivers,

Happy summer reading! As you read with your child over the summer, here are some helpful ways to enrich his or her ability to decode words to help bring meaning to the reading on a weekly basis. This plan allows your child to continue to apply the decoding skills learned this year in class. Each week, you can add a different list of words, books, and poems to make sure your child maintains the decoding skills and enjoys reading every day.

Working with Words Weekly Plan
Monday: Sing the "Where Is Short Vowel?" song (to the tune of "Are You Sleeping?"). Focusing on a different short or long vowel, create the new words that would align with the chosen vowel, and complete the verse. Record in a notebook or on a chart and keep adding to it each week for review and for a completed vowel song book at the end of the summer.

Tuesday: Capture a few word-family words and use shaving cream, whipped cream, or sand to make and break words in the chosen word family. Complete the If/Then Word Family Chart by using this week's selected words. Add to the chart each week with new "if/then" words.

Wednesday: Search through reading materials to find words that can transform from the consonant-vowel-consonant pattern to the pattern of consonant-vowel-consonant + silent *e*. Complete the Vowel Transformers T-Chart and keep adding to it each week.

Thursday: Use the Divide and Conquer Prefix Venn Diagram to analyze words for their parts, such as prefixes and root words:
- What is the prefix, and what does it mean?
- What is the root word?
- How many syllables are in the word? How do you know?
- What parts do the two words have in common?
- What parts do the two words not have in common?
- What does the prefix ___ do when added to a word?

Friday: Play online word work games to practice decoding words, focusing on vowels and prefixes. Here are some free websites:
- Diane Werner's "Short Vowel Sounds" (www.youtube.com/watch?t=19&v=-8s1y3lFVO4)
- Learning Games for Kids (www.learninggamesforkids.com)
- ReadWriteThink.org's "Word Family Sort" (www.readwritethink.org/classroom-resources/ student-interactives /word-family-sort-30052.html)

Sincerely,

[Your child's teacher]

Attached are copies of the following materials for your family's use:
    Where Is Short Vowel?
    If/Then Family Word Chart
    Vowel Transformers T-Chart
    Divide and Conquer Prefix Venn Diagram

Source: Literacy Strong All Year Long: Powerful Lessons for Grades K–2 by Valerie Ellery, Lori Oczkus, and Timothy V. Rasinski. © 2020 ASCD. Readers may duplicate this figure for noncommercial use within their school.

LESSON 4. FLUENCY: PHRASING

Title WEEKLY SUMMER POETRY READING

Trailer Practice, practice, practice. Rehearsing and performing poetry is an excellent way to develop students' reading fluency. A poem can easily be chunked into sentences and phrases that reflect the rhythm of the poem. When students are given opportunities to perform poetry, they have an authentic purpose for developing fluency and reading in meaningful chunks of texts.

Literacy Enhancer Fluency: Phrasing—Chunking Texts into Meaningful Units

Key Academic Vocabulary Vocabulary from a previous lesson is marked with an asterisk (*).

Comma*: A punctuation mark used within a sentence to set off meaningful phrases or other meaningful chunks of text

Period*: A punctuation mark used at the end of a sentence that is a statement

Phrase*: A sequence of two or more words that form a meaningful unit, often preceded and followed by a brief pause when read orally

Poem*: A text in verse form that is often characterized by alliteration, assonance, rhyme, or rhythm to express meaning

Punctuation*: Marks in writing or printing that are used to separate meaningful elements and make the meaning of the text clear

Sentence*: A unit of one or more words that expresses an independent statement, question, request, command, or exclamation

Learning Objectives

- Provide opportunities to read, rehearse, and perform poetry for young children on a weekly basis.
- Identify and read interesting phrases and sentences in poems that students rehearse and perform.

Essential Questions

- What is a poem?
- What are common features found in poetry for young children?
- Why is it important to rehearse and read poems in phrases and sentences?

STEP 1: PREPARATION

Organize Materials

- Hard and electronic copies of approximately 12 poems that are age appropriate
- Chart paper (if working directly with students)
- Computer application for making audio podcasts (e.g., Audacity: www.audacity.com)
- Computer with internet access for the teacher
- Computer with internet access for students
- Literacy notebooks

Here are some options for organizing and differentiating the instructional setting:

- **Small-Group Instruction**
  - Poetry read-aloud modeling phrasing and expressive voice
  - Conversational coaching: Reflecting on rereading
- **Parents or Tutors**
  - Recording a Poem: Podcasting
  - Electronic portfolio of recordings of fluent reading
- **Independent Work**
  - Poetry rehearsal and recording
  - Literacy notebook: Response to independent poetry reading performance

STEP 2: INITIATION

Record a Poem: Podcasting

Use the poem below and then choose one poem for each week of summer vacation. Make a copy of each poem for each student.

Summertime Fun

Summer's here and it's time to play

Outdoors and indoors all through the day

Summer's here but allow me to plead

Summer is also a great time to read

Summertime Fun (with sentence and phrase boundaries added)

Summer's here / and it's time to play //

Outdoors and indoors / all through the day. //

Summer's here, / but allow me to plead. //

Summer is also / a great time to read. //

Create a podcast for each poem chosen. In your podcast, you should do the following:

1. Provide a brief introduction to the poem.
2. Read the poem in an expressive voice, emphasizing reading in appropriate phrases and with good expression. Record your reading as a podcast.
3. Discuss how you read the poem, again emphasizing appropriate phrasing and expression. Also, discuss the nature and content of the poem.
4. Direct students to practice the poem two or three times per day for three days. The practice can be done alone, with a family member, or while listening to the teacher's reading of the poem (see #2 above). On the fourth day, students should record their reading of the poem using a podcast application. The recorded version of each student's reading should be e-mailed to you so you have a record of each reading and the opportunity to evaluate each student's fluency and phrasing.

STEP 3: DEMONSTRATION

Weekly Listen and Read

- Thematically group the poems chosen for summer poetry reading (e.g., summer sports, summer holidays, places to visit).
- Each week, share with students the week's poem and your fluent reading of it. Provide instructions for each student to rehearse and record a personalized reading of the poem over several days.
- Instruct students to listen to your reading of the poem while simultaneously reading along.

STEP 4: COLLABORATION

Rehearse with Others and Conversational Coaching

After listening to the modeled oral rendering and discussion of the weekly poem, have students continue to rehearse the poem for several days. The rehearsals can include reading alone, with family or friends, or while listening to your modeled reading of the poem. Have students engage in the following conversational coaching with you or a parent to provide reflective feedback on the rehearsed readings:

- Compare your poetry readings and discuss how each rereading affected your fluency.
- "After listening to the modeled reading, I noticed _____."
- "Did my reading sound seamless? How was my pacing? How was my phrasing?"
- "Did I use appropriate expression that reflected the meaning?"

- "After listening to the modeled reading, I noticed _____."
- "Did my reading sound seamless? How was my pacing?"

Optional: You can encourage students to do more reading if you provide 12 (or more) poems for them to read over the summer—or you can challenge students to read more complex poetry or other genres. Providing online background and support for the reading will allow students to become successful with even more challenging pieces.

STEP 5: APPLICATION

Student Recordings

After rehearsing the poem over several days, ask each student to record a fluent reading of the poem as a podcast. The recording will serve as a performance of the poem and can be shared for inclusion in an electronic portfolio of students' summer reading. You or your students can harvest interesting words from the poems to use for directed word study.

STEP 6: REFLECTION

Oral Response

After recording the weekly poem, each student should also include a brief oral response to the reading. The oral response should focus on aspects of the reading that the student felt were done well and aspects that may need improvement.

Optional: Students can write, rehearse, and record their own poetry.

Written Response

In addition to a brief oral response after every weekly performance, ask students to respond in writing in their literacy notebooks. The written response may include the student's completion of the following sentence stems:

- I liked or disliked this week's poem because _____.
- I practiced reading the poem _____ times.
- The best part of my reading of the poem was _____.
- The part of poetry reading that I need to work on most is _____.

ADAPTATION/EXTENSION

- Revisit this section in the following lessons for a variety of examples for phrasing:
    - "Phrase Scavenger Hunt" in Chapter 1
    - "Performing Poetry" in Chapter 2
    - "Text Road Signs: Marking Phrase Boundaries" in Chapter 3

- *English Language Learner Suggestion:* Identify and display on a word chart difficult words from the poems that students read. Practice these words with students regularly, remind students of their meaning, and encourage students to use these words in their own oral and written language.
- *Struggling Reader Suggestion:* Engage in additional repeated readings of the poems with your struggling readers. Continue to display and read poems that were introduced in previous days. Be sure to remind students to track the words in each poem visually even if they have the poem memorized. It is only reading if the reader sees the words while reciting them.

EVALUATION

"I Can . . ." Statements

- I can read this week's poem with good expression and phrasing.
- I can understand the content of this week's poem.
- I can explain what I need to focus on when rehearsing my poem.
- I can describe what I need to do when performing and recording my assigned poem.
- I can share features of what makes for a good reading of a poem.

BEHAVIOR INDICATORS

- Independently engages in rehearsal of a weekly poem.
- Records and performs a weekly poem with good fluency and phrasing.
- Identifies common features found in poetry for children.
- Chooses personally interesting words from the weekly poem.
- Provides positive and constructive evaluation and feedback when listening to the podcast recorded reading of the weekly poem.

LESSON 5. COMPREHENSION: CRAFT AND STRUCTURE—PREVIEWING

Title TEXT TRIP TRAVELS

Trailer Driving adventures often include a cell phone with a GPS to guide the route; therefore, students witness adults using maps and directions in their everyday lives. When we teach students to "drive" through wonderful fiction and nonfiction using fiction or nonfiction maps, their comprehension improves. Students move through fiction and nonfiction with their very own "cars" and maps to navigate the text trip to better reading.

Literacy Enhancer Comprehension: Craft and Structure—Previewing and Text Features: Maps

Key Academic Vocabulary Vocabulary from a previous lesson is marked with an asterisk (*).

Author*: The person who wrote the book

Back cover*: The back of a book that often contains information about the book and its author and illustrator

Book cover*: The front of a book that contains the title, author, and illustrator

Character*: The who in the story

Fiction*: The genre that includes stories that are make-believe; may also include poetry

Illustrator*: The person who drew the pictures or illustrations that go with the book's content

Informational text*: A type of nonfiction text

Nonfiction*: The genre that includes factual or real information that is portrayed to answer, explain, or describe

Photographer*: The person who took the photos that go with the book's content

Predict*: To use information from a text to infer what the text will be about or what a reader might learn from it

Problem*: The challenge that the character(s) face and need to overcome

Setting*: Where the story takes place

Story sequence mapping*: Organization of fiction stories around what happens at the beginning of the story, in the middle, and at the end

Text features*: Parts of the text that support the reader in navigating through key characteristics of a text for locating and accessing meaning from the text (e.g., title, headings, photographs, bold words, maps)

***Text walk**:** A preview of a fiction or nonfiction text to see what it is about and gather clues to determine what text features the author has included

***Title**:** The name of the book, which usually tells what it is about or gives clues to the content

Learning Objectives

- Recognize and identify fiction and nonfiction texts.
- Identify the title, author, and illustrator on a book cover.
- Use cover information to predict what the text is about.
- Recognize that fiction texts have a beginning, a middle, an end, a setting, characters, main events, a problem, and a solution.
- Recognize that nonfiction texts have special, distinguishing text features, including headings, photographs, diagrams, maps, graphs, and sometimes an index and glossary.
- Choose a fiction or nonfiction map to use when previewing a text and during the reading process.

Essential Questions

- How can you use a fiction map to preview a text and keep track of events in a story?
- How can you use a nonfiction map to preview a text and keep track of what you are learning when reading a nonfiction text?

STEP 1: PREPARATION

Organize Materials

- Toy car
- Fiction or nonfiction text
- *Fiction Map* reproducible or *Nonfiction Map* reproducible (copies or enlarged for display; available in "We're Going on a Text Trip" lesson, Chapter 3)
- *Nonfiction Road Signs* reproducible (copies or enlarged for display; available in "We're Going on a Text Trip" lesson, Chapter 3)
- Parent Letter for Fiction Texts (copies)
- Parent Letter for Nonfiction Texts (copies)
- Literacy notebooks

Here are some options for organizing and differentiating the instructional setting:

- **Small-Group Instruction**
    - Small-group guided reading
    - Text Trip Travels
- **Parents or Tutors**
    - Parent Letter for Fiction Texts
    - Parent Letter for Nonfiction Texts
- **Independent Work**
    - *In class:* Students fill in the *Fiction Map* reproducible with partners or independently; students work with partners as they drive a toy car over a text to identify the title, author, and illustrator.
    - *At home:* Students read a variety of fiction and nonfiction texts.

STEP 2: INITIATION

Sneak and See 1-2-3

Display either a fiction or nonfiction text. Use the Sneak and See 1-2-3 strategy (see Chapter 1) as students look for the title, author, and illustrator. Explain to students that before good readers dive into a book, they consider the genre. Ask students how they can tell whether a book is fiction or nonfiction. Ask them if they have ever taken a trip where they've needed a map, and talk about how people use maps to drive or walk to where they want to go. Share that students will use a text map to help them "drive" through a book.

STEP 3: DEMONSTRATION

Map Talking: Talking the Text

1. Invite students to think about how an author organizes a text. Display the *Fiction Map* reproducible or the *Nonfiction Map* reproducible, depending on your selected text. Tell students that the map is like a road map in that it helps the reader follow what is going on in the text.
2. Ask students to begin to predict what the text is about from the cover and move into specific text features.
3. *For fiction:* Model by sharing some of your predictions about the characters, setting, problem, or main events.
4. *For nonfiction:* Model how to predict what the text will cover by using text features, such as the table of contents, bold words, pictures, visuals, captions, and maps.

5. *Optional:* Drive the toy car across the text as you study it to guide students in making predictions. Write their answers in the corresponding reproducible.

STEP 4: COLLABORATION

Conversational Coaching

- Before reading, invite students to select a page to predict what they think will happen (fiction) or what they will learn (nonfiction). Encourage students to say, "I predict _____, because _____."
- During reading, encourage students to read the text silently or in pairs, or conduct a shared reading followed by an independent reading. When coaching, rotate to each reading student and encourage "whisper reading" a few sentences.
- Praise and coach the student reader as he figures out new words. Say, "I like the way you (e.g., looked at the beginning sound, checked the picture, sounded it out, read on)."
- *For fiction:* Ask questions and prompt the use of the language from the fiction map. Select one question to ask each student: Who are the characters? Where is the setting? What is the problem? What happened so far? What do you think will happen next?
- *For nonfiction:* Ask questions and prompt the use of the language from the nonfiction map. Select one or two questions to ask each student as you coach: What did you learn at the beginning? Why do you think the author chose this heading? Does the photograph go with the words? How? Can you find a heading, bold word, illustration, or map? What are you learning?
- After students finish reading, fill out the fiction or nonfiction map either as a group or individually. For each portion of the map, ask partners to discuss first, then group share, and then sketch the answers on the map.

STEP 5: APPLICATION

Partner Map Retellings

Invite students to share their favorite parts of the text and the reasons for their thinking. Ask students to reflect on how the map helps guide their reading. Have them turn away from the map and share what they learned or remember from the text with a partner. Make copies of the *Parent Letter for Fiction Texts* and *Parent Letter for Nonfiction Texts* reproducibles (Figure 4.4 and Figure 4.5, respectively) and send one of each home with each student, along with a fiction text and a nonfiction text, to provide guidance to parents for improving their children's reading comprehension.

STEP 6: REFLECTION

Written Response

Invite students to sketch and write about what they learned from the reading in their literacy notebooks. Encourage students to add details to their drawings and their writing.

ADAPTATION/EXTENSION

- Revisit this section in the following lessons for a variety of examples for previewing text:
    - "Sneak and See 1-2-3" in Chapter 1
    - "Is It Make-Believe or Real?" in Chapter 2
    - "We're Going on a Text Trip" in Chapter 3
- *English Language Learner Suggestion*: Choose a fiction or nonfiction text to use to reinforce predicting and previewing. Encourage students to use the language of predicting by providing a frame such as "I predict _____ because _____." Use the same language throughout the reading and encourage students to share with partners.
- *Struggling Reader Suggestion*: Videotape students sharing predicting suggestions and how-tos for their peers. One student may demonstrate how to preview using the cover or a picture preview. Another student may explain how to predict using captions or headings in nonfiction. Use a pretend microphone and encourage students to "ham it up!" Post on the class website (with permission) or show another class.

EVALUATION

"I Can . . ." Statements

- I can identify whether a text is fiction or nonfiction by studying the cover and flipping through the text.
- I can identify the title, author, and illustrator on the cover.
- I can use cover information to predict what the text will be about.
- I can identify fiction map elements (e.g., characters, setting, problem, main events).
- I can identify nonfiction text features (e.g., table of contents, headings, illustrations, maps, diagrams, glossary, index) and explain how using these features helps me understand the text better.
- I can use a fiction or nonfiction map to help me before, during, and after reading.

BEHAVIOR INDICATORS

- Identifies whether a text is fiction or nonfiction by studying the cover and a few pages of the text.
- Identifies the title, author, and illustrator on the cover of a text.
- Uses the information on the cover to make logical predictions about the text.
- Identifies fiction elements (e.g., characters, setting, problem, main events).
- Identifies nonfiction text features (e.g., table of contents, headings, illustrations, maps, diagrams, glossary, index) and explains how they aid in comprehending the text.

FIGURE 4.4
Parent Letter for Fiction Texts

Dear Parents and Families,

Your child is working on learning to better read and comprehend stories. Enclosed you will find a fiction book to read together. Be sure to make this activity fun as you enjoy a book with your child!

Directions for Reading a Fiction Book with Your Child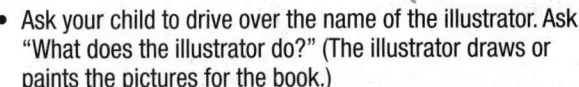

1. **Preview the fiction book with your child before reading:** Tell your child that you are going to preview the text together.

- Using a small toy car, ask your child to drive the car across the cover of the book. Find the title. Read it and study the art on the cover. Discuss what the book might be about.
- Discuss who the characters might be. Ask, "Where do you think the story will take place?"
- Ask your child to drive the car over the name of the author on the cover. Ask, "What does the author do?" (The author writes the book.)
- Ask your child to drive over the name of the illustrator. Ask, "What does the illustrator do?" (The illustrator draws or paints the pictures for the book.)
- Open the book and take a peek at some of the illustrations inside without reading the text yet.
- Now, what do the two of you think the book is about? Invite your child to use this language as you share your ideas: "I think this book might be about _____ because _____."

2. **Read the book with your child:** Choose any of the following ways to read and enjoy the text. Put the car down during reading or use it to follow along under the words on the pages.

- You read the book aloud first, and then your child reads it aloud.
- Take turns reading one page or even one part at a time.
- Echo read. You read a line, and your child repeats it.

3. **Help your child figure out words:** As your child reads, praise and support his or her efforts. When your child comes to an unfamiliar word, try any or all the following prompts. First, quietly wait a few seconds to see if your child can figure it without help. If not, then try these prompts:

- "Does it sound right?"
- "Does it look right?"
- "What would make sense here?"
- "What sound does the word start with?"
- "What sound does the word end with?"
- "Do you see any little parts inside the word that you know?"
- "Check the picture."
- "Read the sentence again."
- "Read on to see if the next sentences help you."

4. **Retell and discuss the book:** After reading, drive the car across the pages of the book and ask your child to tell you what the pages are about. Refer to the illustrations and words to help your child recall the events in the book. Talk about the following:

- "Who are the characters in the story?" (animals? people?)
- "What are their names?"
- "Where does the story take place?"
- "Is there a problem in the story?"
- "What is the problem?"
- "What happened in the beginning?"
- "What happened in the middle?"
- "What happened at the end?"
- "What was your favorite part, and why?"

You may want to use this format as you read other fiction books with your child, too. Be sure to make it enjoyable and more of a discussion than a test!

Sincerely,

[Your child's teacher]

Source: Literacy Strong All Year Long: Powerful Lessons for Grades K–2 by Valerie Ellery, Lori Oczkus, and Timothy V. Rasinski. © 2020 ASCD. Readers may duplicate this figure for noncommercial use within their school.

FIGURE 4.5
Parent Letter for Nonfiction Texts

Dear Parents and Families,

Your child is working on learning to better read and comprehend nonfiction texts. Enclosed you will find a nonfiction book to read together. Be sure to make this activity fun as you enjoy a book with your child!

Directions for Reading a Nonfiction Book with Your Child

1. **Preview the nonfiction book with your child before reading:** Tell your child that you are going to preview the text together.

- Using a small toy car (optional), ask your child to drive the car across the cover of the book. Find the title. Read it and study the art on the cover. Discuss what the book might be about. Ask, "What do you think we might learn from this book?"
- Ask your child to drive over the name of the author on the cover. "What does the author do?" (The author writes the book.)
- Ask your child to drive over the name of the illustrator or photographer if there is one listed on the cover. Ask, "What does the illustrator or photographer do?" (The illustrator draws or paints the pictures for the book. The photographer takes the photographs for the book.)
- Open the book and take a peek at some of the illustrations inside without reading the text yet.
- Now, what do the two of you think the book is about? Invite your child to use this language as you share your ideas: "I think this book might be about _____ because _____."
- Continue driving through the book. Be sure to stop and look at any of the following nonfiction text features to help you and your child preview the book and discuss what the book is about: the table of contents, headings, and bold words. Continue to discuss what you think you will learn from the book.

2. **Read the text with your child:** Choose any of the following ways to read and enjoy the book. Put the car down during reading or use it to follow along under the words on the pages.

- You read the book aloud first, and then your child reads it aloud.
- Take turns reading one page or even one part at a time.
- Echo read. You read a line, and your child repeats the line.

3. **Help your child figure out words:** As your child reads, praise and support his or her efforts. When your child comes to a word that is unfamiliar, try any or all of the following prompts. First, quietly wait a few seconds to see if your child can figure it out without help. If not, then try these prompts:

- "Does it sound right?"
- "Does it look right?"
- "What would make sense here?"
- "What sound does the word start with?"
- "What sound does the word end with?"
- "Do you see any little parts inside the word that you know?"
- "Check the picture."
- "Read the sentence again."
- "Read on to see if the next sentences help you."

4. **Retell and discuss the book:** After reading, drive the car across the pages of the book and ask your child to tell you what the pages are about. Refer to the illustrations and words to help your child recall the events in the book. Talk about the following:

- "What is the beginning about?"
- "What did the author teach us about in the middle?"
- "What did we learn at the end?"
- "What was your favorite thing that you learned, and why?"

You may want to use this format as you read other nonfiction books with your child, too. Be sure to make it enjoyable and more of a discussion than a test!

Sincerely,

[Your child's teacher]

Source: Literacy Strong All Year Long: Powerful Lessons for Grades K–2 by Valerie Ellery, Lori Oczkus, and Timothy V. Rasinski. © 2020 ASCD. Readers may duplicate this figure for noncommercial use within their school.

LESSON 6. COMPREHENSION: KEY IDEAS AND DETAILS—DETERMINING IMPORTANCE AND SUMMARIZING

Title HOME RUN WITH DETAILS

Trailer Home run! What a great feeling it is to knock a ball out of the park! But sometimes you swing and miss and don't get a full connection. How can you hit a homerun? The answer can be found in the concept of a diamond—a baseball diamond, that is. Readers practice retelling, determining importance, and summarizing to get a deeper meaning as they hit a home run with their reading!

Literacy Enhancer Comprehension: Key Ideas and Details: Determining Importance and Summarizing—Retelling Key Details, and Main Topic

Key Academic Vocabulary Vocabulary from a previous lesson is marked with an asterisk (*).

Essential*: Necessary for the meaning and purpose

Gist*: The main point or overall part of a text

Information*: Gathered knowledge; facts or ideas

Key detail*: An important feature, fact, or item that supports the overall meaning

Main topic*: The gist or general thought of the whole concept

Retelling*: Recalling in a sequential order what is happening in a text

Sequencing*: Placing information in a certain order

Sift*: To filter and examine what is most important

Story elements*: Parts (ingredients) of a story: characters, setting, events, plot, problem, and solution

Learning Objectives

- Identify the story elements of characters, setting, and main events in a story.
- Sequence story elements through a retell of what is read.
- Identify interesting and informational facts from text.
- Determine what details are essential for overall meaning.
- Determine key details about the topic being studied.
- Identify the main topic of the content being studied.

Essential Questions

- What is a story element?
- What makes a good retell?
- Why is it important to be able to retell a text?

- What is an essential detail?
- How can you tell the difference between an important fact and an interesting detail?
- What is a key detail?
- How do you determine the main topic?
- What is the relationship between key details and the main topic?

STEP 1: PREPARATION

Organize Materials

- Baseball equipment
- Any materials for this strategy strand from Chapters 1–3
- Multimodal text set for the topic of study
- *Home Run Diamante Poem* reproducible (copies or enlarged for display)
- Literacy notebooks

Here are some options for organizing and differentiating the instructional setting:

- **Small-Group Instruction**
    - Read-aloud modeling how to locate what is essential in text
    - Conversational coaching: The relationship between details and the main topic
- **Parents or Tutors**
    - Summertime Pastime
    - *Home Run Diamante Poem* reproducible
- **Independent Work**
    - Literacy notebook: Independent creation of a diamante poem and a summary of a text

STEP 2: INITIATION

Summertime Pastime

Make a class list of things connected with summertime (e.g., swimming, reading for pleasure, playing baseball). Share how summer is not meant for readers to have a summer slide unless they are referring to baseball, a jungle gym, or a waterslide. (If readers have a summer slide, it means that they have lost reading achievement previously gained.) Share that today's lesson will have a summer baseball twist, with a review of the concepts they know about retelling, sifting, details, and being able to get the gist of a text.

STEP 3: DEMONSTRATION

Sifting Details

- Review that a retell is in sequential order, like procedural steps in a recipe. Compare sequential order with running bases around a baseball diamond (first, second, third, and ultimately home plate).
- Remind students about sifting details and how to determine if something in a text is just interesting information or actually important information. Use baseball terminology (e.g., *ball, base, bat, fans, hot dog, player, stands*) to determine what is important and necessary to play a ball game and what is just there to add "flavor" and interest to the game.
- Review how to use your fingers to point out the strategies in playing baseball (e.g., 1 = hitting, 2 = running the bases, 3 = fielding the ball), and then snap your fingers and say, "I get the gist! It's about baseball."

STEP 4: COLLABORATION

Conversational Coaching

Read aloud Jack Norworth's classic poem "Take Me Out to the Ball Game" and engage in conversational coaching by asking students to discuss the following questions with diverse partners:

- What essential information helps make the author's point?
- How do you determine what is interesting information compared with what is important information?
- What information can you represent on at least three fingers?
- What is happening with that information when you snap your fingers?
- What is the relationship between the details (i.e., fingers) and the main topic (i.e., snap)?

STEP 5: APPLICATION

Diamante Poems

Using the *Home Run Diamante Poem* reproducible (Figure 4.6), have students work in groups or individually to create a diamante poem that highlights details related to the main topic of baseball.

STEP 6: REFLECTION

Written Response

In their literacy notebooks, have students independently create a diamante poem based on a text that they recently heard read aloud or that they independently read. Make sure they remember to determine what's important as they choose words for their poem. Based on the words in their poem, students can then create a summary of the text.

ADAPTATION/EXTENSION

- Revisit this section in the following lessons for a variety of examples for determining importance and summarizing:
    - "Retell Recipe" in Chapter 1
    - "Sifting Details" in Chapter 2
    - "Finding the Topic: It's a Snap" in Chapter 3

- *English Language Learner Suggestion:* Create word choices with images for the Home Run Diamante Poem and have the students select the correct word or image to complete the poem. Here's an example:

    Ice Cream

    delicious, icy

    scoop, lick, eat

    chocolate, strawberry, vanilla, banana

    mix, fix, taste, devour

    yummy, gone

    Summer

- *Struggling Reader Suggestion:* Create task cards for step-by-step format of writing a Diamante Poem. Mix the above Sample "Ice Cream" Home Run Diamante Poem with images and have students place them in order and match to each of the step-by-step format task cards. Example:
    - Format Task Card = *poem*
    - Noun = *ice cream*
    - Adjective = *delicious, icy*
    - Verb = *scoop, lick, eat*

- Related noun = *chocolate, strawberry, vanilla, banana*
- Verb = *mix, fix, taste, devour*
- Adjective = *yummy, gone*
- Noun = *summer*

EVALUATION

"I Can . . ." Statements

- I can identify characters and the setting in a story.
- I can sequence the order of a familiar story through a retell.
- I can use illustrations and details in a story to describe its characters.
- I can identify key details using essential elements in a text.
- I can explain what key details are instead of just interesting information in a text.
- I can answer questions using specific details in a text.
- I can determine three key details about a specific topic.
- I can identify the main topic based on specific details in a text.

BEHAVIOR INDICATORS

- Identifies the characters, setting, and main events in a story.
- Sequences the order of a story through a retell.
- Identifies key details in a text.
- Determines what is just interesting in a text and what is actually important.
- Asks and answers questions about key details in a text: who, what, when, where, and why.
- Uses supporting details in a text to clearly explain the main topic.
- Uses the illustrations and details in a text to describe its key ideas.

FIGURE 4.6
Home Run Diamante Poem

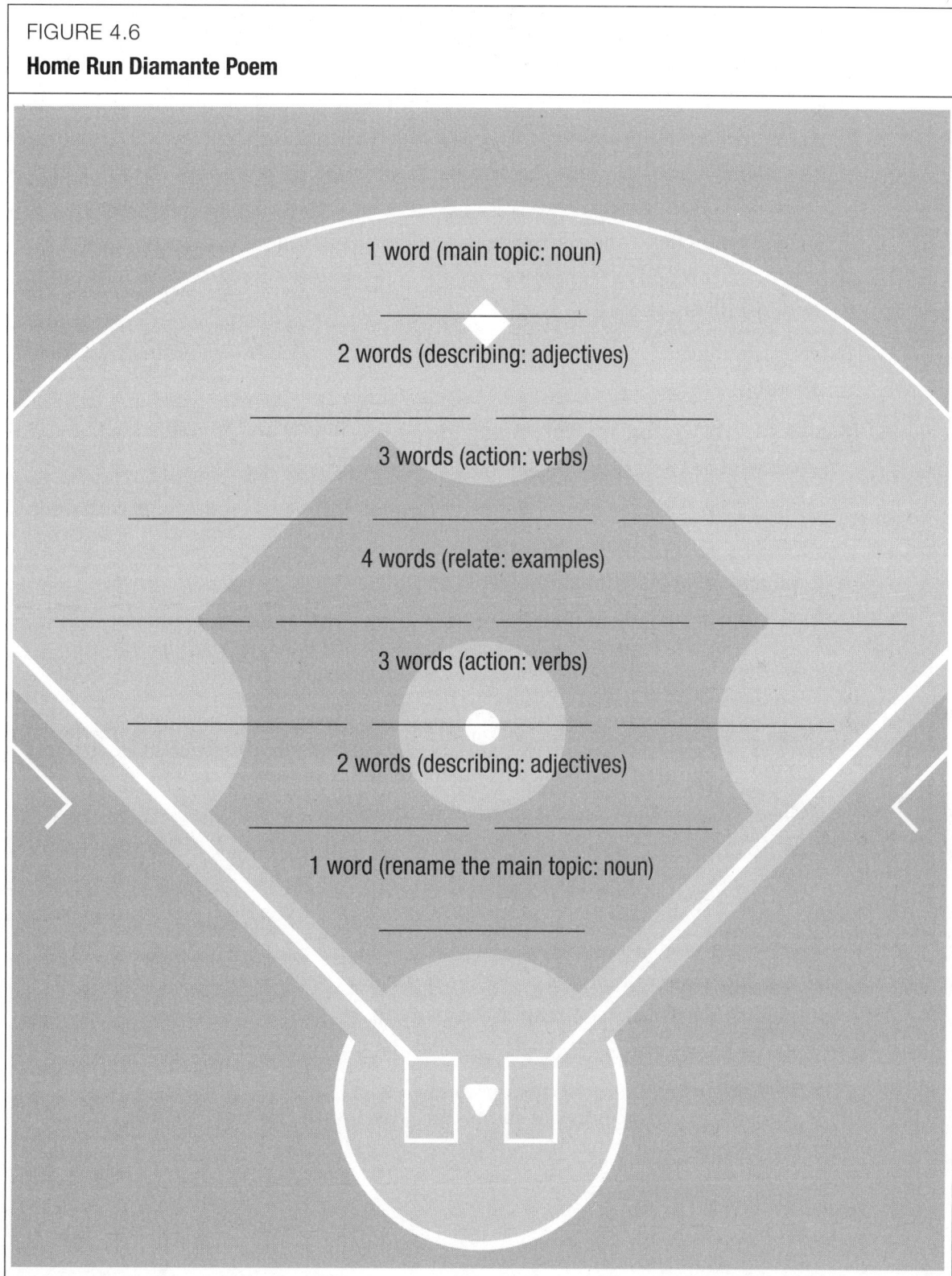

Source: Literacy Strong All Year Long: Powerful Lessons for Grades K–2 by Valerie Ellery, Lori Oczkus, and Timothy V. Rasinski. © 2020 ASCD. Readers may duplicate this figure for noncommercial use within their school.

LESSON 7. COMPREHENSION: KEY IDEAS AND DETAILS—QUESTIONING FOR CLOSE READING

Title MY QUESTION, YOUR QUESTION!

Trailer Albert Einstein said, "The important thing is not to stop questioning." Children enter school brimming with questions. The trick is to harness and encourage this natural curiosity in the classroom. Questioning plays an important role in learning to read; good readers ask questions throughout the reading experience to better comprehend and clarify ideas. Students learn to take turns reading and asking and answering relevant questions that deepen thinking, promote clarification, and inspire discussion.

Literacy Enhancer Comprehension: Key Ideas and Details—Questioning for Close Reading

Key Academic Vocabulary Vocabulary from a previous lesson is marked with an asterisk (*).

Answer clues*: General knowledge information from a text that aligns with *who, what, when, where,* or *why* questions

Character*: A person or animal in a text

How*: A question word that asks for the means, procedure, or quality of something

Question*: A sentence in interrogative form

What*: A question word that asks about the events or things that happened

When*: A question word that asks the time of day or year

Where*: A question word that asks about the place

Who*: A question word that asks about the people or animals in the text

Why*: A question word that asks for a reason

Learning Objectives

- Ask and answer questions about the text before, during, and after reading to predict, clarify, and summarize the learning.
- Ask and answer *who, what, when, where,* and *why* questions about key ideas and details in a text.
- Ask and answer wonder questions to clarify a text's key ideas, details, and vocabulary.

Essential Questions

- What are some questions about key ideas and details in a text that begin with *who, what, when, where, why,* and *how*?
- How does asking questions before, during, and after reading help the reader comprehend a text?
- How do questions help the reader clarify a text's key ideas, details, and vocabulary?

STEP 1: PREPARATION

Organize Materials

- Bag filled with different objects
- Fiction and nonfiction texts
- *Ask a Question Cards* reproducible (copies or enlarged for display)
- *My Question, Your Question Bookmark* reproducible (copies or enlarged for display)
- *Parent Letter for Questioning* reproducible
- Literacy notebooks

Here are some options for organizing and differentiating the instructional setting:

- **Small-Group Instruction**
    - 20 Wonder Questions
    - Read aloud with "The Question Word Song"
    - Ask a Question Cards
    - My Question, Your Question Bookmark
    - Conversational Coaching
    - Question Variations
    - Hold It
    - Jump on It
- **Parents or Tutors**
    - My Question, Your Question Bookmark
- **Independent Work**
    - Ask a Question Cards
    - My Question, Your Question Bookmark

STEP 2: INITIATION

20 Wonder Questions

Ask students to review the question words that they know. Hold up a bag filled with a few different objects and tell students that you want them to guess one of the objects in the bag by asking you questions about it. Students can use the question words to help them figure out what the object is. Give detailed responses to students' questions without giving away the object's identity. (*Note:* This is not a yes/no response game.) See if students can guess the object in five or fewer questions such as these:

- What color is it?
- What do you do with it?
- How big is it?
- Why do people use it?
- Where does it come from?
- How does it work?

If students have trouble asking questions, try writing questions to guide them. Also, try inserting the phrase "I wonder" in front of each question. Repeat the process as students guess the other objects in the bag. Tell students that questions also help us understand what we read.

STEP 3: DEMONSTRATION

The Question Word Song

Ask students to review question words. Display the *Ask a Question Cards* reproducible (Figure 4.7). Tell students that asking questions when they read can deepen their thinking and help them figure out ideas and words in a text that they want to know. Invite students to sing the following tune to review question words:

> **The Question Word Song**
>
> (Sing to the tune of "Bingo." Clap as you sing!)
>
> Who, what, when, where, why?
>
> Who, what, when, where, why?
>
> Who, what, when, where, why,
>
> And how makes a question!

Display or enlarge the *My Question, Your Question Bookmark* reproducible (Figure 4.8) so all students can see it. Read aloud from a fiction text. Pause every few pages to help students think of questions to ask. Fill in the reproducible as you see fit.

Repeat this lesson with a nonfiction text. Highlight text features, such as photographs and headings, to help guide students' questions.

STEP 4: COLLABORATION

Conversational Coaching

Pass out copies of the *My Question, Your Question Bookmark* reproducible and display a copy to use for modeling. Read a familiar text or introduce a new one. Pause every few pages to discuss possible questions. Have students take turns formulating a question, using the bookmark as a guide. Continue reading the entire text, pausing every few pages to model questions and to invite students to share questions. When you are finished reading the text, guide students to turn to specific pages to reread and then write questions. Guide students to question by giving them very specific directions, such as these:

- "Ask a *who* question about the character _____ on this page."
- "Ask a *when* question about this sentence."
- "Ask a *where* question about the picture on this page."
- "Ask a *why* question about what the character _____ said on this page."
- "Ask a *why* question for the reason the author _____."
- "Ask a *why* question for the reason the illustrator _____."

When finished, have partners engage in conversational coaching by quizzing each other, taking turns asking and answering questions from their *My Question, Your Question Bookmark* reproducibles.

STEP 5: APPLICATION

Question Bookmark and Card Games

- Students work independently or in pairs to fill in the questions on their *My Question, Your Question Bookmark* reproducible. Then, they take turns posing their questions to their partner.
- *Hold it:* Make a copy of the *Ask a Question Cards* reproducible for each student. Have students cut the cards apart and put them in an envelope, in a resealable plastic bag, or on a key ring to store them. Have students use the cards to play various games in pairs. As students read a text together, they should pause every few pages to take turns asking questions.
- *Jump on it:* Outside on the asphalt or concrete playground, use chalk to create eight squares, and fill in the squares to look like the *Ask a Question Cards* reproducible. (Variations include using masking tape inside on the floor or carpet or using carpet squares for each question word.) Draw a line outside the boxes,

from where a student can toss an object or jump into a box. Play games in which students actively select question words. Invite students to bring books to use as they ask and answer questions about the text. Here are some variations:
  - A student tosses a beanbag or bean-stuffed animal into one of the squares and asks a question about the text, using the question word in that square.
  - A student chooses a question to ask and jumps on that question word square. The teacher or another student poses the question to the jumper.
  - The teacher or a student provides the answer to a question, and another student jumps to the corresponding question word square.
  - A student jumps onto a square and bounces a ball on it while asking a question that starts with that question word. The student who answers the question may also bounce the ball standing on the starting line or move into that question word square.
- Make copies of the *Parent Letter for Questioning* reproducible (Figure 4.9) and send one home with each student, along with a copy of the *My Question, Your Question Bookmark* reproducible and a selection of books, so parents can help their children better comprehend texts and clarify ideas encountered in them.

STEP 6: REFLECTION

Written Response

Encourage students to write questions in their literacy notebooks before, during, and after reading a text. Use the *My Question, Your Question Bookmark* reproducible as a guide. Ask students to put a star next to their favorite question and share it with the class. Post questions on a bulletin board in the classroom. Discuss what makes a strong question.

ADAPTATION/EXTENSION

- Revisit this section in the following lessons for a variety of examples for questioning:
  - "The Who, What, Where, When Show" in Chapter 1
  - "The Question Game" in Chapter 2
  - "Question the Character" in Chapter 3
- *English Language Learner Suggestion*: Cut apart the *Ask a Question Cards* reproducible and give each student or group one question to focus on. Read a page or two of text aloud and pause to ask students to pose a question verbally for

the class to answer. Guide students with comments that scaffold and direct their efforts as they reread the text to formulate questions.

- *Struggling Reader Suggestion*: Create sets of cards from the *Ask a Question Cards* reproducible and distribute a set to each pair of students. Guide partners as they read a text and pause every page or two to take turns asking questions. Partners may hold the cards in their hands like playing cards or put the cards in a pile, and each partner takes a turn drawing a question card from the other student's hand or the pile. The student who draws the card must ask a question that starts with that word and uses the current page in the text to find evidence to create the question.

EVALUATION

"I Can . . ." Statements

- I can ask and answer questions before I read to help me predict what will happen in the text.
- I can ask and answer questions during reading to help me clarify the text.
- I can ask and answer questions after reading to help me summarize the text.
- I can ask and answer questions using *who, what, when, where, why,* and *how*.
- I can ask and answer questions by using "I wonder."

BEHAVIOR INDICATORS

- Asks questions to help predict before reading and what he wonders about the text.
- Asks questions during reading to clarify events, ideas, or words in the text.
- Asks questions after reading to demonstrate comprehension of the text.
- Asks and answers questions using *who, what, when,* and *where*.
- Asks and answers questions using *why* and *how*.
- Asks "I wonder" questions throughout reading.

FIGURE 4.7
Ask a Question Cards

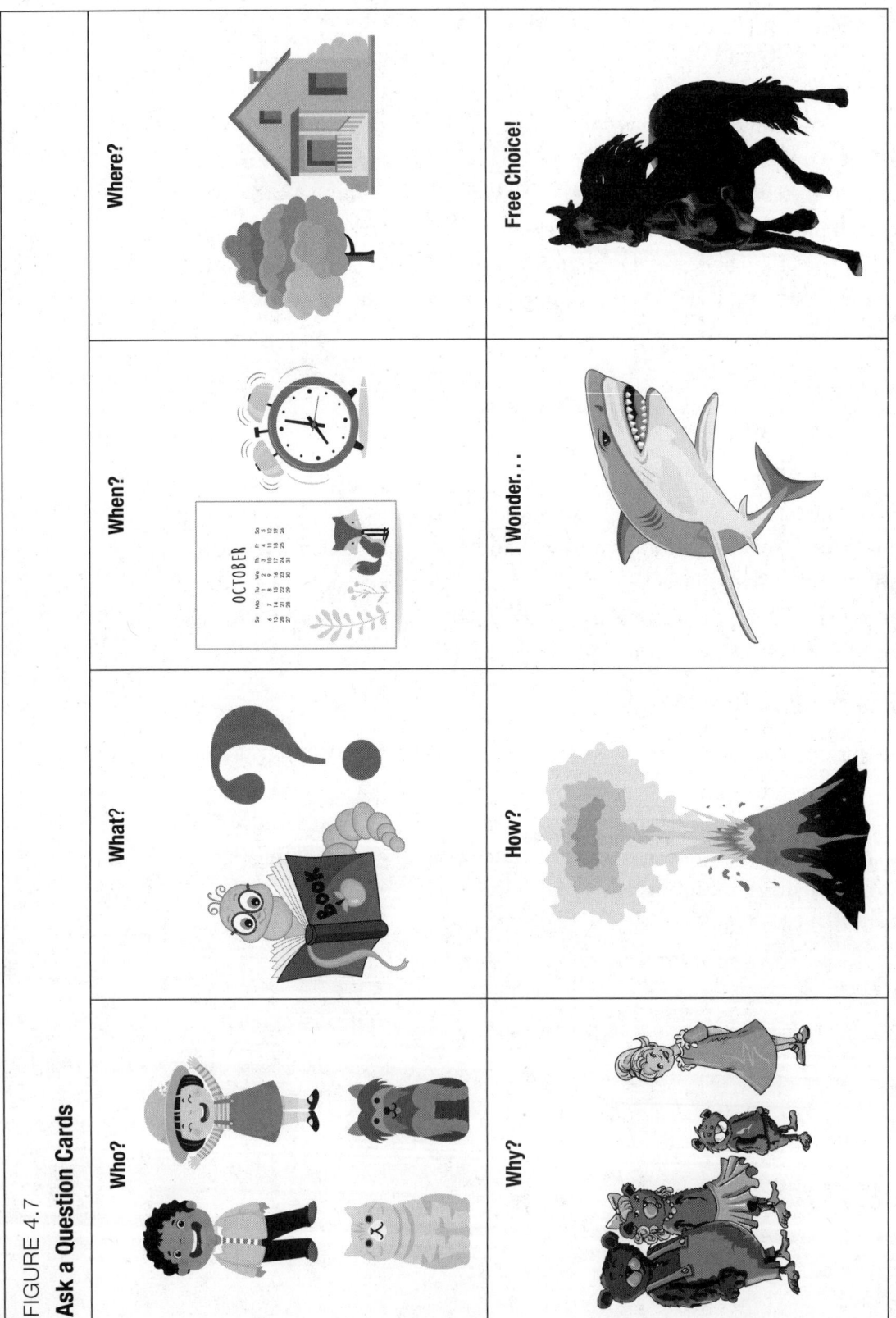

Source: *Literacy Strong All Year Long: Powerful Lessons for Grades K–2* by Valerie Ellery, Lori Oczkus, and Timothy V. Rasinski. © 2020 ASCD. Readers may duplicate this figure for noncommercial use within their school.

FIGURE 4.8
My Question, Your Question Bookmark

Directions: Take turns asking and answering questions.

Who?	What?	When?
Where?	Why?	How?

Who _____
_____?

What _____
_____?

When _____
_____?

Where _____
_____?

Why _____
_____?

How _____
_____?

I wonder _____
_____.

Source: Literacy Strong All Year Long: Powerful Lessons for Grades K–2 by Valerie Ellery, Lori Oczkus, and Timothy V. Rasinski. © 2020 ASCD. Readers may duplicate this figure for noncommercial use within their school.

FIGURE 4.9
Parent Letter for Questioning

Dear Parents,

Albert Einstein once said, "The important thing is not to stop questioning." Fortunately, young children are full of questions. Questioning plays an important role in reading. Good readers ask questions throughout the reading experience to better comprehend the text and to clarify ideas. Practicing asking and answering questions while reading will make your child a stronger reader. Rather than becoming a teacher during this process, your role is to ask questions and wonder along the way, too.

Enclosed is a *My Question, Your Question Bookmark* for you and your child to use as you read together. Here are the basics:

- **Before reading:** Study the cover and title and flip through some of the pages. Take turns asking each other questions such as these: "I wonder, what. . .?" and "I wonder, who. . .?"
- **During reading:** Read aloud or take turns reading with your child. Pause every few pages to take turns asking each other questions such as these: "Why did. . .?" "How does. . .?" and "Who is. . .?" Choose question words from the bookmark.
- **After reading:** Page through the book and take turns quizzing each other by using the question words on the bookmark.

Be sure to make it enjoyable and more of a discussion than a test!

Sincerely,

[Your child's teacher]
Enclosure: My Question, Your Question Bookmark

Source: Literacy Strong All Year Long: Powerful Lessons for Grades K–2 by Valerie Ellery, Lori Oczkus, and Timothy V. Rasinski. © 2020 ASCD. Readers may duplicate this figure for noncommercial use within their school.

LESSON 8. VOCABULARY: ASSOCIATING WORDS

Title DESCRIBE IT IN FIVE!

Trailer Children delight in hearing text filled with rich, playful language and words. Parents and teachers who read aloud to children know about this magical spell. Explicitly teaching students to read closely for a variety of synonyms helps their comprehension deepen and their vocabularies grow. Instead of relying on their usual words, students begin to choose more interesting vocabulary to communicate. In this lesson, students will experience the joy of words through play and activity.

Literacy Enhancer Vocabulary: Associating Words—Synonyms, Adjectives

Key Academic Vocabulary Vocabulary from a previous lesson is marked with an asterisk (*).

Adjective*: A word that describes a noun (a person, place, or thing)

Antonym*: A word that has an opposite meaning of another word

Homograph*: A word that has more than one meaning

Homonym*: Another name for a homograph

Noun*: A person, place, or thing

Opposite*: Two words or concepts that are in some way related but distinctly different in meaning from each other

Shades of meaning*: Words that are synonyms with varying degrees of different meanings

Synonym*: A word that has a similar meaning to another word

Verb*: An action word

Learning Objectives

- Describe a variety of objects using five key attributes—size, color, shape, sense (touch, sight, smell, taste, and hearing), and weight—to guide descriptions.
- Apply a variety of adjectives to describe nouns.
- Share oral and written descriptions that use the five attributes.

Essential Questions

- What are some words that can be used to accurately describe the size, color, shape, sense, and weight of an object?
- How can using the five key attributes help you describe nouns more accurately?

- How does watching for rich language during reading impact your comprehension and writing?

STEP 1: PREPARATION

Organize Materials

- Bag filled with different objects
- Plastic fly swatters
- Fiction or nonfiction text
- *Describe It! Bookmark* reproducible (copies or enlarged for display)
- *I Can Describe It! Bookmark* reproducible (copies or enlarged for display)
- *Describe It in Five!* reproducible (copies or enlarged for display)
- *Parent Letter for Learning Fun Words* reproducible (copies)
- Literacy notebooks

Here are some options for organizing and differentiating the instructional setting:

- **Small-Group Instruction**
    - What's in the Bag?
    - I Can Describe It! Bookmark
    - Describe It in Five!
    - Read-aloud with Swat a Word
- **Parents or Tutors**
    - I Can Describe It! Bookmark
    - Conversational coaching
- **Independent Work**
    - I Can Describe It! Bookmark
    - Describe It in Five!
    - Writing using adjectives

STEP 2: INITIATION

What's in the Bag?

- Fill a bag with objects for students to describe. (Keep the bag handy for use later in this lesson, too.) Include school items such as pencils, paper, and books, but also fill with interesting items from home. Select one of the objects without showing it and encourage students to guess what it is. Display or hand out copies of Figure 4.10, the *Describe It! Bookmark* reproducible. Guide students to ask yes/no questions about size, color, shape, sense, and weight to guess each object in the bag. Prompt as necessary when students are trying to guess the objects.

Tell students that today they will learn how authors use interesting words to better describe things they write about. Have students chant, "Describe it in five!" Together, make the following gestures in the air as you all say each of these words:

- *Size*: Make a small circle and a large one with your hands.
- *Color*: Point to markers or crayons.
- *Shape*: Point to two different shapes in the room.
- *Sense*: Point to something smooth and something rough.
- *Weight*: Point to something heavy and something light.

STEP 3: DEMONSTRATION

Swat a Word

1. Read aloud from a variety of picture books that feature strong descriptive language. Ask students to use one or more of the categories in the *Describe It!* reproducible (Figure 4.10) so they can be on the lookout for words that describe things. Show students a fly swatter and ask them what it is used for. Tell them that you are going to swat wonderful words instead of flies. Project a copy of the text or read from a Big Book. As you read aloud, use the fly swatter to swat adjectives as they occur in the text. Invite students to raise their hands to indicate when they hear an adjective, or describing word, for you to swat. Here are some read-aloud suggestions for picture books that provide opportunities for students to discuss synonyms and descriptive language:
    - *In the Small, Small Pond* by Denise Fleming
    - The Fancy Nancy series by Jane O'Connor
    - *Thesaurus Rex* by Laya Steinberg

2. Display the *I Can Describe It! Bookmark* reproducible (Figure 4.11) to record descriptive words that you swatted in the text. Discuss the five categories. Give each student a copy of the reproducible.

3. Display the *Describe It in Five!* reproducible (Figure 4.12). Select an object from the bag and fill in the reproducible. Draw a picture of the object and model how to select descriptive words to write about it according to size, color, shape, sense, and weight. Here's an example: "The toy truck is small. It is eggshell blue, just like the sky. The shape is a rectangle like an ice-cream sandwich. When I touch it, it feels smooth like a marble. It is light in weight like a spoon."

4. Invite students to turn and talk with partners as they repeat and share responses.

STEP 4: COLLABORATION

Conversational Coaching

Students work in teams, and each team is in charge of one of the five attributes. Give each team an object from the bag. Have teams engage in conversational coaching by asking them to describe their object within their teams and then report their word choices to the class. Next, select an object from a book the class has read. Invite each group to talk about their assigned attribute in relation to the object and share with the class.

STEP 5: APPLICATION

Describe It in Five!

At an independent or partner work center, students can either pull objects out of a bag and fill in the *Describe It In Five!* (Figure 4.12) reproducible or read books and record descriptive words on the reproducible.

Make copies of the *Parent Letter for Learning Fun Words* reproducible (Figure 4.13) and send one home with each student, along with a copy of the *Describe It in Five! Bookmark* reproducible and one or more books, to help parents nurture their children's vocabulary.

STEP 6: REFLECTION

Written Response

Encourage students to write in their literacy notebooks about something they did already over the summer break (e.g., seeing a movie, visiting a friend or relative, playing a game), using descriptive words for size, color, shape, sense, and weight.

ADAPTATION/EXTENSION

- Write descriptive words on inflated balloons. Choose words that indicate size, color, shape, sense, and weight. Then, give one balloon to each student. Students keep their balloons in the air while you play music. When the music stops, each student reads the descriptive word to a partner and uses it in a sentence.
- Using ReadWriteThink.org's student interactive Postcard Creator (www.readwritethink.org/classroom-resources/student-interactives/postcard-creator-30061.html), have students write postcards about their summer break using at least three descriptive words.
- *English Language Learner Suggestion*: Using a copy of the *Describe It in Five!* reproducible fill it in with a small group or draw it onto chart paper. Choose one object from a picture book fiction or nonfiction to draw and describe

- *Struggling Reader Suggestion:* Provide fly swatters and copies of a text for partners to share. Read a page aloud and pause during the reading so students can take turns swatting at the descriptive words. Record words on the *I Can Describe It! Bookmark* reproducible (Figure 4.11).

EVALUATION

"I Can . . ." Statements

- I can draw and describe attributes of an object.
- I can sort words into categories (i.e., size, color, shape, sense, weight).
- I can use common adjectives in my writing.

BEHAVIOR INDICATORS

- Uses adjectives to describe nouns.
- Sorts objects by attributes.
- Applies common adjectives to enhance writing.

FIGURE 4.10
Describe It! Bookmark

Directions: Use this bookmark to help you remember describing words.

Describe It!

Size Words

big, huge, gigantic, enormous   small, little, teeny, tiny

Color Words

red, scarlet, pink, yellow, gold, orange, coral, copper, green, lime, emerald, blue, purple, lavender, violet, black, brown, cream, white

Shape Words

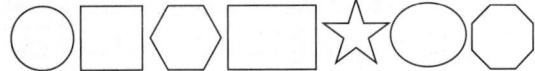

circle, square, hexagon, rectangle, star, oval, octagon

Sense Words

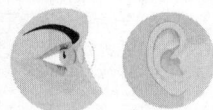 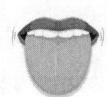  

Weight Words

heavy, light, thick, thin, narrow, wide

Describe It!

Size Words

big, huge, gigantic, enormous   small, little, teeny, tiny

Color Words

red, scarlet, pink, yellow, gold, orange, coral, copper, green, lime, emerald, blue, purple, lavender, violet, black, brown, cream, white

Shape Words

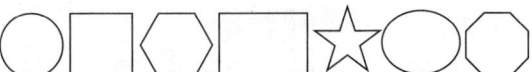

circle, square, hexagon, rectangle, star, oval, octagon

Sense Words

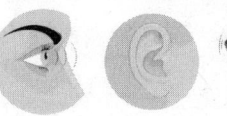   

Weight Words

heavy, light, thick, thin, narrow, wide

Source: Literacy Strong All Year Long: Powerful Lessons for Grades K–2 by Valerie Ellery, Lori Oczkus, and Timothy V. Rasinski. © 2020 ASCD. Readers may duplicate this figure for noncommercial use within their school.

Stopping the Summer Slide

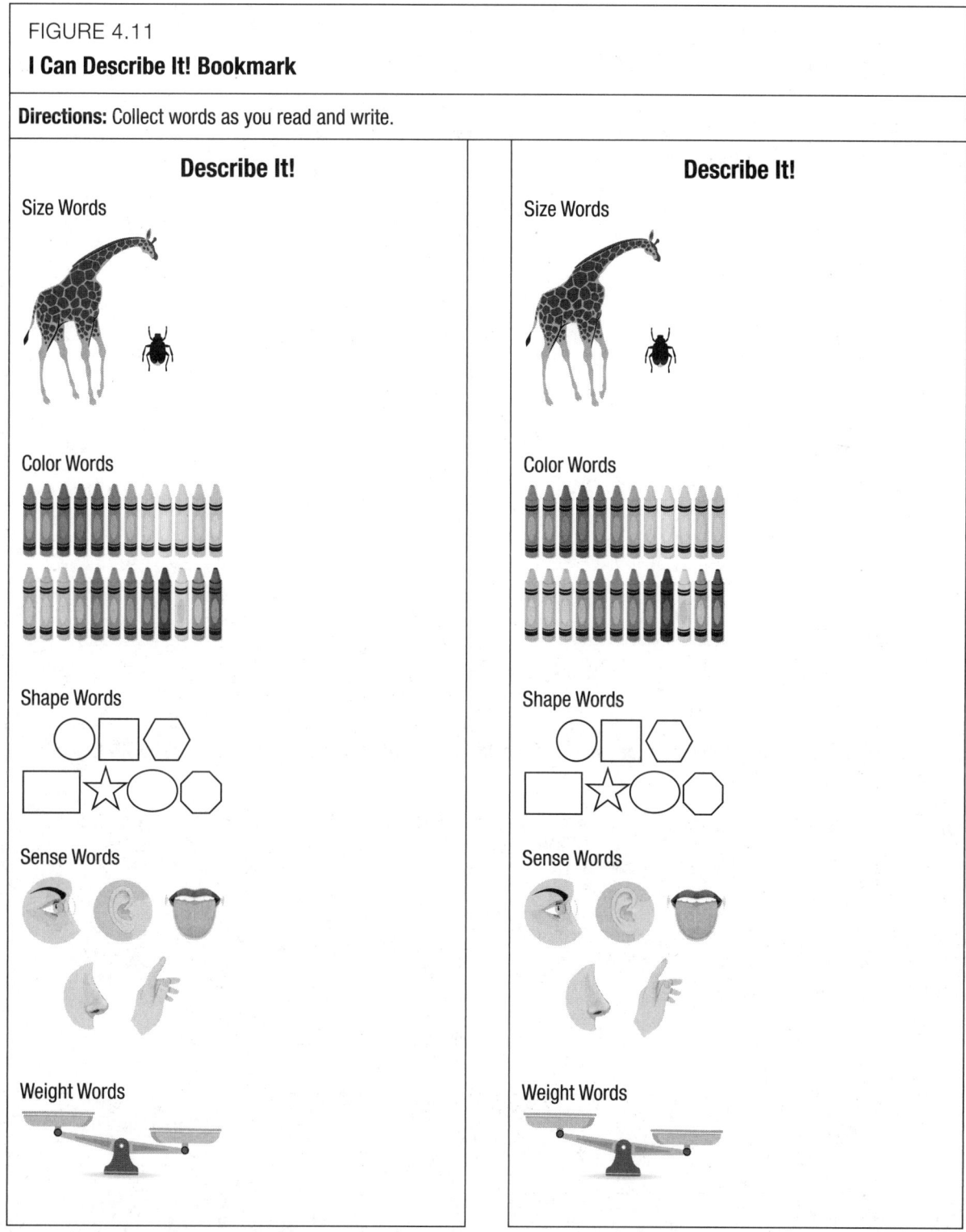

FIGURE 4.11

I Can Describe It! Bookmark

Directions: Collect words as you read and write.

Source: Literacy Strong All Year Long: Powerful Lessons for Grades K–2 by Valerie Ellery, Lori Oczkus, and Timothy V. Rasinski. © 2020 ASCD. Readers may duplicate this figure for noncommercial use within their school.

FIGURE 4.12
Describe It in Five!

I am describing _____ .

1. Draw a simple picture of your object.

2. Write one word in each box that describes your drawing. Use your Describe It! Bookmark. Then, add details to your drawing.

3. Write sentences.

Size: _____ is _____ .

Color: It is the color _____ , just like _____ .

Shape: The shape is _____ like a _____ .

Sense: When I touch it, it feels _____ like _____ .

Weight: It is _____ like a _____ .

Source: Literacy Strong All Year Long: Powerful Lessons for Grades K–2 by Valerie Ellery, Lori Oczkus, and Timothy V. Rasinski. © 2020 ASCD. Readers may duplicate this figure for noncommercial use within their school.

FIGURE 4.13
Parent Letter for Learning Fun Words

Dear Parents,

Reading is a wonderful way to nurture and increase your child's vocabulary. A bigger, richer vocabulary means that your child is a better reader and writer. Reading has a powerful effect on a child's vocabulary and knowledge of words.

Here are two fun activities that you can do with your child as you explore learning words together.

1. **What's in the Bag?** Find a bag (paper or cloth, not plastic) or an empty box. Secretly put a common object, such as a toy, a tool, or an article of clothing, in the bag for your child to guess what it is. Have your child guess what is in the bag by asking yes/no questions. Use the Describe It in Five! reproducible to guide the guesses. Here are some sample yes/no questions:
   - *Size:* Is it large? Is it small?
   - *Color:* Is it red? Is it blue?
   - *Shape:* Is it a circle? Is it a rectangle?
   - *Sense:* Is it rough? Is it smooth?
   - *Weight:* Is it heavy? Is it light?

2. **Word Watch:** As you read and enjoy books together, watch for adjectives (words that describe nouns). Use the *Describe It in Five!* reproducible during and after reading to discuss interesting words that the author used in descriptions. Take turns pointing to words that you enjoyed in the reading.

Sincerely,

[Your child's teacher]
Enclosure: Describe It in Five! (Figure 4.12, p. 296)

Source: Literacy Strong All Year Long: Powerful Lessons for Grades K–2 by Valerie Ellery, Lori Oczkus, and Timothy V. Rasinski. © 2020 ASCD. Readers may duplicate this figure for noncommercial use within their school.

LESSON 9. VOCABULARY: ANALYZING WORDS

Title LITERARY SCRAPBOOKS: FROM PARTS OF SPEECH TO A WHOLE PICTURE OF A TEXT

Trailer Capturing memories in a scrapbook helps us remember trips we've taken. Students can capture memories of their trip through a text as a reader. Students will design a literary scrapbook by focusing on characters, actions, and events from a story. Students will use nouns, verbs, and prepositions in the story to summarize their journey.

Literacy Enhancer Vocabulary: Analyzing Words—Parts of Speech: Nouns, Verbs, and Prepositions

Key Academic Vocabulary Vocabulary from a previous lesson is marked with an asterisk (*).

Common noun*: A nonspecific type of noun that names any regular, ordinary person, animal, place, thing, or idea

Irregular plural noun*: A type of a noun that changes its spelling in the plural form in ways other than what is normal by adding *-s* or *-es* to the end of the noun; can end in a variety of ways, with no consistent pattern (e.g., *foot → feet, man → men, mouse → mice, person → people*)

Irregular verb*: A type of verb that changes its form for the past tense and can also completely change for the past participle, rather than just adding a letter or letters, such as *-ed* or *-d*; can end in a variety of ways, with no consistent pattern (e.g., *sing → sang, go → went*)

Noun*: A part of speech that is a type of naming word that represents a person, animal, place, thing, idea, or concept; there are more nouns in the English language than any other words; usually followed by a verb

Parts of speech*: Categories of words used in English grammar (e.g., nouns, verbs, adverbs, adjectives, prepositions)

Plural*: A form of a word that conveys quantity (more than one)

Preposition*: A part of speech that shows the logical relationship of a noun to the rest of the sentence through words that specify where (spatial), when (temporal), and why (logical) something is taking place (e.g., *at, before, beside, by, to, with*); always followed by a noun or pronoun in a phrase; never followed by a verb, and a verb is never a part of a prepositional phrase

Proper noun*: A specific type of noun that names a particular person, animal, place, thing, or idea and begins with a capital letter

Regular verb: A type of verb whose past tense and past participle forms end by adding a *-d* or *-ed* (e.g., *dance → danced, roll → rolled*)

Verb*: A part of speech that is a type of word that demonstrates an action (physical or mental); tells what the subject (noun) of a simple sentence is doing; without a verb, a sentence would not exist

Learning Objectives

- Identify how parts of speech affect the way we read and write.
- Identify and analyze parts of speech (nouns, verbs, and prepositions).

Essential Questions

- How do words and their use influence language?
- What is the relationship between nouns and verbs?
- How does the author show that a word is demonstrating the past?

STEP 1: PREPARATION

Organize Materials

- Scrapbook artifacts (i.e., documents, memorabilia, photographs) on a given subject
- Scrapbook materials (e.g., camera, magazines, photo album, paper, scissors, tape, markers, stickers)
- Multimodal text sets with scrapbook formats
- *Steps for Creating a Literary Scrapbook* reproducible (copies or enlarged for display)
- *Parent Letter for Analyzing Parts of Speech Weekly Plan* reproducible (copies)
- Literacy notebooks

Here are some options for organizing and differentiating the instructional setting:

- **Small-Group Instruction**
  - Becoming Collectors
  - Scrapbook Genre: Read-aloud with a scrapbook format
  - Steps for Creating a Literary Scrapbook
  - Parent Letter for Analyzing Parts of Speech Weekly Plan

- **Parents or Tutors**
    - Steps for Creating a Literary Scrapbook
    - Parent Letter for Analyzing Parts of Speech Weekly Plan

- **Independent Work**
    - Steps for Creating a Literary Scrapbook reproducible
    - Materials for creating a literary scrapbook
    - Independent reading books

STEP 2: INITIATION

Becoming Collectors

Share documents, memorabilia, and photographs that are all related (e.g., travel trip, summer vacation, sports team, favorite story book). Show students one of the photographs and ask them to describe who they think is in the picture, what they think the person or animal is doing, and where they think the picture was taken. Explain to students that many people save and collect items to remember an event, theme, or concept to highlight a special moment or interesting facts. Explain that students are going to become character collectors as they create literary scrapbooks focused on specific parts of speech: nouns, verbs, and prepositions. Students will be analyzing these parts of speech in favorite literature books to remain literacy strong.

STEP 3: DEMONSTRATION

Scrapbook Genre

1. Read aloud from a text related to scrapbooking. Here are some suggested read-aloud texts:
    - *Zoe Sophia's Scrapbook: An Adventure in Venice* by Claudia Mauner and Elisa Smalley
    - *An Island Scrapbook: Dawn to Dusk on a Barrier Island* by Virginia Wright-Frierson
    - *A Desert Scrapbook: Dawn to Dusk in the Sonoran Desert* by Virginia Wright-Frierson
    - *The Lincolns: A Scrapbook Look at Abraham and Mary* by Candace Fleming
    - *One Small Step: Celebrating the First Men on the Moon* by Jerry Stone
2. Discuss the format of the text and how its purpose is to document experiences, travels, life experiences, characters, and so forth. Examine the text features (i.e., sidebar notes, graphics, travelogue style, photographs, illustrations, captions).

Select a fun summer literature-based read-aloud. Introduce the *Steps for Creating a Literary Scrapbook* (Figure 4.14) reproducible as a guide to create a class literary scrapbook.

STEP 4: COLLABORATION

Hunting for Nouns and Verbs and Conversational Coaching

Invite students to work in groups or with partners to search for souvenirs and other items (nouns) in the text that the main character (noun) from the read-aloud would put into the class literary scrapbook. These objects should reflect events in the story or important aspects of the character. Include an explanation next to each object describing its significance and what the character would be doing (verb) with the items. Have students engage in conversational coaching as they are hunting for the nouns and verbs. Ask students to discuss how they will be able to apply their parts-of-speech finds in the class literary scrapbook. Here are some guiding sample questions for conversational coaching:

- Who is the character?
- What do we know about this character?
- What objects does the character use, want, or have in the story? Why are they significant?
- What are some details about this character's appearance?
- How would you describe the character's actions?
- Where is this character in the story?

STEP 5: APPLICATION

Summer Scrapbooking

Invite students to collect, draw, cut, and paste items into the class literary scrapbook. Have them use scrapbooking materials to create a page for each book they read. Encourage students to use the *Steps for Creating a Literary Scrapbook* reproducible as they write informational captions to label or describe each picture, photograph, or item in the scrapbook.

Make copies of the *Parent Letter for Analyzing Parts of Speech Weekly Plan* reproducible (Figure 4.15), and send one home with each student along with a suggested reading list so parents can help their children continue to practice the parts of speech learned this year while they create a literary scrapbook together over the summer. Also, include one copy of each of these reproducibles, which are discussed in the parent letter:

- Steps for Creating a Literary Scrapbook
- Verb Verifier from the "Hunting to Position Prepositions and Verify Verbs" lesson in Chapter 3
- Positioning Prepositions Cards from the "Hunting to Position Prepositions and Verify Verbs" lesson in Chapter 3

STEP 6: REFLECTION

Oral or Written Response

In their literacy notebooks, have students record a list of all the books they read and include it in the class literary scrapbook. Have them respond to these essential questions through written response (or orally):

- How do words and their use influence language?
- What is the relationship between nouns and verbs?
- How does the author show that a word is demonstrating the past?

ADAPTATION/EXTENSION

- Read *Turtle Summer: A Journal for My Daughter* by Mary Alice Monroe and use the directions in the text to create an informational nature scrapbook.
- Read *P Is for Passport: A World Alphabet* by Devin Scillian and create an alphabet travel scrapbook that highlights nouns in a rhythmic format using alliteration and rhyme.
- *English Language Learner Suggestion:* Create a digital scrapbook with annotations, video, audio, and photographs. Here are some suggested online tools:
    - For photographs: www.pics4learning.com
    - For digital scrapbooking communities: www.pixelscrapper.com
    - For digital scrapbook templates: www.smilebox.com
    - For adding voice to photographs and slideshows: fotobabble.com
- *Struggling Reader Suggestion:* Use Scholastic's Character Scrapbook activity (teacher.scholastic.com/activities/scrapbook) to describe the characters from books being read. Print each character page to form a complete character scrapbook of all the books read over the summer.

EVALUATION

"I Can . . ." Statements

- I can identify nouns and verbs in a text I am reading.
- I can use nouns and verbs correctly when I speak and write.
- I can write captions to highlight nouns, verbs, and prepositions in a text.
- I can explain how the parts of speech affect the way I read and write.

BEHAVIOR INDICATORS

- Analyzes a text for its nouns.
- Analyzes a text for its verbs.
- Writes using nouns, verbs, and prepositions (e.g., captions, journal/diary entries).

FIGURE 4.14
Steps for Creating a Literary Scrapbook

Step 1: Reading and Analyzing Words
- Select and read a story.
- Make a list of nouns from the story.
- Sort the list into common and proper nouns.
- Circle the main character in the list of nouns.
- Make a list of verbs from the story.
- Locate preposition words that describe location, time, and direction.

Step 2: Planning and Prepping
- Gather materials for your scrapbook, such as paper, scissors, glue, magazines, crayons, and markers. *Optional:* Use online tools.
- Search for or create photographs and memorabilia (drawn, cut out of magazines, photographed, or computer generated) of characters and objects that are significant to the story. *Optional:* Use modeling clay to create a character or image from the book and take a picture of it to place on a scrapbook page.
- Create a storyboard layout, outlining features of the book being read and highlighting actions of the characters.

Step 3: Writing Parts
- Write mock-up captions and sentences on index cards to match your images. Include the nouns, verbs, and prepositions that go with each image.
- Write on a separate piece of paper a journal or diary entry from the main character's point of view that reflects a situation with another character, highlights of what the character is doing, or the summary of the story. *Optional:* Use an app or online resource, such as Fotobabble (www.fotobabble.com), to create a digitally recorded voice journal or diary entry.

Step 4: Mounting and Sharing
- Position the pictures, captions, diary entries, stickers and other memorabilia on the page.
- Mount the images and diary entries onto the page and add the captions from the cards underneath or around the images.
- Present your literary scrapbook page as a report about the book you read.
- Add new pages for each book you read until you have a complete literary scrapbook!

Source: Literacy Strong All Year Long: Powerful Lessons for Grades K–2 by Valerie Ellery, Lori Oczkus, and Timothy V. Rasinski. © 2020 ASCD. Readers may duplicate this figure for noncommercial use within their school.

FIGURE 4.15
Parent Letter for Analyzing Parts of Speech Weekly Plan

Dear Parents and Caregivers,

As you read with your child over the summer break, here are some helpful ways to enrich word analysis to build vocabulary and bring meaning to what your child is reading. This weekly plan allows your child to continue to practice the parts of speech learned throughout the school year.

Analyzing Words Weekly Plan

Monday: Hunting nouns Select a fiction or nonfiction text to use throughout the week. If you select an easy reader, it should be practiced daily. If you select a higher-level book, determine how many chapters or pages need to be read daily to finish the book by the end of the week. Read the text with your child. Hunt for the common and proper nouns. Begin to collect nouns for a summer scrapbook page based on text you are reading together. Use the Steps for Creating a Literary Scrapbook reproducible as a guide.

Tuesday: Pluralizing nouns Choose singular common nouns from the text read today and have your child pluralize them. (You may need to provide guidance for irregular plurals, such as mouse → mice.) Ask your child, "How did you make them plural?" Find up to 10 words that are already plurals in the text and sort the common nouns according to how their plurals were made. Decide on the layout for the scrapbook page by highlighting the character and other nouns from the text.

Wednesday: Verifying verbs Read the text and hunt for actions that the main characters performed. Write down the verbs and act them out together (similar to playing a game of Charades). Make two columns and sort the verbs into regular and irregular verb groups using the Verb Verifier reproducible. Highlight various verbs on the scrapbook page.

Thursday: Positioning prepositions While reading the text for the day, hunt for prepositions. Ask your child, "What did the prepositions tell you? How did they help you understand the story or the meaning of the text?" Use the Positioning Prepositions Cards reproducible to sort prepositions found in the text read today. Demonstrate various prepositions from the text on the scrapbook page.

Friday: Parts-of-speech relationships and online games Read the text for the day. Have your child write a sentence using a common noun and a verb from the text that demonstrates their relationship to each other. Have your child say aloud or write the sentence again and add a preposition that will answer when, where, or why. Create captions together using these sentences on this week's scrapbook page. Use free online resources such as these to practice analyzing parts of speech by focusing on nouns, verbs, and prepositions:

- "Noun Town" videos on Grammaropolis: www.grammaropolis.com/videos.php
- "Ice Cream Talk: Nouns and Verbs" game on ABCYa.com: www.abcya.com/nouns_and_verbs.htm
- "Prepositions" game by Turtlediary.com: www.turtlediary.com/grade-1-games/ela-games/prepositions.html

Above all, have fun with your child as you help enrich reading and writing!

Sincerely,

[Your child's teacher]

Enclosures: Steps for Creating a Literary Scrapbook, Figure 4.14, p. 304 • Verb Verifier, Figure 3.17, p. 225 • Positioning Prepositions Cards, Figure 3.18, p. 226

Source: Literacy Strong All Year Long: Powerful Lessons for Grades K–2 by Valerie Ellery, Lori Oczkus, and Timothy V. Rasinski. © 2020 ASCD. Readers may duplicate this figure for noncommercial use within their school.

LESSON 10. MOTIVATION: MOTIVATING READERS

Title SPLASH INTO SUMMER READING!

Trailer While students engage in summer fun, take steps to guarantee that reading also lands on their to-do list. Provide opportunities for students to choose their own reading material and determine their reading rituals. Then, couple choice with opportunities for celebrating and sharing books and build students' reading self-images so they will see themselves as readers. Invite them to splash into summer reading!

Literacy Enhancer Motivation: Motivating Readers

Key Academic Vocabulary Vocabulary from a previous lesson is marked with an asterisk (*).

Author*: The person who wrote the book

Fiction*: The genre that includes stories that are make-believe; may also include poetry

Nonfiction*: The genre that includes factual or real information that is portrayed to answer, explain, or describe

Predict*: To use information from a text to infer what the text will be about or what one might learn from it

Summarize*: To tell what has happened in the text by sharing important points and details

Title*: The name of the text; tells what it is about or gives clues to the content

Learning Objectives

- Set goals for reading at both home and school that include what to read, where to read, when to read, and who to read with.
- Maintain class reading logs and individual reading logs at home and school.
- Participate in book talks and discussions.

Essential Questions

- How can you set goals and routines for reading that include what to read, where to read, who to read with, and when to read?
- How can you use a book log to keep track of your reading and to figure out what to read next?
- What can you say about a book to share it with others?

STEP 1: PREPARATION

Organize Materials

- Hula hoop or masking tape
- Music
- Stuffed animals
- Fiction or informational books
- *Splash into Summer Reading Song* reproducible (copies or enlarged for display)
- *Splash into Summer Reading Plan* reproducible (copies or enlarged for display)
- Parent Letter for Motivation

Here are some options for organizing and differentiating the instructional setting:

- **Small-Group Instruction**
    - Pool Time
    - Teacher as reader demonstration
    - Splash into Summer Reading Song reproducible
    - Splash into Summer Reading Plan reproducible
    - Musical books
    - Problem/solutions response chart

- **Parents or Tutors**
    - *Splash into Summer Reading Plan* reproducible
    - *My Reading Log* reproducible from Chapter 1's "Take Off with Reading! Class Book Club" lesson

- **Independent Work**
    - *Splash into Summer Reading Plan* reproducible
    - Independent reading books

STEP 2: INITIATION

Pool Time

Discuss fun goals for summer activities, such as learning to swim across the pool without stopping, riding a two-wheeled bike, playing baseball, or jumping rope for five minutes straight! Tell students that they may create goals for summer reading, too, when they join the Splash into Summer Reading Club. Create a pool time experience by bringing in a hula hoop to serve as a pretend pool or using masking tape to mark off the floor or carpet for a pool. You may wish to place books in the pool. Invite a student volunteer to pretend to jump into the pool. The swimmer then chooses a book and explains why she picked it.

STEP 3: DEMONSTRATION

Read Aloud and Model Goals

1. Read aloud any book that demonstrates a love of books and learning. Discuss the characters in the books: Where, when, and what do they read? Here are some suggested titles:
   - *I Like Books* by Anthony Browne
   - *Fire Up with Reading!* by Toni Buzzeo
   - *Miss Brooks Loves Books! (and I Don't)* by Barbara Bottner
   - *The Best Time to Read* by Debbie Bertram and Susan Bloom
   - *The Best Book to Read* by Debbie Bertram and Susan Bloom
   - *How Rocket Learned to Read* by Tad Hills

2. Share with students your summer reading goals and routines. You may also want to share some of the appropriate material you are reading and photographs of you reading in different spots. (Make it fun by placing your books in a box or gift bag to reveal during the lesson.) Tell students that they are going to sing a song to find out more about your reading. Display the *Splash into Summer Reading Song* reproducible (Figure 4.16). Hum the tune of "Frère Jacques" with the class before singing the song together. Tell the class that you'll sing just the teacher parts by yourself so they can learn more about your reading habits.

3. Display the *Splash into Summer Reading Plan* reproducible (Figure 4.17) and fill it in with your plan as you sing the song together again.

4. Invite a student volunteer to either fill in the *Splash into Summer Reading Plan* reproducible with you or sing the song with responses in the teacher parts. Discuss with students the many options for each of these questions:
   - What do you read?
   - Where do you read?
   - When do you read?
   - Who do you read with?

5. Talk about variety in where one reads and what one reads. Share the distractions of different reading locations and the importance of making reading every day a habit.

6. Distribute the *Splash into Summer Reading Plan* reproducible and have students fill in the *what*, *where*, and *when* parts. Call on student volunteers to act out

some of the information that they wrote on the reproducible (e.g., under a tree, in a tent in the living room on a rainy day).

STEP 4: COLLABORATION

Conversational Coaching

Have students engage in conversational coaching by discussing the essential questions from step 3 of this lesson with diverse partners. If necessary, use the verses on the *Splash into Summer Reading Song* reproducible to prompt students to discuss their reading routines.

Musical Books

Share book titles with students in a spin-off of musical chairs. Arrange six or more pairs of chairs in a row back to back and place a book under each chair. (Before starting this activity, make sure to model and reinforce behavior rules for it.) Invite the same number of students as chairs to come up and walk around in a circle while music plays. When you stop the music, the walkers sit in the chair closest to them, retrieve the book under it, and flip through the book for a short amount of time to see if they'd like to read it. Signal the players to place the books back under the chairs and walk around to the music again to repeat the activity. After several turns, invite students to share their thoughts with the class about the books they flipped through.

STEP 5: APPLICATION

Books That Students Like to Read

Have students draw pictures of themselves reading in the who part of *the Splash into Summer Reading Plan* reproducible. Next, have students identify books they'd like to read in the bottom box of the reproducible.

Bring a Reading Buddy

Select a date to invite students to bring stuffed animals to read with during class. Allow students to read on the rug, in the pretend pool area, or all over the room. Make it a fun reading celebration! You may need to provide small stuffed animals for students who don't bring one from home.

Make copies of the *Parent Letter for Motivation* reproducible (Figure 4.18) and send one home with each student, along with one or more books and the *My Reading Log* reproducible from the "Take Off with Reading! Class Book Club" lesson in Chapter 1, to provide suggestions to parents about how to motivate their children to read every day.

STEP 6: REFLECTION

Oral Response

Have students discuss their responses to the *Splash into Summer Reading Plan* reproducible. Ask them to interview one another in small groups and use their responses on the reproducible as reminders. Invite students to answer these questions:

- Why are these titles and locations your favorites?
- What problems do you have when trying to read independently at home or at school?

Then, chart a list of student responses and solutions to reading problems. Here is a sample chart:

Problem	Response Example	Solutions
What to read	"I can't find any books I like."	• Ask a friend, teacher, or librarian for suggestions. • Read other books by an author you like.
Where to read	"My house is too noisy."	• Try reading under your blanket with a flashlight or make a tent somewhere in your house or backyard. • Shut the door to your room when you read.
When to read	"I forget to read every day."	• Choose a time and read at that time every day. • Write yourself a note and post it on your bedroom door or mirror as a reminder.
Who to read with	"My parents are busy."	• Read aloud with an older sibling. • Read aloud to a younger sibling or your pet.

ADAPTATION/EXTENSION

Revisit this section in the following lessons for a variety of examples for motivating readers:

- "Take Off with Reading! Class Book Club" in Chapter 1
- "Take Off and Partner Book Talks!" in Chapter 2
- "Ready, Set, Read!" in Chapter 3
- *English Language Learner Suggestion*: Fill out the Splash into Summer Reading Plan together. Talk about each section and encourage students to act out various possible responses and then sketch their choices.
- *Struggling Reader Suggestion:* Revisit the Splash into Summer Reading Song in a small group setting. As you sing each verse, encourage students to record their responses on their Splash into Summer Reading Plan. Share your own plans for what you plan to read and model how to fill out the plan.

EVALUATION

"I Can . . ." Statements

- I can identify books that I want to read.
- I can tell where and when I read.
- I can share who reads with me.

BEHAVIOR INDICATORS

- Names titles of specific books that he is reading at home and at school.
- Identifies places where he reads at home and at school.
- Reads daily at home at a given time of day.
- Reads to and with others at home and at school.

FIGURE 4.16
Splash into Summer Reading Song

Sing to the tune of "Frère Jacques"

Students and Teacher: WHAT are you reading? WHAT are you reading?
Please tell us now. Please tell us now.

Teacher: I'm reading a _____ (genre or author) book.
I'm reading a _____ (repeat or add another genre or author you're reading) book.
That's what I'm reading now. That's what I'm reading now.

Students and Teacher: WHERE do you read? WHERE do you read?
Please tell us now. Please tell us now.

Teacher: I read at home _____ (e.g., on my porch, on my couch, or in my chair). I read at school _____ (e.g., at my desk, in my chair, or at the library). That's where I read. That's where I read.

Students and Teacher: WHEN do you read? WHEN do you read?
Please tell us now. Please tell us now.

Teacher: I read _____ (e.g., during lunch, before dinner, or before I go to bed).
I read _____ (repeat or add another time you read). That's when I read. That's when I read.

Students and Teacher: WHO do you read with? WHO do you read with?
Please tell us now. Please tell us now.

Teacher: I read _____ (e.g., by myself, with my children, or with you).
I read _____ (repeat or add someone else you read with). That's who I read with. That's who I read with.

Source: Literacy Strong All Year Long: Powerful Lessons for Grades K–2 by Valerie Ellery, Lori Oczkus, and Timothy V. Rasinski. © 2020 ASCD. Readers may duplicate this figure for noncommercial use within their school.

FIGURE 4.17
Splash into Summer Reading Plan

Name: _____

What to Read

Draw a picture of the types of books you like.

Where to Read

Draw a picture of where you like to read.

When to Read

Draw a picture of the time you read.

Who to Read With

Draw a picture of you reading with someone or by yourself.

 **Books I Want to Read**

1. _____

2. _____

Source: Literacy Strong All Year Long: Powerful Lessons for Grades K–2 by Valerie Ellery, Lori Oczkus, and Timothy V. Rasinski. © 2020 ASCD. Readers may duplicate this figure for noncommercial use within their school.

FIGURE 4.18
Parent Letter for Motivation

Dear Parents,

Here are some ways to help your child practice and enjoy reading every day.

Four Ways to Motivate Your Child to Read

1. **Books to read:**
   - Go to the library.
   - Read books borrowed from school.
   - Check online for book suggestions in your child's favorite genre or by his or her favorite authors. Here are two good websites to check:
     - Scholastic Summer Reading Challenge: www.scholastic.com/ups/summer/home (You can sign your child up for the challenge to earn rewards for reading.)
     - Spaghetti Book Club: www.spaghettibookclub.org (These are book reviews by kids for kids!)
   - Use your library card to download ebooks and audible ebooks on the spot.
   - Build a custom audible library.

2. **Where to read:**
   - Read in bed or with a flashlight under the covers!
   - Read in a cozy chair.
   - Read in a tent you make with blankets.
   - Read outside under a tree, on the porch, or at the park.

3. **When to read:**
   - Read every day for 15–30 minutes or longer!
   - Choose one or more times to read, such as bedtime, in the afternoon, or before or after dinner.
   - Read at the same time every day.

4. **Whom to read with:**
   - Read with a parent or older sibling.
   - Read to a grandparent or an older community member.
   - Read to a younger sibling.
   - Read to a pet!

Keeping Track of Reading
Ask your child to keep track of reading progress by filling out My Reading Log. Assist your child in filling in the information for each book and include the date, a drawing of the cover, the title, the author and illustrator, and a rating for the book. Ask your child to explain if the book was good, and why or why not. Please sign your child's Reading Log at the end of the summer and give it to your child's next teacher!

Sincerely,

[Your child's teacher]
Enclosure: My Reading Log (Figure 1.18 p. 74)

Source: Literacy Strong All Year Long: Powerful Lessons for Grades K–2 by Valerie Ellery, Lori Oczkus, and Timothy V. Rasinski. © 2020 ASCD. Readers may duplicate this figure for noncommercial use within their school.

Appendix: Rubrics to Assess Student Competencies

As you implement the various techniques that support the lessons in this book, use the behaviors identified as a guide to assess your students' abilities. These strategy *assessments* are embedded within each lesson, and you can use them to evaluate students' strengths and weaknesses (behavior indicators). This information will help you keep the results in mind to support the lesson's big ideas.

In this section, we offer compiled rubrics for evaluating observable behaviors for each strategy strand. These rubrics are resources for monitoring your students' progress on each of the competencies covered in this book.

Isolating and Identifying Sounds

Student: _____

Chapter 1: Need to Know Names				
Observable Behavior Indicators	Not Yet	Rarely	Often	Always
Isolates and identifies initial sounds by positioning the mouth, lips, jaw, and tongue to correspond with appropriate single-syllable words.				
Compares the beginning sounds in words and determines if they can make an alliteration.				
Identifies the initial sound in a word and pronounces additional words that begin with the same sound to create an alliteration.				
Chapter 2: Mingle and Jingle with Vowels				
Observable Behavior Indicators	Not Yet	Rarely	Often	Always
Isolates and identifies short-vowel sounds by positioning the mouth, lips, jaw, and tongue to correspond with appropriate short vowels in single-syllable words.				
Isolates and identifies long-vowel sounds by positioning the mouth, lips, jaw, and tongue to correspond with appropriate long vowels in single-syllable words.				
Distinguishes long- from short-vowel sounds in spoken single-syllable words when reading regularly spelled, one-syllable words.				
Chapter 3: Digraph Hero Teams				
Observable Behavior Indicators	Not Yet	Rarely	Often	Always
Isolates and identifies selected digraphs by positioning the mouth, lips, jaw, and tongue to correspond with the appropriate digraph in single-syllable words.				
Distinguishes consonant digraphs in words when reading regularly spelled, one-syllable words.				
Generates words with similar digraphs.				
Chapter 4: I Spy! Capturing Sounds				
Observable Behavior Indicators	Not Yet	Rarely	Often	Always
Isolates and identifies selected sounds by positioning the mouth, lips, jaw, and tongue to correspond with a chosen word for the sound.				
Distinguishes specific sounds in words.				
Categorizes objects by a specific sound and justifies why they are together.				

Source: Literacy Strong All Year Long: Powerful Lessons for Grades K–2 by Valerie Ellery, Lori Oczkus, and Timothy V. Rasinski. © 2020 ASCD. Readers may duplicate this figure for noncommercial use within their school.

Blending and Segmenting

Student: _____

Chapter 1: The Blending Dance				
Observable Behavior Indicators	**Not Yet**	**Rarely**	**Often**	**Always**
Listens to a sequence of sounds (onsets and rimes) of single-syllable words and combines them to form the word.				
Identifies the onset and rime in a word.				
Substitutes the onset or rime in a word to form a new word.				
Chapter 2: Making Word Smoothies				
Observable Behavior Indicators	**Not Yet**	**Rarely**	**Often**	**Always**
Orally produces single-syllable words by segmenting and blending sounds.				
Distinguishes the sounds in spoken single-syllable words.				
Identifies the vowels in single-syllable words.				
Chapter 3: The Blend Factor				
Observable Behavior Indicators	**Not Yet**	**Rarely**	**Often**	**Always**
Produces a word by blending sounds, including consonant blends.				
Identifies the number of syllables in a word.				
Determines the vowel in each syllable.				
Chapter 4: The Sweet Blend of Sounds				
Observable Behavior Indicators	**Not Yet**	**Rarely**	**Often**	**Always**
Determines the number of sounds in a word by segmenting the word.				
Identifies the digraph(s) in a word.				
Produces a word by blending sounds, including consonant blends.				

Source: Literacy Strong All Year Long: Powerful Lessons for Grades K–2 by Valerie Ellery, Lori Oczkus, and Timothy V. Rasinski. © 2020 ASCD. Readers may duplicate this figure for noncommercial use within their school.

Decoding

Student: _____

Chapter 1: Vowel Changers				
Observable Behavior Indicators	Not Yet	Rarely	Often	Always
Associates the short sounds with the common spellings (graphemes) for the five major vowels.				
Decodes regularly spelled, one-syllable CVC words.				
Distinguishes short vowels when reading regularly spelled, one-syllable words.				
Chapter 2: Vowel Transformers				
Observable Behavior Indicators	Not Yet	Rarely	Often	Always
Associates the long and short sounds with the common spellings (graphemes) for the five major vowels.				
Identifies final-*e* and common vowel team conventions for representing long-vowel sounds.				
Distinguishes long and short vowels when reading regularly spelled, one-syllable words.				
Chapter 3: Fixated on Prefixes: Divide and Conquer				
Observable Behavior Indicators	Not Yet	Rarely	Often	Always
Decodes two-syllable words following basic patterns by breaking the words into syllables.				
Identifies the prefix and the root word.				
Determines the meaning of a newly formed word when a common prefix is added to a root word.				
Chapter 4: Working Words Weekly Summer Plan				
Observable Behavior Indicators	Not Yet	Rarely	Often	Always
Follows a weekly plan to practice decoding words.				
Decodes words following basic patterns by breaking the words into syllables.				
Decodes regularly spelled words with short and long vowels.				
Determines the meaning of a newly formed word when a common prefix is added to a root word.				

Source: Literacy Strong All Year Long: Powerful Lessons for Grades K–2 by Valerie Ellery, Lori Oczkus, and Timothy V. Rasinski. © 2020 ASCD. Readers may duplicate this figure for noncommercial use within their school.

Phrasing

Student: _____

Chapter 1: Phrase Scavenger Hunt				
Observable Behavior Indicators	**Not Yet**	**Rarely**	**Often**	**Always**
Identifies a phrase in written text.				
Identifies a sentence in written text.				
Provides a reasonable definition of a phrase in written text.				
Provides a reasonable definition of a sentence in written text.				
Identifies a period and its purpose in written text.				
Identifies a comma and its purpose in written text.				
Explains the importance of chunking text into phrases and sentences when reading.				
Chapter 2: Performing Poetry				
Observable Behavior Indicators	**Not Yet**	**Rarely**	**Often**	**Always**
Independently engages in rehearsal of a poem.				
Performs a poem with good fluency and phrasing.				
Identifies common features found in poetry for children.				
Listens attentively as an audience member when poetry is being read aloud.				
Provides positive and constructive feedback when listening to a classmate read a poem.				
Chapter 3: Text Road Signs: Marking Phrase Boundaries				
Observable Behavior Indicators	**Not Yet**	**Rarely**	**Often**	**Always**
Independently engages in rehearsal of a narrative text.				
Performs a narrative text with good fluency and phrasing.				
Identifies phrase boundaries in narrative texts that are not marked by punctuation.				

continued

Source: Literacy Strong All Year Long: Powerful Lessons for Grades K–2 by Valerie Ellery, Lori Oczkus, and Timothy V. Rasinski. © 2020 ASCD. Readers may duplicate this figure for noncommercial use within their school.

Phrasing (continued)

Chapter 3: Text Road Signs: Marking Phrase Boundaries (continued)				
Observable Behavior Indicators	Not Yet	Rarely	Often	Always
Listens attentively as an audience member while another person reads orally.				
Provides positive and constructive feedback when listening to a classmate read a narrative passage.				
Chapter 4: Weekly Summer Poetry Reading				
Observable Behavior Indicators	Not Yet	Rarely	Often	Always
Independently engages in rehearsal of a weekly poem.				
Records and performs a weekly poem with good fluency and phrasing.				
Identifies common features found in poetry for children.				
Chooses personally interesting words from the weekly poem.				
Provides positive and constructive evaluation and feedback when listening to the podcast recorded reading of the weekly poem.				

Source: Literacy Strong All Year Long: Powerful Lessons for Grades K–2 by Valerie Ellery, Lori Oczkus, and Timothy V. Rasinski. © 2020 ASCD. Readers may duplicate this figure for noncommercial use within their school.

Previewing

Student: _____

Chapter 1: Sneak and See 1-2-3				
Observable Behavior Indicators	**Not Yet**	**Rarely**	**Often**	**Always**
Identifies the title on a book cover.				
Applies the term *title* when identifying the title on a book cover.				
Identifies the author's name on a book cover.				
Applies the term *author* when identifying the author's name on a book cover.				
Explains the author's role in writing a book.				
Identifies the illustrator's name on a book cover.				
Explains the illustrator's role in illustrating a book.				
Applies title and cover art when sharing logical predictions about what the text might be about.				
Identifies the back cover.				
Explains the content of the back cover.				
Chapter 2: Is It Make-Believe or Real?				
Observable Behavior Indicators	**Not Yet**	**Rarely**	**Often**	**Always**
Identifies fiction books using a wide range of examples.				
Gives one reason why a book is fiction.				
Shares two or more reasons why a book is nonfiction.				
Identifies nonfiction books using a wide range of examples.				
Gives one reason why a book is nonfiction.				
Shares two or more reasons why a book is nonfiction.				
Names several types of fiction texts (e.g., poems, Readers Theater scripts, adventure stories, mysteries).				

continued

Source: Literacy Strong All Year Long: Powerful Lessons for Grades K–2 by Valerie Ellery, Lori Oczkus, and Timothy V. Rasinski. © 2020 ASCD. Readers may duplicate this figure for noncommercial use within their school.

Previewing (continued)

Chapter 2: Is It Make-Believe or Real? (continued)				
Observable Behavior Indicators	**Not Yet**	**Rarely**	**Often**	**Always**
Names several types of nonfiction texts (e.g., how-to, explanations).				
Sorts a stack of books into fiction and nonfiction.				
Chapter 3: We're Going on a Text Trip				
Observable Behavior Indicators	**Not Yet**	**Rarely**	**Often**	**Always**
Identifies a fiction book by looking at the cover and taking a text walk.				
Identifies fiction elements in a fiction book (i.e., characters, setting, problem, main events).				
Identifies the story sequence in a fiction book (i.e., beginning, middle, end).				
Identifies a nonfiction book by previewing the cover and taking a text walk.				
Distinguishes at least three text features in a nonfiction book (e.g., table of contents, headings, photographs, maps, bold words, glossary, index).				
Applies nonfiction text features to locate information in a nonfiction book.				
Chapter 4: Text Trip Travels				
Observable Behavior Indicators	**Not Yet**	**Rarely**	**Often**	**Always**
Identifies whether a text is fiction or nonfiction by studying the cover and a few pages of the text.				
Identifies the title, author, and illustrator on the cover of a text.				
Uses the information on the cover to make logical predictions about the text.				
Identifies fiction elements (e.g., characters, setting, problem, main events).				
Identifies nonfiction text features (e.g., table of contents, headings, illustrations, maps, diagrams, glossary, index) and explains how they aid in comprehending the text.				

Source: Literacy Strong All Year Long: Powerful Lessons for Grades K–2 by Valerie Ellery, Lori Oczkus, and Timothy V. Rasinski. © 2020 ASCD. Readers may duplicate this figure for noncommercial use within their school.

Determining Importance and Summarizing

Student: _____

Chapter 1: Retell Recipe				
Observable Behavior Indicators	**Not Yet**	**Rarely**	**Often**	**Always**
Identifies the characters, setting, and main events in a story.				
Sequences the order of a story through a retell.				
Sequences and relates a series of events in a logical order for a retell.				
Chapter 2: Sifting Details				
Observable Behavior Indicators	**Not Yet**	**Rarely**	**Often**	**Always**
Identifies key details in a text.				
Determines what is interesting and what is important.				
Asks and answers questions about key details in a text: who, what, where, when, and why.				
Chapter 3: Finding the Topic: It's a Snap!				
Observable Behavior Indicators	**Not Yet**	**Rarely**	**Often**	**Always**
Uses supporting details from a text to clearly explain the main topic.				
Asks and answers questions about key details in a text: who, what, when, where, why, and how.				
Uses the illustrations and details in a text to describe its key ideas.				
Chapter 4: Home Run with Details				
Observable Behavior Indicators	**Not Yet**	**Rarely**	**Often**	**Always**
Identifies the characters, setting, and main events in a story.				
Sequences the order of a story through a retell.				
Identifies key details in a text.				
Determines what is just interesting in a text and what is actually important.				

continued

Source: Literacy Strong All Year Long: Powerful Lessons for Grades K–2 by Valerie Ellery, Lori Oczkus, and Timothy V. Rasinski. © 2020 ASCD. Readers may duplicate this figure for noncommercial use within their school.

Determining Importance and Summarizing (continued)

Chapter 4: Home Run with Details (continued)				
Observable Behavior Indicators	Not Yet	Rarely	Often	Always
Asks and answers questions about key details in a text: who, what, when, where, and why.				
Uses supporting details in a text to clearly explain the main topic.				
Uses the illustrations and details in a text to describe its key ideas.				

Source: Literacy Strong All Year Long: Powerful Lessons for Grades K–2 by Valerie Ellery, Lori Oczkus, and Timothy V. Rasinski. © 2020 ASCD. Readers may duplicate this figure for noncommercial use within their school.

Questioning for Close Reading

Student: _____

Chapter 1: The Who, What, Where, When Show				
Observable Behavior Indicators	**Not Yet**	**Rarely**	**Often**	**Always**
Asks questions about key ideas and details using the question words *who*, *what*, *where*, and *when*.				
Answers questions using complete sentences.				
Answers questions about key ideas and details using the question words *who*, *what*, *where*, and *when* with text evidence.				
Chapter 2: The Question Game				
Observable Behavior Indicators	**Not Yet**	**Rarely**	**Often**	**Always**
Answers questions about key ideas and details using the question words *who*, *what*, *when*, *where*, and *why* with text evidence.				
Answers questions using complete sentences to demonstrate understanding of key details in a text.				
Asks questions about key ideas and details using the question words *who*, *what*, *when*, *where*, and *why* that align with answer clues given.				
Chapter 3: Question the Character				
Observable Behavior Indicators	**Not Yet**	**Rarely**	**Often**	**Always**
Poses questions to characters in a text, focusing on key ideas and details and using the question words *who*, *what*, *when*, *where*, *why*, and *how*.				
Answers questions in complete sentences to clarify comprehension.				
Answers questions while role playing as a character in a text and uses evidence from the text to answer questions that begin with *who*, *what*, *when*, *where*, *why*, and *how*.				
Infers what a character thinks, feels, and does by using text evidence and connections to his or her own life, other books, and the world.				

continued

Source: Literacy Strong All Year Long: Powerful Lessons for Grades K–2 by Valerie Ellery, Lori Oczkus, and Timothy V. Rasinski. © 2020 ASCD. Readers may duplicate this figure for noncommercial use within their school.

Questioning for Close Reading (*continued*)

Chapter 4: My Question, Your Question!				
Observable Behavior Indicators	**Not Yet**	**Rarely**	**Often**	**Always**
Asks questions to help predict before reading and expresses what he or she is wondering about the text.				
Asks questions during reading to clarify events, ideas, or words in the text.				
Asks questions after reading to demonstrate comprehension of the text.				
Asks and answers questions using *who*, *what*, *when*, and *where*.				
Asks and answers questions using *why* and *how*.				
Asks "I wonder" questions throughout reading.				

Source: Literacy Strong All Year Long: Powerful Lessons for Grades K–2 by Valerie Ellery, Lori Oczkus, and Timothy V. Rasinski. © 2020 ASCD. Readers may duplicate this figure for noncommercial use within their school.

Associating Words

Student: _____

Chapter 1: Up and Down with Opposites!				
Observable Behavior Indicators	Not Yet	Rarely	Often	Always
Identifies the meaning of each word in a pair of verbs that are opposites.				
Matches a common verb to its opposite.				
Names the opposite of a given verb.				
Identifies the meaning of each word in a pair of adjectives that are opposites.				
Matches a common adjective to its opposite.				
Names the opposite of a given adjective.				
Chapter 2: Meaning Madness Time: What Else Does It Mean?				
Observable Behavior Indicators	Not Yet	Rarely	Often	Always
Provides the definition of a multiple-meaning word.				
Explains two meanings for the same word.				
Provides sentences, drawings, or dramatizations for two different meanings of a word.				
Chapter 3: Shades of Meaning				
Observable Behavior Indicators	Not Yet	Rarely	Often	Always
Identifies, names, and categorizes synonyms for emotions.				
Orders emotion words according to level of intensity.				
Identifies, names, and categorizes synonyms for common verbs.				
Orders common verbs according to meaning.				

continued

Source: Literacy Strong All Year Long: Powerful Lessons for Grades K–2 by Valerie Ellery, Lori Oczkus, and Timothy V. Rasinski. © 2020 ASCD. Readers may duplicate this figure for noncommercial use within their school.

Associating Words (*continued*)

Chapter 4: Describe It in Five!				
Observable Behavior Indicators	Not Yet	Rarely	Often	Always
Uses adjectives to describe nouns.				
Sorts objects by attributes.				
Applies common adjectives to enhance writing.				

Source: Literacy Strong All Year Long: Powerful Lessons for Grades K–2 by Valerie Ellery, Lori Oczkus, and Timothy V. Rasinski. © 2020 ASCD. Readers may duplicate this figure for noncommercial use within their school.

Analyzing Words

Student: _____

Chapter 1: We're Going on a Word Hunt: Nouns and Verbs				
Observable Behavior Indicators	Not Yet	Rarely	Often	Always
Demonstrates the ability to identify nouns.				
Demonstrates the ability to identify verbs.				
Determines the difference between a noun and a verb.				
Uses singular nouns with matching verbs in basic sentences.				
Chapter 2: Oh, A-Hunting We Will Go: The Path to Plurals				
Observable Behavior Indicators	Not Yet	Rarely	Often	Always
Transforms a regular noun into its plural form.				
Uses singular nouns with matching verbs in basic sentences.				
Identifies frequently occurring irregular plural nouns in basic sentences.				
Chapter 3: Hunting to Position Prepositions and Verify Verbs				
Observable Behavior Indicators	Not Yet	Rarely	Often	Always
Demonstrates the ability to identify prepositions in sentences.				
Demonstrates the ability to identify irregular verbs in sentences.				
Correctly forms and uses the past tense of irregular verbs while speaking and writing.				
Chapter 4: Literary Scrapbooks: From Parts of Speech to a Whole Picture of a Text				
Observable Behavior Indicators	Not Yet	Rarely	Often	Always
Analyzes a text for its nouns.				
Analyzes a text for its verbs.				
Writes using nouns, verbs, and prepositions (e.g., captions, journal/diary entries).				

Source: Literacy Strong All Year Long: Powerful Lessons for Grades K–2 by Valerie Ellery, Lori Oczkus, and Timothy V. Rasinski. © 2020 ASCD. Readers may duplicate this figure for noncommercial use within their school.

Motivating Readers

Student: _____

Chapter 1: Take Off with Reading! Class Book Club				
Observable Behavior Indicators	Not Yet	Rarely	Often	Always
Identifies the title of a book on the cover.				
Identifies the author's name on a book cover.				
Identifies different types of books.				
Rates a book and gives at least one reason using the text.				
Records the title, author, and personal rating on a book log.				
Consistently maintains a book log to keep track of independent reading.				
Chapter 2: Take Off and Partner Book Talks				
Observable Behavior Indicators	Not Yet	Rarely	Often	Always
Participates in discussion with a partner by making eye contact, actively listening, and adding related comments.				
Predicts what a book will be about before and during reading.				
Provides reasons for predictions.				
Summarizes what a book is about during and after reading by sharing a favorite part and a summary of the text, including the beginning, middle, and end.				
Provides text evidence for the summary.				
Identifies unknown words throughout the reading process.				
Chapter 3: Ready, Set, Read!				
Observable Behavior Indicators	Not Yet	Rarely	Often	Always
Identifies a goal for reading more books by setting a goal with a number of books and a timeline for reading them.				
Identifies a goal for reading different kinds of books.				
Names genres or types of books to read in a given time frame.				

Source: Literacy Strong All Year Long: Powerful Lessons for Grades K–2 by Valerie Ellery, Lori Oczkus, and Timothy V. Rasinski. © 2020 ASCD. Readers may duplicate this figure for noncommercial use within their school.

Chapter 3: Ready, Set, Read! (continued)				
Identifies a goal for spending more time reading by setting minute goals for home and school.				
Identifies a goal for reading more challenging books by identifying what makes them challenging: more words on the pages, more pages, or chapters.				
Sets a goal to read more challenging books in a given time frame.				
Chapter 4: Splash into Summer Reading!				
Observable Behavior Indicators	Not Yet	Rarely	Often	Always
Names titles of specific books that he or she is reading at home and at school.				
Identifies places where he or she reads at home and at school.				
Reads daily at home at a given time of day.				
Reads to and with others at home and at school.				

Source: Literacy Strong All Year Long: Powerful Lessons for Grades K–2 by Valerie Ellery, Lori Oczkus, and Timothy V. Rasinski. © 2020 ASCD. Readers may duplicate this figure for noncommercial use within their school.

Study Guide

This guide is designed to enhance your understanding and application of the information contained in *Literacy Strong All Year Long: Powerful Lessons for Grades K–2*, 2nd edition. You can use this study guide before or after you have read the book, or as you finish each chapter. The questions provided are not meant to cover all aspects addressed in the book, but, rather, to address specific ideas that might warrant further reflection.

Most of the questions contained in this study guide are ones you can think about on your own, but you might consider pairing with a colleague or forming a study group with others who have read this book.

Objectives for individual or group book studies of *Literacy Strong All Year Long: Powerful Strategies for Grades K–2*:

- To encourage student growth in literacy to become "literacy strong."
- To adopt strategies that spiral across the year to strengthen student growth and close the achievement gap.
- To reflect on student needs and adjust practice to differentiate instruction for all students, including struggling readers and English language learners.
- To explore, discuss, and reflect on research-based lesson design to increase student achievement in the following areas of literacy: phonics and phonemic awareness, fluency, comprehension, vocabulary, and motivation.
- To increase student achievement using an interactive lesson design that engages and supports students as they become strong, independent, and motivated readers.

Introduction

1. **Prioritize Effective Primary Grade Approaches.** What are some effective research-based approaches that educators can use to keep literacy strong and promote growth in the intermediate grades? Why do these practices matter? Which are most important for the population you serve?

2. **Spiral Instruction to Promote Growth.** How does literacy growth for intermediate students change throughout the school year? How does instruction need to increase in complexity and spiral to meet student needs?

3. **Teach Important Skills and Strategies.** How does the development of skills and strategies in the areas of word study, fluency, comprehension, vocabulary, and motivation affect intermediate student achievement? How would you prioritize this list for your current students? Explain.

4. **Select and Rank Lessons.** Study Figure 1, page xx, that lists the 40 lessons within this book. Notice the progression of lessons across the seasons of the school year. Identify and note the lessons or strands your students need the most. Discuss with your group. How will you monitor growth in these areas?

5. **Differentiate Instruction with Lesson Features.** Study and discuss the lesson design features found in every lesson (listed for your convenience). Reflect on each feature. Discuss how your lesson choices will help students become independent and literacy strong learners.

Preparation (Before Teaching)

- Lesson Trailer
- Literacy Enhancer
- Materials

Gradual Release Steps

- Initiation
- Demonstration
- Collaboration
- Application
- Reflection

Differentiation and Evaluation Options

- Adaptation/Extension
- Evaluation

6. **Select and Teach Lessons.** Select a lesson to teach to your students or select and plan a lesson as a group. Be prepared to share your students' response after teaching the lesson. Discuss what you learned and what you'd like to do next to further student progress and understanding.

Study Guide: Chapter 1. Starting the Year Literacy Strong

1. **Prioritize Beginning-of-the-Year Essentials.** Brainstorm a list of must-dos for the beginning of the school year. Compare your list to those listed in the chapter opener. Which of the ideas in the chapter opener appeal most to you? How do such literacy routines help develop independence in your students?

2. **Gather Initial Formative Assessment.** Discuss which informal and formative assessment procedures are most helpful to you at the start of the school year. How can you gather literacy baselines quickly and how will you use the information to design instruction?

3. **Set Up Procedures for Read-Aloud and Independent Reading.** What are the benefits of reading aloud to students on the first day or in the first days of school? What titles work well for reading aloud at your grade level? How can you engage students during read-alouds to promote better comprehension? Discuss the importance of independent reading and practical ways to encourage students to read on their own.

4. **Build Community.** How can you use singing, poetry, chants, and art to build community during the first weeks of school? Why is this important for primary children and their literacy development?

5. **Differentiate Instruction.** Discuss the role of small-group instruction and formative assessment in the primary grades. Look through the lessons in Chapter 1. How can you differentiate instruction by delivering some of the instruction to small groups? How can you differentiate to meet the needs of English language learners and struggling readers? Choose one lesson and work as a team to discuss ways to teach the lesson or parts of it to small groups. Which students will you target and why?

6. **Match Lessons to Your Curriculum.** Select and rank the lessons you wish to teach at the beginning of the year. Discuss why you've selected these lessons and how you will deliver them to your class. How do the lessons mesh with your district curriculum? Explain how you use the lessons to supplement or supplant the curriculum you teach.

7. **Select and Teach Lessons.** Work with a team to select one lesson from Chapter 1 to study, plan, and deliver to students. Report back and share how students

responded. Discuss and share your findings. What do you need to do next to meet student needs?

Study Guide: Chapter 2. Beating the Midyear Blahs

1. **Prioritize Midyear Essentials.** Brainstorm a list of literacy must-dos as you enter the middle of the school year. Compare your list to the one from the beginning of the year. How have things changed? Where do you need to focus your instructional attention in continue strengthening your students' literacy capacity?

2. **Check out the Literacy Scenarios.** Read over the *Take Off and Partner Talks Bookmarks* and *Meaning Madness Time* scenarios at the beginning of Chapter 2. How might you use the lessons in either of these scenarios to promote midyear literacy development? Read the *Is It Make-Believe or Real?* scenario and think about ways you can help your students better understand the differences between fiction and nonfiction texts. What will you share with your students so they can implement the techniques from these scenarios when they read on their own?

3. **Interactive Strategies for Fluency, Vocabulary, and Comprehension.** What strategies help promote growth in fluency? How do close reading lessons with poetry help students to grow in fluency and comprehension? How can you incorporate a word wall and a text feature wall in your classroom? Describe some cooperative learning techniques, especially with partners, that help promote literacy in primary grades.

4. **Select and Teach Lessons.** Work with a team to select several lessons from Chapter 2 to study, plan, and teach to students. Report back and share how students responded. Discuss and share your findings. What do you need to do next to meet student needs?

5. **Spiral Lessons and Align to Your Curriculum.** Review the lessons you implemented in Chapter 1. Notice the Literacy Enhancement Strategy and identify how the next lesson in the same strategy spirals from it. How do the lessons align with your district curriculum? Explain how you may use the lessons to supplement or supplant the curriculum you teach.

6. **Gauge Student Response to Literacy Lessons.** Reflect on your students' word journals or oral and written responses. Were there any lessons or features of lessons that they particularly enjoyed or found effective? How will you use your own observations plus student responses to change and improve your literacy instruction?

Study Guide: Chapter 3. Ending the Year Literacy Strong

1. **Prioritize End-of-the-Year Essentials.** Brainstorm a list of literacy must-dos as you enter the final months of the school year. Compare your list to the list you made at the beginning of the year. How have things changed? Where do you need to be focusing your instructional attention to end the year literacy strong?

2. **Review the Literacy Scenarios.** Read over the literacy scenarios at the beginning of the chapter. Which one appeals most to you (and your students)? What are some ways you can enhance fluency development by using songs and other performance texts in your classroom? How will you assess student growth in fluency? Create a plan to make any of the chapter opener scenarios work in your classroom.

3. **Assess Students You Are Most Worried About.** Use the informal, formative assessment procedures you chose at the beginning of the school year to check on the progress of your most worrisome students. Have they made sufficient progress from your baseline assessment? If not, what will you do to meet these students' literacy needs?

4. **Maintain a Strong Parent Connection.** As the end of the school year approaches, it is easy for parents to drift away from family literacy. How might you help parents continue working with and supporting their children at home in reading? Consider an end-of-the-year parent conference to share ideas and titles to keep literacy going strong in the last months of the school year and into the summer break. How else might you communicate with parents? What information and ideas from the lessons do you want to share with parents?

5. **Continue to Promote Student Independence.** As the school year ends, students should be well engaged in independent reading in school and at home. How can you reinforce the importance of independent reading during the last months of the school year?

6. **Gauge Student Response to Literacy Lessons.** Were there any lessons or features of lessons that students especially enjoyed or found effective? How will you use your observations plus student responses to change and improve your literacy instruction?

7. **Move Beyond the Lessons.** The lessons in this book are meant to serve as models for your own lessons. How can you adapt the gradual release model from these lessons to make other lessons you teach more engaging? What do you notice about the engagement techniques in the lessons such as singing jingles, chants, and active movements? In what ways do these active techniques help make lessons

more engaging and memorable? Try using the format or some of the techniques you've learned from the Literacy Strong lessons with other lessons you need to deliver. Share and discuss with colleagues.

Study Guide: Chapter 4. Stopping the Summer Slide

1. **Review the Literacy Scenarios.** Read over the *Describe It in Five!*, *Splash into Reading*, and *Summer Poetry Reading* scenarios at the beginning of Chapter 4. Explain which ideas you would like to try and share why they appeal to you. What will you have to share with parents for them to implement ideas from the summer scenarios?

2. **Assess Students One More Time.** Just before vacation begins, assess your students informally to determine the progress they have made. Analyze your data to determine recommendations you can make to parents and next year's teacher. Based on your analysis, are there any literacy competencies that need additional attention in your curriculum?

3. **Keep in Touch with Parents and Families.** As the school year ends and students head into summer, make plans for ways to stay in touch with them and their parents. Make a list of what might you share with parents and children—articles on the importance of reading, specific tips and strategies, recommended books and texts for summer reading, information on summer reading programs, and even personal letters of thanks and encouragement.

4. **Send Them Off with a Book.** What better way to start summer than to provide your students with a great book! By now you know your students well. Based on their interests, what books do you think individual students would like to read? How might you acquire books to give your students? Would you want to pair or put in small groups students with the same book? Make a list of activities that students could do in response to reading their books.

5. **Review the School Year and Anticipate the Next.** Before you leave for the summer, take stock of the successes you have achieved in helping students to become literacy strong. How can you make these achievements even better next year? Did you have concerns about any lessons you implemented in the past year? What changes need to be made so students experience more growth?

6. **Choose Lessons Wisely.** It is likely that not all the lessons in Chapter 4 will or can be implemented by families. Summers are busy. With that in mind, prioritize a list of the lessons that you feel will have the greatest positive effect on your students

given your end-of-year assessments. Then, make a plan for delivering these lessons to parents.

7. **Monitor Summer Lessons.** The lessons in this chapter are designed for use in summer school or for families to implement together. Make a plan for how you will monitor the lessons that you send out to your students and their families. Will you send periodic reminders or suggestions to parents? Will you ask parents or students to respond to the lessons with evidence that they were implemented?

8. **Connect to the Coming School Year.** The lessons in Chapter 4 can segue into the following school year. For example, singing patriotic songs and reading patriotic poetry on the 4th of July may lead to other uses of song and poetry throughout the school year. Study and choose lessons for the summer and brainstorm ways to move the ideas across grade levels into the fall.

References and Resources

Allington, R. L., & McGill-Franzen, A. (Eds.). (2013). *Summer reading: Closing the rich/poor reading achievement gap.* New York: Teachers College Press.

Anderson, O. R. (2009). The role of knowledge network structures in learning scientific habits of mind: Higher order thinking and inquiry skills. In I. M. Saleh & M. S. Khine (Eds.), *Fostering scientific habits of mind: Pedagogical knowledge and best practices in science education* (pp. 59–82). Rotterdam, The Netherlands: Sense.

Beck, I. L., Perfetti, C. A., & McKeown, M. G. (1982). Effects of long-term vocabulary instruction on lexical access and reading comprehension. *Journal of Educational Psychology, 74*(4), 506–521. doi:10.1037/0022-0663.74.4.506

Boss, S., & Larmer, J. (2018). *Project-based teaching: How to create rigorous and engaging learning experiences.* Alexandria, VA: ASCD

Caine, R. N., & Caine, G. (2013). The brain/mind principles of natural learning. In T. B. Jones (Ed.), *Education for the human brain: A road map to natural learning in schools* (pp. 43–62). Lanham, MD: Rowman & Littlefield.

Carlo, M. S., August, D., McLaughlin, B., Snow, C. E., Dressler, C., Lippman, D. N., & White, C. E. (2004). Closing the gap: Addressing the vocabulary needs of English-language learners in bilingual and mainstream classrooms. *Reading Research Quarterly, 39*(2), 188–215. doi:10.1598/RRQ.39.2.3

Clay, M. M. (2000). *Concepts about print: What have children learned about the way we print language?* Portsmouth, NH: Heinemann.

Dweck, C. (2012). *Mindset: How you can fulfill your potential.* London: Robinson.

Ellery, V. (2011). *Equipping the warrior woman: Strategies to awaken your purpose, strength, and confidence.* Sisters, OR: Deep River.

Ellery, V. (2014). *Creating strategic readers: Techniques for supporting rigorous literacy instruction* (3rd ed.). Newark, DE: International Reading Association.

Ellery, V., & Rosenboom, J. L. (2011). *Sustaining strategic readers: Techniques for supporting content literacy in grades 6–12.* Newark, DE: International Reading Association.

Fresch, M. J., & Harrison, D. L. (2013). *Learning through poetry: Long vowels.* Huntington Beach, CA: Shell Education.

Hiebert, E. H., & Taylor, B. M. (1994). *Getting reading right from the start: Effective early literacy interventions.* Boston: Allyn & Bacon.

Hildrew, C. (2018). *Becoming a growth mindset school* (1st ed.). New York: Routledge.

Hoyt, L. (2002). *Make it real: Strategies for success with informational texts.* Portsmouth, NH: Heinemann.

Hoyt, L. (2009). *Revisit, reflect, retell: Time-tested strategies for teaching reading comprehension* (Rev. ed.). Portsmouth, NH: Heinemann.

Jensen, E., & Nickelsen, L. (2008). *Deeper learning: 7 powerful strategies for in-depth and longer-lasting learning.* Thousand Oaks, CA: Corwin.

Kelley, M. J., & Clausen-Grace, N. (2008). *R5 in your classroom: A guide to differentiating independent reading and developing avid readers.* Newark, DE: International Reading Association.

Kim, J. S., & White, T. G. (2011). Solving the problem of summer reading loss. *Phi Delta Kappan, 92*(7), 64–67. doi:10.1177/003172171109200714

Lanning, L. A. (2013). *Designing a concept-based curriculum for English language arts: Meeting the Common Core with intellectual integrity, K–12.* Thousand Oaks, CA: Corwin.

Marzano, R. J., & Simms, J. A. (2013). *Vocabulary for the Common Core.* Bloomington, IN: Marzano Research Laboratory.

McEwan-Adkins, E. K. (2012). *Collaborative teacher literacy teams, K–6: Connecting professional growth to student achievement.* Bloomington, IN: Solution Tree.

Miller, D. (2009). *The book whisperer: Awakening the inner reader in every child.* San Francisco: Jossey-Bass.

Mraz, M., & Rasinski, T. V. (2007). Summer reading loss. *The Reading Teacher, 60*(8), 784–789. doi:10.1598/RT.60.8.9

National Governors Association Center for Best Practices & Council of Chief State School Officers. (2010). *Common Core State Standards for English language arts and literacy in history/social studies, science, and technical subjects.* Washington, DC: Authors.

National Research Council. (2012). *Education for life and work: Developing transferable knowledge and skills in the 21st century.* Washington, DC: National Academies Press.

Oczkus, L. (2009). *Interactive think-aloud lessons: 25 surefire ways to engage students and improve comprehension.* New York: Scholastic.

Oczkus, L. D. (2012). *Best ever literacy survival tips: 72 lessons you can't teach without.* Newark, DE: International Reading Association.

Oczkus, L. (2014). *Just the facts! Close reading and comprehension of informational text.* Huntington Beach, CA: Shell Education; Newark.

Padak, N., & Rasinski, T. (2005). *Fast Start for Early Readers: A research-based, send-home literacy program with 60 reproducible poems and activities that ensures reading success for every child.* New York: Scholastic.

Padak, N., & Rasinski, T. (2008). *Fast Start: Getting ready to read.* New York: Scholastic.

Rasinski, T. V. (2010). *The fluent reader: Oral and silent reading strategies for building fluency, word recognition and com- prehension* (2nd ed.). New York: Scholastic.

Rasinski, T., & Cheesman Smith, M. (2018). *The megabook of fluency.* New York: Scholastic.

Rasinski, T., & Griffith, L. (2011). *Fluency through practice and performance.* Huntington Beach, CA: Shell Education.

Rasinski, T., & Oczkus, L. (2015a). *Close reading with paired texts level 1.* Huntington Beach, CA: Shell Education.

Rasinski, T., & Oczkus, L. (2015b). *Close reading with paired texts level 2.* Huntington Beach, CA: Shell Education.

Rasinski, T., & Oczkus, L. (2015c). *Close reading with paired texts level K.* Huntington Beach, CA: Shell Education.

Rasinski, T.V., & Padak, N. (2005). *3-minute reading assessments: Word recognition, fluency, and comprehension: Grades 1–4.* New York: Scholastic.

Rasinski, T. V., Padak, N. D., & Fawcett, G. (2009). *Teaching children who find reading difficult* (4th ed.). New York: Pearson.

Rasinski, T., & Stevenson, B. (2005). The effects of Fast Start Reading: A fluency-based home involvement reading program, on the reading achievement of beginning readers. *Reading Psychology, 26*(2), 109–125. doi:10.1080/02702710590930483

Rasinski, T., & Zutell, J. (2010). *Essential strategies for word study: Effective methods for improving decoding, spelling, and vocabulary.* New York: Scholastic.

Reutzel, D. R., & Clark, S. (2011). Organizing literacy classrooms for effective instruction: A survival guide. *The Reading Teacher, 65*(2), 96–109. doi:10.1002/TRTR.01013

Reutzel, D. R., & Fawson, P.C. (2002). *Your classroom library: New ways to give it more teaching power.* New York: Scholastic.

Roth, L. (2012). *Brain-powered strategies to engage all learners.* Huntington Beach, CA: Shell Education.

Routman, R. (2003). *Reading essentials: The specifics you need to teach reading well.* Portsmouth, NH: Heinemann.

Scholastic. (2015). *Kids and family reading report* (5th ed.). New York: Author.

Sousa, D. A. (2011). *How the brain learns* (4th ed.). Thousand Oaks, CA: Corwin.

Strobel, J., & van Barneveld, A. (2009). When is PBL more effective? A meta-synthesis of meta-analyses comparing PBL to conventional classrooms. *The Interdisciplinary Journal of Problem-Based Learning, 3*(1). doi:10.7771/1541-5015.1046

Topping, K. (1995). *Paired reading, spelling and writing: The handbook for teachers and parents.* New York: Cassell.

Torgesen, J. K. (2004). Avoiding the devastating downward spiral: The evidence that early intervention prevents reading failure. *American Educator, 28*(3), 6–19.

Wiggins, G., & McTighe, J. (2011). *The understanding by design guide to creating high-quality units.* Alexandria, VA: ASCD.

Wolfe, P. (2010). *Brain matters: Translating research into classroom practice* (2nd ed.). Alexandria, VA: ASCD.

Wong, H. K., & Wong, R. T. (2009). *The first days of school: How to be an effective teacher.* Mountain View, CA: Harry K. Wong.

Yopp, H. K., & Yopp, R. H. (2011). *Purposeful play for early childhood phonological awareness.* Huntington Beach, CA: Shell Education.

Other Suggested Readings

Adams, M. J. (2011). The relation between alphabetic basics, word recognition, and reading. In S.J. Samuels & A. E. Farstrup (Eds.), *What research has to say about reading instruction* (4th ed., pp. 4–24). Newark, DE: International Reading Association.

Ardoin, S. P., Morena, L. S., Binder, K. S., & Foster, T. E. (2013). Examining the impact of feedback and repeated readings on oral reading fluency: Let's not forget prosody. *School Psychology Quarterly, 28*(4), 391–404. doi:10.1037/ spq0000027

Bear, D. R., Invernizzi, M., Templeton, S., & Johnston, F. (2011). *Words their way: Word study for phonics, vocabulary, and spelling instruction* (5th ed.). Boston: Pearson.

Beck, I. L., McKeown, M. G., & Kucan, L. (2008). *Creating robust vocabulary: Frequently asked questions and extended examples.* New York: Guilford.

Blachowicz, C., & Fisher, P. J. (2014). *Teaching vocabulary in all classrooms* (5th ed.). Boston: Pearson.

Brassell, D., & Rasinski, T. (2008). *Comprehension that works: Taking students beyond ordinary understanding to deep comprehension.* Huntington Beach, CA: Shell Education.

Cunningham, P. M. (2012). *Phonics they use: Words for reading and writing* (6th ed.). Boston: Pearson.

Gambrell, L. B., & Morrow, L. M. (Eds.). (2015). *Best practices in literacy instruction* (5th ed.). New York: Guilford.

Kelley, M. J., & Clausen-Grace, N. (2013). *Comprehension shouldn't be silent: From strategy instruction to student in- dependence* (2nd ed.). Newark, DE: International Reading Association.

Morgan, D. N., Mraz, M., Padak, N. D., & Rasinski, T. (2009). *Independent reading: Practical strategies for grades K–3*. New York: Guilford.

Rasinski, T. (2005). *Daily word ladders, grades 2–3*. New York: Scholastic.

Rasinski, T. (2008). *Daily word ladders, grades 1–2*. New York: Scholastic.

Rasinski, T. (2011). *Daily word ladders, grades K–1*. New York: Scholastic.

Rasinski, T. V., & Padak, N. D. (2012). *From phonics to fluency: Effective teaching of decoding and reading fluency in the elementary school* (3rd ed.). Boston: Pearson.

Rasinski, T., & Zimmerman, B. (2013). What's the perfect text for struggling readers? Try poetry! *Reading Today, 30*(5), 15–16.

Samuels, S. J., & Farstrup, A. E. (Eds.). (2006). *What research has to say about fluency instruction*. Newark, DE: International Reading Association.

Children's Literature

1 Hunter by Pat Hutchins
Add It, Dip It, Fix It: A Book of Verbs by R. M. Schneider
Amanda's First Day of School by Joan E. Goodman
A, My Name Is . . . by Alice Lyne
The Berenstain Bears' Graduation Day by Mike Berenstain
The Best Book to Read by Debbie Bertram and Susan Bloom
The Big Test by Julie Danneberg
Blueberries for Sal by Robert McCloskey
Boo to a Goose by Mem Fox
Born to Read by Judy Sierra
Brand-New Pencils, Brand-New Books by Diane deGroat
Brown Bear, Brown Bear, What Do You See? by Bill Martin, Jr.
The Cat with Seven Names by Tony Johnston
Curious George Goes to an Ice Cream Shop edited by Margret and H. A. Rey
David Goes to School by David Shannon
A Desert Scrapbook: Dawn to Dusk in the Sonoran Desert by Virginia Wright-Frierson
Don't Let the Pigeon Drive the Bus! by Mo Willems
The Dove Dove: Funny Homograph Riddles by Marvin Terban
Exactly the Opposite by Tana Hoban
Farm Animals by Daniel Nunn
Feet and Puppies, Thieves and Guppies: What Are Irregular Plurals? by Brian P. Cleary
Fire Up with Reading! by Toni Buzzeo
First Day Jitters by Julie Danneberg
The Foot Book by Dr. Seuss
Fortunately by Remy Charlip
The Grouchy Ladybug by Eric Carle
Hop on Pop by Dr. Seuss
How Do Dinosaurs Go to School? by Jane Yolen
How I Became a Pirate by Melinda Long

How Rocket Learned to Read by Tad Hills
I Am Amelia Earhart by Brad Meltzer
I Am Abraham Lincoln by Brad Meltzer
I Am Rosa Parks by Brad Meltzer
I Am Albert Einstein by Brad Meltzer
Ice Bear: In the Steps of the Polar Bear by Nicola Davies
The Ice Cream King by Steve Metzger
If You Give a Mouse a Cookie by Laura Joffe Numeroff
If You Were a Noun by Michael Dahl
I Like Books by Anthony Browne
In the Small, Small Pond by Denise Fleming
An Island Scrapbook: Dawn to Dusk on a Barrier Island by Virginia Wright-Frierson
It's Back to School We Go! First Day Stories from Around the World by Ellen Jackson
It's Time for School, Stinky Face by Lisa McCourt
I Wanna Iguana by Karen Kaufman Orloff
I Wonder When? by Mary Elizabeth Salzmann
Last Day Blues by Julie Danneberg
A Light in the Attic by Shel Silverstein
The Lincolns: A Scrapbook Look at Abraham and Mary by Candace Fleming
A Mink, a Fink, a Skating Rink: What Is a Noun? by Brian P. Cleary
Miss Bindergarten Celebrates the Last Day of Kindergarten by Joseph Slate
Miss Brooks Loves Books! (and I Don't) by Barbara Bottner
Monkey and Duck Quack Up! by Jennifer Hamburg
Mrs. Spitzer's Garden by Edith Pattou
Never Ride Your Elephant to School by Doug Johnson
The Night Before Summer Vacation by Natasha Wing
Olivia's Opposites by Ian Falconer
Ook the Book by Lissa Rovetch
One Fish Two Fish Red Fish Blue Fish by Dr. Seuss
One Small Step: Celebrating the First Men on the Moon by Jerry Stone
Opposites by Sandra Boynton
Peanut Butter and Jelly: A Play Rhyme illustrated by Nadine Bernard Westcott
A Picture Book of Helen Keller by David A. Adler
A Picture Book of Jackie Robinson by David A. Adler
A Picture Book of Sitting Bull by David A. Adler
P Is for Passport: A World Alphabet by Devin Scillian
Polar Bear's Underwear by Tupera Tupera
Quentin Quokka's Quick Questions by Barbara deRubertis
The Relatives Came by Cynthia Rylant
School Around the World by Dona Herweck Rice
Sheep in a Jeep by Nancy Shaw
Should I Share My Ice Cream? by Mo Willems
Summer Days and Nights by Wong Herbert Yee
Swirl by Swirl: Spirals in Nature by Joyce Sidman
Testing Miss Malarkey by Judy Finchler

Thesaurus Rex by Laya Steinberg
Time of Wonder by Robert McCloskey
To Root, to Toot, to Parachute: What Is a Verb? by Brian P. Cleary
Turtle Summer: A Journal for My Daughter by Mary Alice Monroe
What's Up, Duck? A Book of Opposites by Tad Hills
Wemberly's Ice-Cream Star by Kevin Henkes
Your Foot's on My Feet! and Other Tricky Nouns by Marvin Terban
Zoe Sophia's Scrapbook: An Adventure in Venice by Claudia Mauner and Elisa Smalley
Zoola Palooza: A Book of Homographs by Gene Barretta
The Amelia Bedelia series by Peggy Parish
The Fancy Nancy series by Jane O'Connor

Children's Literature by Strand

Thanks to the experts at Booksource.com for organizing this bibliography of children's literature.

Phonemic Awareness
Each Peach Pear Plum by Janet Ahlberg and Allan Ahlberg
Sheep in a Jeep by Nancy Shaw
Skippyjon Jones by Judy Schachner
Three Little Kittens by Paul Galdone

Phonics
Alison's Zinnia by Anita Lobel
Sheep on a Ship by Nancy Shaw
The Cat on the Mat Is Flat by Andy Griffiths

Comprehension
Elephants Swim by Linda Capus Riley
Mud by Mary Lyn Ray
This Is Not My Hat by Jon Klassen

Fluency
Bat Loves the Night by Nicola Davies
Button Up! by Alice Schertle
Love the Baby by Steven L. Layne
Saturdays and Teacakes by Lester L. Laminack

Writing
Little Red Writing by Joan Holub
The Day the Crayons Quit by Drew Daywalt
The Plot Chickens by Mary Jane Auch

Motivation to Read
The Incredible Book Eating Boy by Oliver Jeffers
We Are in a Book! by Mo Willems
Wild About Books by Judy Sierra

About the Authors

Valerie Ellery has dedicated 30 years to the field of education in various roles as a National Board Certified Teacher, curriculum specialist, mentor, reading coach, international educational consultant, and best-selling author for 10 years. Her books *Creating Strategic Readers* and *Sustaining Strategic Readers* have been used internationally in classrooms and universities to inspire educators to motivate and engage today's learners. She authored 10 student readers for Saint Mary's Press with guiding questions, vocabulary, and retell it cards. In addition, she coauthored two secondary curriculums in the area of self-worth and human trafficking, *Bodies Are Not Commodities* and *Shine Hope* (A21campaign.org and Hillsong.com), which will be used to influence young adults in 37 nations. Using innovative, interactive, and informative methods, Valerie models best practices in classrooms and motivates staffs globally to create strategic thinkers and readers. She lives in Florida with husband, Gregg, and has four adult children and two beautiful grandchildren. For more information or to reach Valerie for professional development, visit http://www.ValerieEllery.com.

Lori Oczkus is a literacy coach, best-selling author, and popular international speaker. Tens of thousands of teachers have attended her motivating, fast-paced workshops and read her practical, research-based professional books and articles. Lori has experience working as a bilingual elementary teacher, intervention specialist, staff developer, and literacy coach. She works with students in classrooms every week and knows the challenges that teachers face in teaching students to read. Lori has been inducted into the California Reading Association Hall of Fame for her many contributions to the field of reading. Her travels to provide literacy trainings in other countries include trips to Canada, London, and Trinidad. Lori is the author of seven best-selling professional books. Her latest publications include *Just the Facts: Close Reading and Comprehension of Informational Text* and *Close Reading with Paired Texts*, a K–5 series coauthored with Tim Rasinski. Lori's *Reciprocal Teaching at Work: Strategies for Improving Reading Comprehension* is a best seller. She also is the coauthor of several reading programs, including *Talk About Books*, a K–2 guided reading series and *Exploring Reading*, a K–8 intervention kit for teacher-created materials. Lori lives in California with her husband, Mark, and has three young adult children. For more information or to reach Lori for professional development, visit http://www.LoriOczkus.com.

Timothy V. Rasinski is a professor of literacy education at Kent State University. He has written more than 200 articles and has authored, coauthored, or edited more than 50 books or curriculum programs on reading education. His best-selling book on reading fluency, *The Fluent Reader*, is now in its second edition. His scholarly interests include reading fluency, word study, and readers who struggle. His research on reading has been cited by the National Reading Panel and has been published in journals such as *Reading Research Quarterly*, *The Reading Teacher*, *Reading Psychology*, and the *Journal of Educational Research*. Tim is the lead author of the fluency chapter for the *Handbook of Reading Research*. Tim has served on the board of directors of the International Reading Association and was coeditor of *The Reading Teacher*, the world's most widely read journal of literacy education. He has also served as coeditor of the *Journal of Literacy Research*. Tim is past president of the College Reading Association and was inducted into the International Reading Hall of Fame in 2010. Prior to teaching at Kent State, Tim taught literacy education at the University of Georgia. He taught for several years as an elementary and middle school classroom and Title I teacher in Nebraska. For more information or to reach Tim for professional development, visit http://www.timrasinski.com or e-mail at trasinsk@kent.edu.

Related ASCD Resources: Literacy

At the time of publication, the following resources were available (ASCD stock numbers in parentheses).

Print Products

Building Student Literacy Through Sustained Silent Reading by Steve Gardiner (#105027)

Climbing the Literacy Ladder: Small-Group Instruction to Support All Readers and Writers, PreK–5 by Beverly Tyner (#118012)

A Close Look at Close Reading: Teaching Students to Analyze Complex Texts, Grades K–5 by Diane Lapp, Barbara Moss, Maria Grant, and Kelly Johnson (#114008)

Effective Literacy Coaching: Building Expertise and a Culture of Literacy by Shari Frost, Roberta Buhle, and Camille Blachowicz (#109044)

Engaging Minds in English Language Arts Classrooms: The Surprising Power of Joy by Mary Jo Fresch, Michael F. Opitz, and Michael P. Ford (#113021)

Literacy Strong All Year Long: Powerful Lessons for Grades 3–5 by Valerie Ellery, Lori Oczkus, and Timothy V. Rasinski (#118013)

Literacy Unleashed: Fostering Excellent Reading Instruction Through Classroom Visits by Bonnie D. Houck and Sandi Novak (#116042)

Read, Write, Lead: Breakthrough Strategies for Schoolwide Literacy Success by Regie Routman (#113016)

For up-to-date information about ASCD resources, go to www.ascd.org. You can search the complete archives of Educational Leadership at www.ascd.org/el.

ASCD myTeachSource®

Download resources from a professional learning platform with hundreds of research-based best practices and tools for your classroom at http://myteachsource.ascd.org/

For more information, send an e-mail to member@ascd.org; call 1-800-933-2723 or 703-578-9600; send a fax to 703-575-5400; or write to Information Services, ASCD, 1703 N. Beauregard St., Alexandria, VA 22311-1714 USA.

DON'T MISS A SINGLE ISSUE OF ASCD'S AWARD-WINNING MAGAZINE,

EL EDUCATIONAL LEADERSHIP

If you belong to a Professional Learning Community, you may be looking for a way to get your fellow educators' minds around a complex topic. Why not delve into a relevant theme issue of *Educational Leadership*, the journal written by educators for educators.

Subscribe now, or buy back issues of ASCD's flagship publication at **www.ascd.org/ELbackissues.**

Single issues cost $7 (for issues dated September 2006–May 2013) or $8.95 (for issues dated September 2013 and later). Buy 10 or more of the same issue, and you'll save 10 percent. Buy 50 or more of the same issue, and you'll save 15 percent. For discounts on purchases of 200 or more copies, contact **programteam@ascd.org**; 1-800-933-2723, ext. 5773.

To see more details about these and other popular issues of *Educational Leadership*, visit **www.ascd.org/ELarchive.**

LEARN. TEACH. LEAD.

1703 North Beauregard Street
Alexandria, VA 22311-1714 USA

www.ascd.org/el